USES OF TELEVISION

'Always challenging and irresistibly ambitious, Hartley's prose aims for nothing less than spectacular success, embracing risk, defying gravity, and spurning a net. From his own highly original perspective, Hartley outlines the kind of work broadcast television performs for its audiences, for its critics, for modernity and for democracy. The result is a fertile, rich and optimistic account of television as a "transmodern teacher", pointing to new and productive directions for Television Studies.'

Graeme Turner, Professor of English, University of Queensland

'An immensely innovative, thought-provoking, iconoclastic and ambitious book on the history and meaning of television and television studies . . . it both expands and clarifies the academic field.'

Mica Nava, Reader, Department of Cultural Studies, University of East London

Taking inspiration from Richard Hoggart's classic The Uses of Literacy, John Hartley considers the usefulness of both television and television studies. He re-reads the history of broadcast TV's earliest moments, tracing the critical reception it received from that day to this. Uses of Television asks 'improper questions' about what television, and TV Studies, have been for: about the effect of the vast, unknowable audience on television; about the role of television in promoting 'cultural citizenship' by means of 'transmodern teaching'; and about the effects of knowledge produced in the formal study of television.

Via a consideration of neglected aspects of media and domestic history, from the 1930s film Housing Problems to Clarissa Explains It All, from the fridge to Umberto Eco's daughter, Hartley argues that this much-maligned medium can be reassessed in a more positive light. 'Democratainment' and 'do-it-yourself citizenship' are the latest manifestations of a civic and cultural education that TV performs even as it entertains.

John Hartley is Professor and Head of the School of Journalism, Media and Cultural Studies at Cardiff University, and Director of the Tom Hopkinson Centre for Media Research.

USES OF TELEVISION

John Hartley

London and New York

Someone has to teach you all you know.

Thanks Tina.

First published 1999
by Routledge
11 New Fetter Lane, London EC4P 4EE

Simultaneously published in the USA and Canada
by Routledge
29 West 35th Street, New York, NY 10001

Typeset in Joanna and Bembo by
J&L Composition Ltd, Filey, North Yorkshire
Printed and bound in Great Britain by
Biddles Ltd, Guildford and King's Lynn

British Library Cataloguing in Publication Data
A catalogue record for this book is available
from the British Library

Library of Congress Cataloging in Publication Data
A catalogue record for this book has been requested

ISBN 0–415–08508–X (hbk)
ISBN 0–415–08509–8 (pbk)

CONTENTS

v

CONTENTS

FIGURES

ACKNOWLEDGEMENTS

Thanks to Richard Hoggart for giving so generously of his time and conversation in 1997 in both Cardiff and London; and for taking the trouble to read the manuscript of this book. I am especially grateful for his generous comments about Chapter 15. Needless to say he is of course quite innocent of any association with the contents. Whether he sees it as homage, pastiche or plagiarism, I hope he doesn't mind.

Thanks to Paula Amad, Kate Bowles, Tara Brabazon, Abigail Bray, Will Brooker, Geoff Craig, Mark Gibson, Sara Gwenllian Jones, Catharine Lumby, Alan McKee, Steve Mickler, Eva Vieth, McKenzie Wark; the next generation whose talent and goodwill bode well for the future of cultural and media studies. They're alarmingly skilful in doing what I can only observe with admiration. Still, like all good TV viewers, I like to watch, and look forward with warm anticipation to being taught a thing or two.

Thanks to Bobby Allen, Tony Bennett, Frances Bonner, Stuart Cunningham, Chris Lawe Davies, Stephanie Donald, James Donald, John Frow, Lawrence Grossberg, Terence Hawkes, Mark Hobart, Amanda Hopkinson, Henry Jenkins, Stephen Knight, Risto Kunelius, Norm Leslie, Li Zhurun, Niall Lucy, Daniel Meadows, Toby Miller, Meaghan Morris, Mica Nava, Tom O'Regan, Roberta Pearson, Robyn Quin, Krishna Sen, Brian Shoesmith, Roger Silverstone, Esa Sirkkunen, Keyan Tomaselli, Sue Turnbull, Graeme Turner, Eva Warth, Zhao Bin and the staff, both academic and administrative, in the School of Journalism, Media and Cultural Studies at Cardiff University, for being such congenial colleagues and helping me to mature the ideas for this book.

I have to single out for special thanks Mark Gibson of Edith Cowan University and Toby Miller of New York University, both of whom not only put me up on my travels, but also read the MS when there was still time to do something about the dreadful things they found lurking there; it was tremendously helpful and I think the book is the better for their insights. Thanks also to the staff and students of New York University, the Massachusetts Institute of Technology, the University of Utrecht and Edith Cowan University for listening and responding to some of the arguments while they were in preparation. Thanks especially to Richard Allen and George Yudice (NYU), Henry Jenkins

(MIT), Eva Warth (Utrecht) and Norm Leslie (ECU) for the material support in getting me there.

Thanks so much to:

- *Meanjin*, Melbourne, for first publication of 'Suburbanality (in Cultural Studies)'. Special thanks to Jenny Lee and Meaghan Morris.
- Arnold, London, for first publication of sections of 'Housing Television: the textual tradition in TV and cultural studies', in Christine Geraghty and David Lusted (eds), *The Television Studies Book*, published in 1997. Special thanks to Dave Lusted.
- Titus Films, Sidney and the Australian Film Commission for use of the section on the fridge, which results from work commissioned by them. Special thanks to Nick Adler.

Extra special thanks to Rebecca Barden at Routledge – *sine qua non*. Last, as ever, Tina Horton and the sprogs: Karri, Rhiannon, Sophie. Teachers 'in the best sense', all.

1 (PRE-SCRIPT)

PER-SONA

Selves, knowledge, books

> Dim moon-eyed fishes near
> Gaze at the gilded gear
> And query: 'What does this vaingloriousness down here?'
>
> (Thomas Hardy, 1930: 289)

KNOW BUSINESS LIKE SHOW BUSINESS

In 1958, Penguin Books issued the popular (Pelican) edition of Richard Hoggart's *The Uses of Literacy: aspects of working-class life with special reference to publications and entertainments*. Twenty years later John Fiske and I published *Reading Television*. Both of these books are still in print and, while Hoggart's is much the more important in its social reach and its intellectual achievement, both books were trying to make sense of contemporary popular-cultural media from the point of view of the 'reader' or audience; both are about media 'literacy' in a period of social change and democratization, and both were written by authors trained in literary and textual techniques of analysis, rather than in the methodology of the social sciences. As I write this, it is twenty years later again. In the two decades between Hoggart's and ours (1958 to 1978) very few books were published that tried to take television seriously in textual terms (Newcomb, 1974; Williams, 1974), although there was a branch of sociological analysis that sought to describe the 'uses and gratifications' of 'mass media' for individual viewers (Blumler and McQuail, 1968; McQuail, Blumler and Brown, 1972; Blumler and Katz, 1974; Blumler and Katz, 1975). But in the two decades since then (1978 to 1998), books about television have become much more common, and there is, as there was not twenty or forty years ago, something that might be called 'television studies'.

In 1978 it was easy to justify a new general book on TV. Now, when the cup of the student of television studies is getting close to overflow, it is easier to ask why (yet) another one is needed.

On textbooks

The reason is partly institutional or entrepreneurial: to maximize sales academic publishers encourage textbooks rather than more specialized monographs (they prefer teaching to research); while, for their part, institutions of higher education need to be able to direct students to books for basic instruction and guidance. The democratization of higher education in the period since Hoggart has meant that such introductory teaching cannot always be afforded in the traditional form of live tutors and lecturers with specialist skills. Now teaching must be provided on an industrial scale to knowledge 'consumers' whose disciplinary 'literacy' cannot be assumed in advance, but whose individual needs have to be catered for. As always, one answer to this problem is technology; teaching is done by 'virtual' means, including textbooks.

Textbooks themselves serve different purposes. Generally, a textbook calls a readership into being to promote a branch of knowledge or a specialism, and it explains what the new field of study ought to look like. Classically a textbook identifies its object of study, gives a theoretical rationale and a survey of major theorists from the scholarly archive, outlines methodology and arguments, presents an archive of research documents, information or findings, and suggests useful further reading. Usually, the assumed reader of such a thing is the beginning student; someone it would be tactless to assume had an already-tutored ear for the specialist language, the disciplinary conversations or the received wisdom of the specialism in question.

However, in the early period of a particular branch of learning, such a textbook can be as original and innovative as the most erudite scholarly monograph, particularly if the readership it calls into being is made up of other writers, researchers and critics who go on to rework the topic and apply it to their own specialist interests. Such has proven to be the case in television studies. Some of the most influential writings in TV studies' own prehistory have been textbooks, from Ferdinand de Saussure's *Course in General Linguistics* (1974) and Roland Barthes's *Elements of Semiology* (1968) to Richard Hoggart's *The Uses of Literacy* (1958) (written to assist tutors working in adult education), or Terence Hawkes's *Structuralism and Semiotics* (1977) and Fiske's and my *Reading Television* (1978). Books like these served as essays – *trials* of a new vehicle of thought. They are not instruments of standardization and normalization of knowledge, but of exploration and experiment.

Later, when a topic is institutionalized in the way that cultural, media and communication studies have established in formal education the meaning-based study of television, many more textbooks come to the market, and these may take on the more familiar form of an introductory simplification of an existing field of knowledge for institutional apprentices such as first-year undergraduates (and their graduate instructors).

Now, in these days of Research Assessment Exercises, Research Activity Indices and other forms of public monitoring of academic research productivity, a textbook is not a 'research returnable' document. This means that there's little incentive for 'research active' academics to write them, since they are categorized as mere digests of existing knowledge, rather than as contributions to the dynamic development of inter- and post-disciplinary intellectual innovation. So here's another reason why another textbook has to be justified; you get no institutional credit for doing it.

Nevertheless this hasn't stopped people writing them. Introductory texts in TV studies have proliferated so much since 1978 that publishing another one cannot be justified only by reference to the object of study itself. The importance of the *subject matter* is already understood. The credentials of the *analyst* (or the analytical approach) are not in question. In a crowded field a new book must justify itself by reference to a third party; it must prove itself *useful* to the 'end user' — to the *reader*.

It is here that I believe the present book differs from others. It is interested in readers, readerships and in what counts as 'useful' in that context. It is interested in how 'useful' TV is for its own 'end users,' especially the public-as-audience, but not forgetting my own constituency — those in intellectual, academic, critical or governmental positions who 'use' television for thinking about other problems, such as the state of culture, politics and modernity.

More importantly even than these users, however, this book is interested in the 'usefulness' of television seen from a long-term historical and broad social perspective: what is the use of television to the species? What has it been 'for'? Part of the answer to such improbably large questions lies outside of television itself. Television has been put to uses determined beyond its own institutional and semiotic forms, and counted as useful (or not) according to criteria established elsewhere, often before it was even invented. And so this book is curious not only about the 'uses of television' but also about the 'uses of TV studies', and thence about the 'usefulness' of TV studies to its readers, who are themselves all 'readers' of television.

TV studies is taken to be a social and historical fact just as much as is television itself; so there's a triangular relationship between television, readers and television studies, and potential utility in each axis of this relationship:

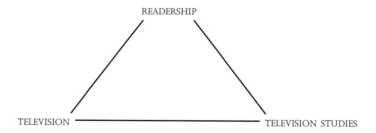

In fact, television producers, TV studies and TV audiences are converging towards one another; no longer are they mutually unknowable and incomprehensible alien beings, but increasingly porous to one another's ideas, personnel and interests.

On gathering new readers

Academic textbooks must nowadays be user-friendly, reader-oriented, population-gathering initiatives. In this respect, they have become more and more like their object of study, television itself, whose overriding characteristic is its need to *gather* populations (audiences or ratings), bringing together people and groups who may have little in common with each other beyond their co-presence as the audience of a given media performance, be it textbook or talkshow. Such 'users' have no prior commitment to engage with that text, no training in 'reading' it, no acculturated 'professional' predisposition to maintain a 'critical' curiosity about unfamiliar material; they have no resources beyond their found demographic propensities and individual preferences. How to get non-committed 'audiences' to take a 'tutored' look at things they don't like or haven't seen before – where 'tutored' ought to mean impersonal, non-subjective, scrupulous, systematic, sustained, non-intuitive, non-anecdotal, non-magical, critical, informed, practised understanding? This is a problem for TV, as for other popular media like journalism; and nowadays it's a problem for ordinary jobbing academics who want to write about television. Indeed, it's a problem of *teaching*.

However, it is not a new problem. Modern print culture is strewn with names of those who've dedicated themselves to improving knowledge, critical thinking and methodical reading or analytical practices among wide or popular readerships, from Peter Ramus in the sixteenth century onwards (Ong, 1958). While popular media literacy is improved by serious media popularizers – from editors like Tom Hopkinson to TV-stars like David Attenborough – it also falls to the writers of textbooks to holler for new recruits to the pleasures of literacy in a given cultural form and its analysis, curiosity about how things work in the world, and thence to the practice of systematic thinking in new subject areas.

Such potential recruits are much more plentiful in 1998 than they were in 1958 because of the increase in the number of people going on from school to take degree courses in higher education. In fact, the media and the academy have now begun to compete seriously for the *same* hearts and minds. The democratization of culture, taste, literacy and knowledge has developed over more than a century. In the period between 1958 and 1998 it has rolled on past popular politics and media into new areas, including fashion, travel and, at last, higher education itself. When I went to university in the late 1960s and early 1970s, I remember frequent mention being made of the 'fact' that students were the 'top' 2 or 3 per cent of the British population; a figure that has since multiplied tenfold to 30 or 40 per cent, in line with more enlightened countries. Before this expansion, academic specialists were confident that they and their students could speak *about* a general population to which they themselves in no cultural sense belonged – 'dons' tutored their students in the tradition (and often in the very language) of the imperial officer-class and administrator-sahibs. By now, in contrast, we are not studying to lead or to manage society, but to join it. Now we are what we analyze; products of and participants in the popular-knowledge-producing apparatus of internationalized consumer society. Scholarship and specialist knowledge are no longer enough; part of the challenge of this sort of popularization is to get readers to see the connections between what they are studying, the institutions and techniques by means of which they are studying it, and their own identities, everyday lives and personal circumstances.

To be useful in this context turns out to be quite a delicate and difficult trick, for we are studying nothing other than ourselves. It may seem that little is 'useful' about that − no matter how interesting it may be. But in fact the convergence between the formerly very distinct and often mutually hostile worlds of intellectual inquiry and popular culture is part of the justification for television studies. Indeed, it is a matter of family resemblance: the triad 'author/book/reader' is structurally similar to 'lecturer/subject matter/student', and in a period of 'mass' higher education both are coming to resemble a familiar triad belonging to the object of study − 'producer/"text"/audience'.

AUTHOR	BOOK	READER
PRODUCER	TEXT	AUDIENCE
LECTURER	TALK	STUDENT

Higher education is part of a much larger cultural and economic sector which can be called the knowledge or information industry; a sector that includes the information-gathering and communicative functions of government. On a global and historical scale of analysis, even if it doesn't feel like it in a tutorial room, the 'know-business' is getting more like 'show-business.'

CONVERGENCE (OF THE TWAIN)

On convergence

This is a process that in the foreign currency business is called 'sustainable convergence'. The present is a period of historic convergence, not only between cultural/knowledge producers and audience/reader consumers, and not only between communications technologies, as telephony, television and computers begin to integrate, but also at the socio-institutional level, between three large-scale social institutions that have previously been understood as distinct, even hostile to each other:

- government
- education
- media

There is a growing family resemblance between academic author and TV producer, between textbook and TV show, between student and audience. Commercially catered knowledge-for-entertainment leads the way; computer encyclopaedias like Encarta or Dorling Kindersley habituate even very young children to a screen-based visualization and segmentation of knowledge, and a click-link mode of information exploration. There's a very intense dialogue between print and screen media in this context, with educational books for children showing more and more convergence with TV characteristics: the Dorling Kindersley (DK) ranges of Eyewitness or Action Books and CDs, for instance, are 'authored' like a TV show, with a special credit for the writer(s), but a final product resulting from the work of a team of editors, designers, photographers, picture researchers, illustrators and picture engineers, and a WWW address, all subservient to the corporate 'author' with the real name-recognition, DK itself. Within such books, there is an inter-active, illustrative, informative atmosphere, based not on the word but on brilliant photographs, illustrations and design, to which the words are an attractive adjunct. Readers are conducted through the books not by authors but, in the case of the DK Action Book *Discover the Titanic*, published just ahead of the Hollywood film (Kentley, 1997), by three 'expedition leaders'. Afterwards 'readers' (who become makers) get to assemble a 'spectacular, easy-to-make 3D model' of the liner, complete with iceberg, supplied with the book; it's got 'pull-out and lift-the-flap sections' that will 'help children explore'. Readers are tutored not in narrative or print literacy but in visual/tactile screen and computer literacy, and in action-learning con-ducted through hand–eye co-ordination, even while they read a book:

> You have been selected to go on a salvage trip to the wreck of the *Titanic*. Join the team that will take you on an amazing journey down to the bottom of the ocean. **Find** the wreck by satellite navigation. **Travel** down to the wreckage site in a submersible. **Learn** about the history of the *Titanic* as you explore. **Raise** and restore the *Titanic*'s treasures.
>
> Supports the National Curricula for England, Wales, Scotland and Northern Ireland.
>
> (Kentley, 1997: cover blurb)

The habits of commercial media consumption are 'tutored' as a literacy, while simultaneously literacy is represented as an exciting pleasure. Media and educa-tion coalesce, and the government is in there too, promoting officially-sanctioned knowledge for schools, and hence helping DK to promote books that 'support' the National Curriculum. More traditional educational textbooks are competing in the same market, as are governmental discourses, from party manifestos to tax returns.

Since this convergence is *in process*, rather than historically complete, it would be useful to understand how the three great social institutions that have grown up around the sites of knowledge-production and meaning-exchange are themselves converging:

GOVERNMENT   MEDIA   EDUCATION

Each needs to be analyzed within sight of the others these days, since their activities are inexplicable viewed in isolation. The great social functions of government, media and education are insitutionalized forms of self-realization:

DEMOCRACY	DRAMA	DIDACTICS
PARTICIPATION	PERFORMANCE	PEDAGOGY
DECISION-MAKING	SHOWING	EXPLAINING
SELF-REPRESENTATION	COMMUNICATION	TEACHING

In other words, the public part of the self, the part that in classical Greek political science was held to inhere within each free person and so to constitute them as selves, has been ex-somatized, taken out of the body; and socialized, erected into institutions. Each aspect of self-realization has been institutionalized separately in a functional division of labour that has historically produced what look like quite distinct and mutually untranslatable phenomena — government, media, education. But nowadays, at the latter end of the democratic era of modernity, it seems that these aspects of the social self are re-converging.

However, they are not re-converging on the physical selves of the assembled citizens; instead these aspects of self-representation are virtualized — and the place where one can observe the process most directly is where it 'hinges', as it were, where the relations can most readily be observed, where the convergence is most sustained. This place is the media.

On transmodernity

Convergence of democratic will-formation, drama and public education is taking place in the most 'postmodern' context of new media technologies, consumer communications, entertainment industries and virtual reality. But, simultaneously, the convergence in question marks a return to a decidedly 'pre-modern' concept of citizenship, derived from the political theory of the ancient Hellenic city state, where (at least for free, male, adult natives — i.e. citizens) democracy, drama and didactics were one and the same thing, practised in the same place by and for the same people, whose assembly in sight of each other *constituted* the polity, and whose collective action of hearing orators, actors and leaders *constituted* the audience. It has only been during 'modernity' — historically a small matter of 400 years at most — that these functions of government, education and media have become decisively disarticulated from one another. Television, in reuniting them, is thus a '*transmodern*' *medium* — pre-modern and postmodern all at once.

The more militantly modernist institutions of government and education have found this transmodern tendency in the media hard to accept, which accounts for some of the suspicion and hostility felt by governmental and educational figures towards popular media especially. They see convergence in a modernist, death-defying but doom-desiring poetics, exactly like those of Thomas Hardy, for whom the concept of global convergence was summed up not by 'virtualization'

7

but by 'vaingloriousness' in the metaphor of the slow, fateful coming together of an iceberg and the SS *Titanic* in a poem called 'The convergence of the twain (lines on the loss of the *Titanic*)' (Hardy, 1930: 288–9). However, the spectacular, myth-inspiring sinking of the *Titanic* did not stop transatlantic travel; it did not reduce but rather encouraged global communications, both symbolic and physical. The cold collision of pre-modern fear of the future ('iceberg') with vainglorious virtualization of the modern (the *Titanic*) makes fear of, but commitment to, modernity the very model of transmodernity, especially in its recent, postmodern manifestations as attention turns from the sinking to the finding of the mythical vessel, and thence the spate of books, films, TV specials and anniversarial re-narrations of the story in visual, Dorling-Kindersley form. As in Hardy, so in Hollywood, where in James Cameron's *Titanic* the convergence is between mytho-logized democratization and pre-modern class, where the death-defying, doom-desiring 'modern' is a teenaged American boy; he can be 'king of the world', romantically if not literally, tying together pre-modern aristocracy (the girl), modern technology (the ship) and postmodern power (the movie), sealed by a kiss *and* death. As in Hardy and Hollywood, so in television.

It is exactly the transmodern tendencies of television that make it interesting to study; a 'useful' experimental 'laboratory' in which to observe what may turn out to be much more general tendencies of *convergence* of pre- and postmodern technologies of social selfhood into what Hardy called 'the intimate welding of their later history'; the place where government, education and media coalesce not so much in a 'convergence of the twain' as a 'ménage à trois'. 'And,' as Hardy put it, 'consummation comes, and jars two hemispheres.'

On integration: internationalization and globalization of the species

As it happens, I personally think the tendency towards 'sustainable convergence' is much more general than the policy-driven rhetoric of 'internationalization' and 'globalization' seems to suggest. In everyday journalism and corporate usage such terms tend to be reserved for developments within the business system of capital investment and commercial expansion, being restricted to the 'internatio-nalization' of technologies and the 'globalization' of markets; currently all the talk is about the integration of television with telephony and computer technologies, and the internationalization of the ensuing integrated market. But there are hints and suggestions that even these large-scale efforts may be part of something much larger, diffused, pervasive and human. In a generation's time, television's social impact will prove not to have been at the level of individual behaviour at all, good or bad. TV is much more interesting than that. It is among those global devel-opments that suggest we are on the path towards the re-integration of our species.

Whether humanity's origin turns out to be in the savannah of Africa (we're the walking species), the warm shallows of the Persian Gulf (we're a swimming species) or the ancient plains of Australia (we're a species that dreams and sings), the fact is that humanity, like many other species, has multiplied, spread far and wide, and diversified. The forms of human culture, industry, organization and behaviour could hardly be more various. Even our diseases began to specialize. Communities were isolated, each playing host to their own infections, to which they developed enough resistance to survive. We adapted to savannah and shallows, arctic and arid, and we walked, swam and sang – marching through millennia to the beat of differentiating drums, dreaming and singing ever more fragmented songs. It seems that over the past few thousand years the human species has been most readily characterized by dis-integration – dispersal to six of the seven continents. We have 'taken root' in different geographical contexts with very different social, cultural and even genetic specializations.

But despite the wild imaginings of our best storytellers, such as Kurt Vonnegut in his novel *Galapagos* (1987), we have yet to take that next evolutionary step, where isolated pockets of a species adapt to their local environment so well that they turn into a distinct new species. We have specialized but not *speciated*. Instead of evolving into post-human amphibians in the wake of nuclear destruction or ecocidal pollution, it seems in fact that humanity is going in the opposite direction. We are re-integrating ourselves as a unified species. Over the last 200 years, commerce and communication have chased empires and diseases across the globe, each vying for dominance as the species proliferates to plague proportions. Suddenly, one community's common cold is another's genocide, one country's commerce is another's collapse, and for a while – most of the nineteenth and twentieth centuries – it seems that contact between segments of our diversified species is invariably disastrous for all. But there is another side to this story. Over the 'modern' period, the age-old dispersal has been fundamentally reversed; previously undisputed barriers have been washed away in an increasing flood of contagion, commerce, communication, conquest and concubinage that has left communities riddled with each other's diseases, counting-systems, commodities, languages, cosmologies and children. For a time such influxes may seem dangerous, even lethal. Global communication can take the 'influences' to populations who have no resistance to them, so one ship from Chile to Easter Island, or from continental Europe to Iceland, can bring flu-deaths in plague proportions to previously isolated populations while hardly affecting the carriers. The influenza that spanned the world in 1918 (and again in the 1950s when I caught it) is well-known to have killed more people than the hostilities of the Great War itself. Both because of and despite these pathological forms of human communication, communities that literally for ages have placed their strongest collective faith in isolation, defensiveness, security and mutual hostility have found that 'modern' commerce and communication are more important than war; 'contagions' of culture, sex and death have served progressively to re-integrate the species. After the shock and mutual damage of first contact, populations have become adapted, resistant and even immune, and channels of communication that caused the problem in the first place (commerce, conquest, sex) have become routine, two-way and increasingly intensive for all parties.

9

In the early modern period, when European cities were in the habit of setting their clocks by the sun, a place like Cardiff was 10 minutes behind London because of its longitude, and this was understood to be natural and proper. The invention of communications technology – in this case the railway – put paid to such authenticist-isolationist notions of time, which abdicated in favour of the time*table*. Contemporary doom-theorists thought this would be the end of life as they knew it, and thankfully they were right; we've acclimatized to the integration of time into internationally standardized zones, and lived to tell the tale. Right across the spectrum of human enterprise, activities have become detached from their local-isolated-authenticist 'gold standard': 'virtualization' began with Columbus if not Marco Polo. Nowadays, it is not surprising to find that the language of medical exchange in Mongolia is English; that the most passionate and public advocate of the philosophy of world integration, and not just at the commercial-sexual level, is an Italian clothes company (Benetton); that traditional communities in Papua New Guinea leapt from the pre-modern 'stone age' to the postmodern 'air age' at a single bound (without going through a modern 'machine age'); that while a butterfly in the Amazon may not change the course of human history, a kiss in Uganda may have serious outcomes in San Francisco.

New patterns emerge – it has transpired that at a higher level of integration the vista is not of universal sameness, but of new patterns of difference. While nations, states and government policies remain territorial, especially in point of principle, and while local communities retain strong affinities with land and location, populations themselves have virtualized in both semiotic (sense-making) and somatic (bodily) communications. Mobility, migration, medical conditions – and media – are all causing human consciousness to converge. Travel and television have actually fulfilled their most clichéd function – they have literally 'broadened the mind' of our dispersed, combative and boundary-loving species. This is a transmodern tendency; it began before modernity and will continue after it. Studying TV is a 'useful' way of checking out what's happening. Instead of speciating, and instead of pursuing policies of Mutually Assured Destruction to their logical conclusion, humanity has hearkened to a Mandelan, Gorbachevian, Dianan, televisual tune; it looks to *gather* populations, not to defeat them. Now, with Mandela (the man who ended apartheid without revenge) as fashion icon in *Vogue* or as straight-man to the Spice Girls, and with Gorbachev (the man who saved the world by letting go) as front man for global fast-food chain Pizza Hut, or as one of the BBC's 75th-anniversary celebrity endorsers, and with Princess Diana (the woman who made love, hugs and touch into a political force as the 'queen of people's hearts'), cordialization of the species has reached epidemic proportions. We're all converging on one another like there's no tomorrow. We've dropped the 'err' from 'Kissinger'. . . . Well, even if this cordialization of politics is not as euphoric as I've just made it sound, and, of course, cordialization is not always appropriate, nevertheless I think it is reasonable to argue that TV must share some of the credit for the process having gone as far as it has so far been able to go; television has been 'useful' in making us aware of positive potentials in our collective selves.

USEFUL KNOWLEDGE: 'KNOW THYSELF'

But studying 'ourselves', however construed, seems at first glance to be quite different from other kinds of study. For instance, new recruits are not expecting to find out 'who they are' when joining a training scheme for a technical, professional or managerial skill, let's say in journalism, media production or corporate communication. Knowing how to marshall the resources necessary to record sound or pictures, or research programme ideas and audience preferences, or make a TV show, or manage a TV station, or regulate the industry; these are considerable skills, often a lifetime in the getting and very hard to 'transfer' (i.e. teach). But they seem to tell us very little about our 'selves'. Impersonal (i.e. professional or technical) skills and corporate knowledge may seem irrelevant in this context. However, the study of any large-scale social activity, like making and watching TV, or of any textual system as pervasive as TV-programming, can teach us about 'ourselves' in important ways, not least by showing how dispersed the 'self' turns out to be.

On the self

The 'self' may be understood narrowly or broadly as:

1 **individual personality** (unique capacities, creativity and ways of performing the self);
2 **social identities** or **subjectivity** (self, gender, family, age, class, nationality, ethnicity);
3 **humanity** with **global** characteristics common to or relevant to the **species** (language, law, learning).

It is frequently thought 'useful' to prepare people for careers in a chosen job (often one chosen by someone else); less so to teach them more general aspects of social organization, and less 'useful' still to teach about general human activity. Nevertheless, there are three 'genres' of TV-media studies that correspond to the above distinctions:

1 **technical studies of media** – corresponding with the individual/personal dimension of the self;
2 **social studies of the media** – corresponding with the social/identity dimension of the self;
3 **philosophical studies of the media** – corresponding with the human/global dimension of the self.

Their *vocational* 'usefulness' is often said to be in inverse proportion to their generality, but it may be argued that their 'usefulness' in understanding *'ourselves'* is in inverse proportion to their technical specialization. The trick is, then, to keep all three aspects in touch with each other; to remain conscious that impersonal skills are part of the operation of selfhood, that the most general philosophical questions are raised in the details of everyday life and conduct, that who we are is partly decided by what we do 'for a living'.

On useful knowledge

The 'philosophical', 'social' and 'technical' aspects of media are not generally taught by departments of philosophy, social studies and technology respectively. Nor are the three corresponding aspects of selfhood – individual, social and human – divided up into subject areas for specialist teaching. Instead, it is within TV studies as such that different kinds of self, skill and utility are at stake:

1   It is widely held to be 'useful' to learn the specialized technical or professional skills (producer, programmer, performer, etc.) that will make someone employable in a given industry. These are *personal* skills, in the sense that individual people either can hold a camera steady (or a company together or an audience in the palm of their hand) or they can't; but they're *impersonal* skills in the sense that knowing how-to techniques tells the knower little about him or herself.

2   It is 'usefulness' of a different kind to study the impact of TV on the audience, and more generally of the media on contemporary society. Knowing how to do large-scale sampling, quantitative and qualitative research methods, interpretation of data, and how to understand demographic variables; these skills are 'useful' in vocational terms, whether directly in research, marketing or polling agencies, or indirectly in managerial positions somewhere in the media, their regulators or in corporate communication more generally. But such skills have a more diffused utility which exceeds their technical/vocational applicability. Being able to 'read' populations in terms of their cultural choices, sense-making habits, and knowing something about the attitudes, opinions, beliefs and preferences of people in different categories, will inevitably tell you more than you need to know in order to do a specific job; it will tell you something about society, and hence about yourself as a member of and in relation to that society. Such leakage of self-reflexivity into technical knowledge is not always counted 'useful', however; in traditional social sciences the selfhood of the student or researcher is rigorously excluded, along with other statistical distortions.

3   The philosophical branch of TV studies is interested not in how to make TV, nor in how to measure its impact on audiences understood as 'others' (consumers who buy, citizens who vote), but in TV as evidence of how 'we' – as a species – make culture, knowledge, sense, and how we relate to

each other. There are few jobs in such a line of study, but (inversely) the resulting knowledge is 'useful' to an understanding of ourselves as human beings. It's the kind of knowledge more commonly associated with philosophy than with media studies, which is perhaps why media studies attracts bemused and often hostile attention in parliament and the press: a subject that at first sight seems to belong to the category of technical, 'craft' utility, turns out to be about as 'useful' as philosophy; indeed, despised and denigrated though it frequently is, media studies may even *be* the philosophy of the information age. I certainly think it is.

On the person – 'per sona'

We are in an era when higher education is increasingly required to demonstrate its utility in vocational and technical rather than social or philosophical terms. In media studies the three different kinds of usefulness are inevitably mixed up, because to understand the media adequately does require attention to all three levels of technical, social and philosophical knowledge. It is in the broadcast, electronic, popular, 'mass' media, and here television is still the number one medium in terms of its popular global acceptance, that we can begin to trace the most general and fundamental questions about: how our species makes sense of (a) the world, (b) other people and (c) the self; how humanity uses images and language, stories and sights, genres and forms, discourses and texts. Language, image, communication and sense-making do not take place in an abstract, individualized context, but in a social environment which is subject to historical change. TV studies can help in the effort to understand how the human species makes sense in conditions of (post)modernity, which include:

1 **capitalization** of entertainment and leisure, and extensive division of labour in text-making of all types;
2 **internationalization** of trade in information, communications and entertainment;
3 **privatization** (domestication and feminization) of the public sphere, and suburbanization of both family and civic life;
4 **virtualization** of power – the conversion of governmental power from direct to 'virtual', from armies to information, control of land to control of airwaves.

These and other very large-scale *historical, political, social* and *semiotic* developments are the reason why TV is important as an object of study, even though they are hardly likely to impress a corporate recruiting officer. Indeed, what makes television an especially complex and satisfying object of study is that it is possible to think through large-scale issues while taking due account of the detailed technical processes and social organization of the popular media. And to square the circle of justifications, it has to be said that the converse also applies; the most successful

13

and universally popular entertainment, from *Star Trek* to *Mr Bean*, always looks for 'universal' social and philosophical themes in the midst of technical details. At the bridge of the USS *Enterprise* or at the wheel of a lime-green Mini, we glimpse the 'human condition'. While corporate recruiting officers may be looking for people who can speak and spell well, and who display corporately useful personal characteristics like ambition, leadership or computer literacy, the truth is that without some understanding of larger issues, the philosophical and social dimensions of the media, no one can do creative work successfully. Hence, in media like television, where creativity, artistry and an original imagination are all at a premium, the ability to observe and understand society and humanity, and to enact or envision some of their peculiarities, whether as comedy, drama, documentary or sport, are at the very heart of the enterprise.

And so 'the self' turns out to be very much at stake in every aspect of television and television studies. At this point it's worth recalling that such a situation is older than modernity itself. In medieval cosmology, itself borrowing from ancient classical knowledge systems, whence we get our very world for the 'self' — the word *person* — these issues have left their monument. The word *person* comes from the Latin *persona*. It was one of a pair of terms, the other being *anima*. They correspond to the medieval conception of a separation between body and soul, the true spirit and life of an individual being associated with the *anima*, with the *persona* as a mere corporeal covering. In medieval terms, then, the soul might be glimpsed as through a theatrical mask, and the person may be understood as such a mask through which the soul speaks to the world. The salient features of a theatrical mask are, first, that it differs from the 'self' that it hides, and second that in order to perform a character, the actor has to make their words 'sound through' it. The Latin for 'sound through' is *per sona*.

2

WHAT ARE THE USES OF TELEVISION STUDIES?

A modern archaeology

Video, ergo sum.

(Faux Réné Descartes)

WHAT ARE THE USES OF TELEVISION (STUDIES)?

Richard Hoggart asked a 'useful' question; in a country where mass education had produced a literate population, what exactly did the large majority *do* with their literacy; what was it for? His question was a challenging one, for he was interested not in the *professional* or *technical* but in the *cultural* uses of literacy; the social and philosophical issues arising from the impact of printing in modernity, especially among the popular classes. Hoggart's move was original, and it has become the hallmark of cultural studies ever since. He shifted analytical attention from the production (political/economic) to the consumption (social/cultural) side of modern society. Instead of inquiring about the uses of literacy as a productive force, he was interested in how people used it as consumers. Classic sociological inquiry would have traced the division between mental and manual labour (workers by brain and workers by hand); the productive force of literacy would have been understood to be concentrated among workers by brain (from white-collar employees to 'knowledge-class' professionals), or in those aspects of manual labour which required literacy. Hoggart's rather perverse innovation was to focus on those people and on those parts of people's lives where literacy was neither required nor expected: he ignored the 'uses of literacy' among the middle classes and in the workplace, and asked what was its cultural 'use' – as a communicative force unique to modern, industrialized, urban life – for people whose investment in it was 'human' rather than technical or functional. He did the working classes the honour of treating them in exactly the same way that critics have traditionally treated the aristocratic and leisured classes; 'culture' was not assumed to be 'what you do when you get home from work', but a central component of existence. What mass literacy lent to popular culture was a question that had never been asked until Hoggart; but at the heart of his question lies an interest not in vocational, technical, professional or productive issues as such

15

(Hoggart is not a modernizing technocrat), but in philosophical and 'human' issues with no immediately pragmatic, practical or utilitarian outcomes. Hence, cultural studies, from its founding text, has tended to focus on 'useless' knowledge (from this workaday perspective) even where it is most interested in the lives and pursuits of working people.

Since Hoggart's day a substantial proportion of those working people have followed him; they've shifted out of the world of the family kitchen into the not-so-lofty halls of higher education; not only to better their chances of being employed in an increasingly knowledge-based economy, but also to get some sort of grip on the world and people around them, and their own place within that world. While the media perform the function of popular philosophers for audiences and readers around the world, those who use the resources of institutions of formal learning to understand the media are, in consequence, performing some of the role previously reserved for philosophers as such.

Hoggart's work connects with important debates of its time; debates about the democratization of culture. *The Uses of Literacy* remains a valuable book – a major word-hoard in the archaeology of knowledge – not only for the reason most frequently advanced, that it is one of the two or three founding texts of cultural studies as we have come to know it, but equally for the opposite reason, namely that it marks one point of culmination in a long-standing series of developments that are by now rather opaque, forgotten, deleted. J.B. Priestley, the BBC Light Programme, *Picture Post*, suburbia, ordinariness, non-aligned middle-ground politics, social democracy, G.B. Shaw . . . these markers (and they're my list, not Hoggart's) of the semio-history of ordinariness have been somewhat lost, or clouded at least, in the adversarial Left–Right politics of politicized academic study in the 1970s and 1980s; in the invention of cultural studies as a theorized form of identity politics; in the methodological disputes between so-called realists and so-called textualists, social sciences and humanities, modernists and postmodernists, rationalists and romantics. Cultural studies in the 1990s has begun to forget its commitment to ordinariness as a positive civic goal. Hoggart is one route back to that 'usefulness'; TV studies is useful as a systematic inquiry into the personal, ordinary sense-making practices of a modern democratizing society. It links textmakers and readers, high and popular culture, in a way that Hoggart himself couldn't have predicted even as he embodied it. He worried about the 'striking and ominous' feature of the time being 'the division between the technical languages of the experts and the extraordinarily low level of the organs of mass communication' (1958: ix). He thought, like other professionalized knowledge-class writers, that the way to 'bridge' the gap would be to have 'laymen' cross over to the 'expert' side. In fact the movement has not been all one-way, and the popularization (populism) of the knowledge professions has not been disastrous. The 'usefulness' of TV studies is that by means of its very specific history, television can let us meditate on the processes involved in the 'expansion of difference' in contemporary culture.

ON A COMPLEX OBJECT OF STUDY

Television is far too big as a textual system, far too complex in all its facets of production, programming and reception, far too varied across time and place, to be studied as a single entity. It is too chaotic an object of study to be described detail by detail. As a result, many books that introduce the general study of television tend to abandon any attempt to describe a coherent entity or phenomenon. Instead they offer:

- **Interdisciplinary analysis**. Contributing disciplines have been located in the humanities (literary, textual, semiotic, cultural, historical and visual-arts based approaches) and social sciences (sociological, political-economy, psychological, anthropological approaches). It is highly desirable that individual studies should be aware of the inter-disciplinarity of the field, and curious about or at least tolerant of alternative approaches. However, it is difficult for any one analysis to attend to all the disciplinary archives, methodological preferences and current hot topics that might illuminate their project. So it is not uncommon to read reviews of books published in one disciplinary tradition that are criticized for not giving sufficient priority to another one, rather than being assessed for what their specialist contribution may be.

- **Intellectually distinct problems**. Television is studied in relation to such issues as power, social change, aesthetics, meaning, economics, marketing, identity, technology. None of these is necessarily or causally related to any of the others. While it is useful to understand how TV might work in relation to technological developments, or power, or aesthetics, it is unwise to assume that one such issue has anything at all to say about the others. Indeed, a long-standing problem of television *studies* is the influence of 'economic-power' arguments *over* others, so that the textual form of TV, and the audience response to it, are both said to be determined by its economic mode of production; its textual impact equated with its social impact, and its social impact equated with power or domination of one group by another. In fact, the question of television's 'textual power' is of a different order from questions of its social power. Whether, and indeed *how*, social power can be observed at work in texts, and textual power understood, is a continuing problem for the field; it is unwise to assume as self-evident that economic or social 'power' can be transmitted directly through texts to the brains of unsuspecting audiences. So much so, that if you trace the problem back the other way, as I do hereafter, you may have to rethink that whole idea of social and economic power.

- **Incommensurate phenomena**. What is chosen for study is loosely connected only by the analysis; there's no 'essential' aspect of television that all studies must attend to. Some concentrate on production, some on programmes, some on audiences. But audiences cannot be explained by analysing production;

programmes cannot be explained by investigating audiences; production cannot be understood by looking at programmes. If I were to write a book, as indeed I have, claiming to explain a great textual system such as journalism by reference to its textuality, I would be taken to task, as indeed I have been, by those for whom journalism is best explained by reference to the intentions and actions of the textmakers, or the opinions and attitudes of the readers. Nevertheless, the present object of study – 'television' – is not so easily claimed by any such faction, including my own; it is desirable to understand how all the bits and pieces fit together, or how they don't, but unwise to place proprietorial fingers on other people's bits. . . .

The object of study is colossal, chaotic, complex. There seems to be no such 'thing' as 'Television', whose natural properties can be described by scientific methods, or whose activities can be explained by causal sequence. TV is irreducible to science. As a result, for those who wish to introduce the formal study of television into the 'discipline' of formal learning, the best that we can hope for is not the academic discipline of 'Television', but the more modest 'television studies'.

Television studies has been characterized not only by the fragmentation or dispersal of the object of study, but also by the specialization of modes of analysis, and by an inability of people working in the field to understand what the others are doing. There's no unity in the *study*, any more than there is in *television*, since analysts speak different disciplinary languages, use different methods, in pursuit of different questions about different bits of the overall phenomenon. So while claims made are often general, actual studies get more specialist; 'television' is usually described by drawing attention to one of the separate 'moments' of production, text, audience and history; looking at the institutionalization, discourse, political economy and social impact of the industries, technologies and practices involved. It is symptomatic of a field with such a fragmented but pervasive object of study that it should display a tendency for claims to be made from time to time, by those working in one corner on one fragment, to understand the whole thing. So political economists, policy-analysts, behavioural psychologists and also (I must admit) textualists have occasionally asserted a general theory of television based on their peculiar insights. TV is, it seems, fully explained by looking at this or that component (as if you can explain the space-shuttle by looking at the O-ring in its fuel-line), making spectacular claims about a mundane field.

TELEVISION AS CULTURAL POLICY . . . ?

However, it is possible to adopt an analytical framework that recognizes the complexity, diversity and even incoherence of the object of study while remaining itself a very simple device. This tactic too has been deployed many times, especially by those writers who would argue that a case can be mounted against television for one or more crimes against the contemporary world. The indictment-list is long: TV has stood accused of various ideological atrocities (Ray, 1995: 7) against cultural standards, sexual decency, respectable language, behavioural propriety; or from another perspective it is accused of abuses in the struggle for political freedom, social change, economic equality. It is investigated for promoting pathological conditions in individuals and societies, from stupidity to consumerism. It has been denounced for maltreatment of various vulnerable, victimized or innocent parties defined by an aspect of their identity, be it gender, class, age, sexuality, family-type, regional identity, nationality, ethnicity or language-group. It's bad for boys and girls, workers and elites, blacks and whites, gays and straights, radicals and conservatives.

The tactic is not unlike that used in old movie thrillers. Some incoherent, good-for-nothing wastrel whose life is in a mess and whose actions are not easily explained even to him- or herself is pushed into a hard chair down at the local police headquarters and given the classic third-degree questioning. Under the unblinking eye of a hostile interrogator, in the harsh light of the academic equivalent of the police cell, the suspect is roughed up a little – nothing that leaves too serious a scar, mind – in order to elicit answers about its supposed crimes. The tactic of interrogation using a single line of questioning certainly produces startling results, and occasionally even a confession. TV executives and programme-makers are among the first people to worry (parentally) about the 'effect' of TV violence, for instance, or (liberally) the representation of minority-groups on screen, or (conservatively) the need to protect family values.

The result of single-line questioning can be revealing – we find something out we hadn't previously suspected or understood. But equally it can be quite unjust – the academic equivalent of 'verballing' – 'fitting up' television to make it appear guilty of some predetermined offence, and reducing its identity to a version of the interrogator's obsessions and nightmares. Unfortunately, it's often hard to untangle the revelation from the nightmare, the 'verballing' from the 'true confession'. Television's ideological atrocities may be real or imagined, but imagining them is itself real, so whether or not TV makes adolescent boys act aggressively, for instance, the belief that it does is a powerful 'fact' both of analysis and in the organization of the industry – it is a belief/fact that has an effect on what shows are made, what is done in them, when they are shown, and what people think about them.

The analytical desire to cut through the crap of complexity to the simple pleasure of forcing reality to conform to an already-held theory about it (as in: 'Confess! [Thwack!] You're the one whodunit! [Ker-pow!]') has an academic history as well a B-movie and comic form. When cultural studies was itself in process of formation, from the 1950s through to the 1970s, some of the most influential work was done by analysts who used a single framework of explanation to slice through surface illusion ('Swoosh!') to the gritty reality within ('Thunk!'). In those days the undisputed theoretical superhero was *class*; from this was derived perhaps the most important founding 'simple' question of cultural studies: 'What about the workers?' Culture, media, sense-making, style, aesthetics, genre, literacy and the relations between textmakers in any medium and their audiences; all were interrogated according to questions of *class*, and class was understood as antagonistic, i.e. from a Marxist rather than from a functionalist or hierarchical perspective. Later the questions were converted to *gender*, though the presumption of structural antagonism remained. Later again: *ethnicity*, understood as binary antagonism as between 'white' and 'black', no matter that ethnic variety is not easily reduced to 'two' 'colours', other than for the purpose of preserving structural opposition. Next: *sexual* orientation, led by gay and lesbian activists, for whom the class model worked only to make a sense of structural oppression legible, since sexual orientation is not socially distributed along class lines. Meanwhile, *national* (e.g. first peoples) and *language* (e.g. Welsh-language) minorities stood in line, not patiently, tapping their persuaders, taking adversarial rhetorics and 'class'-type politics from the class model, even though the explanatory efficacy of 'class' in relation to nations and speech communities is necessarily reduced to something approaching zero, since such communities *encompass* classes, however they're construed, and however antagonistic they may be. But by now the framework was set; there was infinite potential for any 'identity' to queue up and ask 'What about us?' And queue up they did.

At this point, it became clear that the 'simple' question based on revealing class struggle within any semiotic or social system was no longer simple. There was the 'problem of the ampersand' in media and cultural studies: analysis was getting to be more complex than the complex field whose crap it was supposed to cut. Instead of careful descriptions of working-class culture there was 'the ampersand': analysis of (insert object of study here – film, TV series, cultural form) according to questions of class & gender & ethnicity & sexual orientation & nationality & language-community & age & size & disability & & &. As a rather jaundiced critic has recently pointed out, this way madness lies:

> Though Cultural Studies was seemingly expanding to fill out the world with its nuances and representations, there's an inherent problem in this non-conflictual drive towards universality. Lewis Carroll once jokingly hypothesised about a country that, in a fit of one-upmanship, commissioned a map so detailed that it was to be drawn on a scale of 1:1. Of course, it could never be unfolded without plunging the entire nation into darkness. The more representation approaches the complexity of reality, the more redundant it becomes. You might as well listen to the real thing.
>
> (Matt ffytche writing in *The Modern Review*, No. 2, November 1997: 67–8)

There's certainly a problem here, though its consequences are not so inevitably disabling as the Modern Reviewer suggests: 'In the process of turning away from the certainties of *en bloc* narratives such as Marxism and feminism, academics have lost the possibility of having any effective standpoint from which to criticise society . . . the political wishes of researchers have become the "love that dare not speak its name"' (ffytche, 1997: 68).

The recognition of complexity in the object of study, and the abandonment of claims to general explanation, does not necessarily lead to a mad search for 1:1 proportional representation, or to unspeakable socio-political desires (though Matt ffytche does have a point). Most importantly, the recognition of hybridity, and modesty about explanatory schemes, mean that academic research has withdrawn somewhat from front-line ideology; it has a different attitude towards its readers, and in fact addresses and attracts different readers. It no longer speaks to, for and about the *general population*, but tends to speak to more specialized audiences of fellow-professionals in government and business. During the 1980s media and cultural researchers began to retreat from simple cultural theories addressed to non-specialist students whose consciousness they wished to recruit to radical Leftism, and began instead to abandon the field to the 'policy-wallahs'. There was a tendency to begin to favour 'administrative' over theoretical research. TV studies has shared this history of abandoning grand claims – scientificity, 'grand' theory, general claims on whole populations or readerships – and turning to policy, the mundane, the banal.

This analytic modesty, promoted most militantly by Ian Hunter, Tony Bennett (see for instance Hunter, 1988; Bennett, 1992) and their circle of influence in the Centre for Cultural and Media Policy in Brisbane, may be appropriate in the context of the abandonment of claims. And it is doubtless 'useful' in quite straightforward ways to make cultural theory, media studies and textual research answer questions posed by producers, regulators and (but rarely) audiences, especially when confidence is shaken about the sanity of the preferred theoretical discourse and the speakability of the analyst's own preferences. Easier by far to get on first-name terms with practical people who know what they want. Furthermore, there was a sophisticated *theoretical* justification for this turn to policy, allowing those who were good at it the delicious pleasure of demolishing the pretensions of 'grand theory' *with* grand theory. This is in fact a move that can be counted as foundational in cultural studies, since it is exactly what Raymond Williams did with the 'elitist' tradition of literary criticism in his book *Culture and Society* (1958) – arguing the minoritarian culturalists to a standstill on their own turf. In the present case the work of Michel Foucault, in particular the concept of 'governmentality' derived from his later writings, was used by the proponents of 'cultural policy studies' to show how culture, discourse and even criticism itself were instruments of knowledge-power whose operation served the purposes of population management. For the policy-wallahs, cultural studies was a governmental discourse, and critical intellectuals were deluding themselves if they thought they could stand outside of the processes, power-relations and mundane 'policies' of population management they criticized in others. There is of course much to think about in these issues, and, although 'cultural policy studies' remained strongly identified with Tony Bennett and therefore with an Australian-based debate, the intervention was of general significance to cultural studies, posing a general challenge to the heroic but unworldly adversarialism of cultural criticism of both Right and Left up to that time.

The turn to 'policy' was in its sometimes rather hectoring way a turn back to the interest in ordinary life, usefulness and a public beyond the academy after a decade or so during which cultural studies had worked through successive encounters with ever more abstract theorizing, mostly with a French accent, from semiotics and structuralism, through psychoanalysis, Althusserianism, deconstruction and Gramscian cultural Marxism, to postmodernism and beyond. While the founders of cultural studies in the 1950s were preocupied with trying to 'translate' ordinary experience into the language of the academy, so as to make it the subject of serious intellectual work and hence a proper object for public policy, the cultural studies of the 1970s was preoccupied with translations of a very mixed group of Francophone intellectuals and philosophers, so as to produce a theoretical *lingua franca* by means of which cultural studies itself could be recognized, communicated and taught: from Lévi-Strauss, Barthes and Althusser, via Lacan, Irigaray and Kristeva, to Derrida, Deleuze and Guattari, and on to Foucault, Baudrillard and Lyotard.

But the 'policy-wallahs' had also read all this stuff; their turn to policy was an outcome of theoretical work, and perhaps evidence of a desire to move from the writerly rhetoric of 'French' theory to a more 'German' version of social theory (not to the idealism of Hegel, or the sociologism of Durkheim and Weber, but to cultural questions derived from philosophical writings, from Herder and Kant to Nietzsche, Heidegger and Wittgenstein). But in any case, not for 'cultural policy studies' the naïve pragmatism of the 'English' founders of cultural studies, especially Richard Hoggart − despite his own lifelong involvement in policy questions, Hoggart was neglected if not actively criticized for his atheoretical empiricism and literary residualism.

Indeed, the most militant of the policy-wallahs, including Tony Bennett himself, Stuart Cunningham and others, were led to make on behalf of 'governmentality' the very same general claims they criticized in others; 'cultural policy studies' was promoted in the late 1980s and 1990s not as an alternate or 'regional' approach within cultural studies, but as its definitive replacement. 'Useful' work could and should be done in relation to television by investigating its own 'policy' issues − from regulation (and deregulation) of both the industry and the content of television, to audience surveys, the impact of technological changes, and questions of international trade.

. . . OR TELEVISION *AS* CULTURE AND *AS* POLITICS?

However, and this is where I think the turn to policy was not an advance for utility and ordinariness over self-important 'high' theory, despite the importance of understanding and following developments in the regulatory, industrial, technological and commercial forms of television, it is precisely these forms that have always been uncontroversially open to study – turning back to such issues was nothing new, and left the ideological positioning of television within public discourse unchallenged. Where television had been and still is a 'recalcitrant' object of study is in the two areas where cultural studies has most at stake: culture and politics.

TV has never won acceptance in intellectual or public culture *as* culture, and nor has it been accepted *as* politics. This is not to say that its impact on culture and its political force have not endlessly been discussed; on the contrary, I'm suggesting that the interminable stream of fearful, critical and promotional commentary on television's effect on culture and politics is evidence of how these spheres are still understood to be 'elsewhere', as it were, with television ever the interloper or *arriviste*, spoiling culture, corrupting politics, sensationalizing the public sphere and commercializing the cultural sphere. A turn to questions of technlogy, industry, regulation and survey in this context is, perhaps, a return to the very rhetoric that has for decades hindered a complete understanding of television. Because of its large-scale capital investment, its massive social reach, its popular address to an essentially unknowable audience, and its ever-imminent renewal or replacement by newer technologies, television is all too easily confined to questions of population management (precisely, of 'governmentality'). It can readily be reduced to questions of commodity management too, where the provision of technology, commercial products and 'content' is thought of essentially as an attempt to bring supply into optimum alignment with demand (with government regulation to monitor the marketplace).

But none of this encourages public understanding of television from the point of view of the audiences themselves, for whom television needs to be seen *as* culture and *as* politics. Perhaps it is not insignificant that 'culture' and 'politics' (along with war) are traditionally the pursuits of the aristocratic and ruling classes; and despite the manifold democratizations of the nineteenth and twentieth centuries, the consequences have still not been fully assimilated into critical, intellectual and 'governmental' discourses. Television is still in need of its 'grand theory', especially in the public (mediated) domain, where a mixture of commercial promotion, 'public service' critique and 'literary' disdain teaches the public very little indeed about what television has been, is, and could be for, and about their own relationship to that. Television has successfully been used to teach the public about the culture and politics of past elites, with very informative shows about kings and cathedrals, but it gets very little encouragement to analyze its own cultural and political place in the contemporary world, nor that of its own audiences. It tries as hard as it can to pretend that, as a cultural form and political force in its own right, it isn't there. Audiences can be supposed to be swayed by commercial messages and by technological-behavioural influences, but not by culture and politics as such.

But television is not simply a resource supplied commercially to a market. As the early critics of cultural studies, especially Richard Hoggart, understood in their unsystematic, pragmatic, 'English' way, it is culture and politics, not just technology and commerce. TV needs to be imagined in this large-scale, general way, and its importance 'as' culture and politics needs to be established, or at least asserted, before a return to more mundane issues can be properly situated and understood. And the articulation of culture with politics is still the definitive opening gambit, the enabling move, of cultural studies. For instance, here's George Lipsitz:

> Politics and culture maintain a paradoxical relationship in which only effective political action can win breathing room for a new culture, but only a revolution in culture can make people capable of political action. . . . Culture exists as a form of politics, as a means of reshaping individual and collective practice for specified interests, and as long as individuals perceive their interests as unfilled, culture retains an oppositional potential.
>
> (Lipsitz, 1990: 16)

This is the rhetoric of modernist intervention — 'revolution', 'action', 'interests' and 'opposition'. Such rhetoric has most frequently been applied to television — it is held to be among the things that need 'reshaping', one of the 'interests' that prevents 'effective political action'. However, if, as a cultural practice among its audiences, television itself is a 'culture that exists as a form of politics', then perhaps some of the rhetoric and the assumptions about politics, interests and action need rethinking. Can television be understood as culture articulated with politics without immediately reaching for the revolver of revolution, the modernist gesture of adversarial opposition? In fact Lipsitz and others, notably in this context the African American scholar of television Herman Gray in his book *Watching Race: Television and the Struggle for 'Blackness'* (1995), are arguing for precisely this move:

> At their best, [representations of African American culture on television] fully engage all aspects of African American life and, in the process, move cultural struggles within television and media beyond limited and narrow questions of positive/negative images, role models, and simple reversals to the politics of representation.
>
> (Gray, 1995: 92)

Gray calls for a 'politics of representation' that engages with television on the one side and a specific cultural identity on the other (and he professes himself hopeful about the prospects too — see Gray, 1995: 175–6). But to get to this point he has had to rely on a conceptualization of television that derives not from 'policy' but from arguing through what television as culture and as politics (in general) might mean for a specific community. Only then can the question of *which way to turn* in the 'turn to policy' be answered. So it may transpire that the abandonment of general claims is premature. It may be that television needs to be subject not only to ever-more finely dissected administrative research, but also to an ambitious attempt to set it within general historical contexts, conditions and changes. It needs not to be seen in *categorical* terms as, for instance, an instrument of capitalist exploitative expansionism, class struggle, gender supremacism, colonial oppression, ideological hegemony, psycho-sexual repression, nationalist power, cultural control, always doing something to someone, always negatively, and usually in a combination of two or more of the above, but in *historical* and 'evolutionary' terms – how TV can be understood as a product, a part and a promoter of historical changes of very long duration in the previously strictly reserved areas of culture and politics.

Meanwhile, the habits, changes and histories of analytical, theoretical and critical discourses about television, media and culture need to be seen increasingly as part of the historical milieu which needs explaining, rather than as some safe haven of scientific truth for academics to use as that mythical 'effective standpoint from which to criticize society'. The Marxist moment, grand theory, and conversations with feminism, queer theory, post-colonial critique or postmodernism, the 'third-degree' interrogation of television are themselves symptoms of knowledge-production – a part of the socio-textual landscape that needs explaining. And so is 'policy' analysis, the self-presentation of the analyst and the attempt to be 'useful'.

CAVEAT LECTOR

Once these problems have been set out, the way to moving on has already shown itself. While it is not possible to imagine 'television' as a singular object of study, and not wise to reduce it to a single characteristic, it is possible to take a simple analytical approach by changing the question to one that is fundamentally historical. Not: WHAT IS TELEVISION? But: WHAT IS TELEVISION FOR? WHAT ARE THE USES OF TELEVISION? This is the 'research question' of this book.

Of course, it's not innocent; it is already an allusion or homage to – or plagiarism of – Richard Hoggart's most celebrated publication. Approaching the media of popular entertainment as a Left-Leavisite, Hoggart wanted to apply to them the language of literary appreciation, but was also critical of them for not often enough bringing their readers and audiences 'the best that has been thought or said', as Matthew Arnold's term was then understood. So to the question 'what are the *uses* of literacy?' Hoggart made two answers simultaneously – he was able to show that popular literacy *had* uses, which were as he pointed out rooted in the culture of the people whose lives were under investigation, not under the control of those who taught them the literacy; and at the same time he was able to maintain a critical, independent eye on the media products themselves, to see what their 'use' was from that perspective. In the internal tension of his book, the dialogue between the 'cultural' use and the 'critical' use, both understood to have political consequences, lies the origin of cultural studies.

Cultural studies is my own 'disciplinary' training, and the dialogue between 'cultural' and 'critical' uses of television will be the 'conversation' that ensues in this book. From this perspective, I have an answer to the question, WHAT ARE THE USES OF TELEVISION? Mind you, I warn you in advance that the answer won't make all that much sense until you've let me explain it, which will of course take up the remainder of the book. But nevertheless, so you know where I'm coming from, here's my answer: I am going to suggest that the uses of television are best understood by means of the concept of TRANSMODERN TEACHING. And that what television has been used for is the formation of CULTURAL CITIZENSHIP.

3

TV STUDIES AS CROSS-DEMOGRAPHIC COMMUNICATION

I have committed (though in an incompetent way) most of the faults
I am describing in others.

(Richard Hoggart, 1970: 169)

Richard Hoggart's 'literary analysis' of the organs of mass communication was to some extent out of his own control. As originally conceived, it was a standard Left-Leavisite attack on the 'regrettable' influence of the entertainment media over the reading habits and culture of the popular classes. Its intended title was ***Ab**-uses of Literacy* (it was saved from this dreadful fate by Chatto's libel lawyers). As originally conceived, it had no 'front half' – it was a 'reading' of popular print media for the instruction of teachers in adult education without the opening chapters on working-class community. Hoggart allowed what he knew personally to wash through this otherwise 'academic' project and, by letting go of its 'schoolmasterly' aspect, turned it into great teaching. By situating popular literacy in the sympathetically imagined context of his own upbringing, where he placed his own critical self-formation, Hoggart produced not instruction but something more like an anthropology of the everyday, a semio-history of ordinariness. His serious but accessible purpose was directed at the 'lay reader' – the very figure at the heart of the analysis. His critical but mild-mannered conclusions were not directed *against* popular culture, but towards engaging with it in a practical way; towards understanding it from within, in common with the population whose culture it was, so as to effect changes that everyone would agree were for the better, rather than for the benefit of the better off. This was academic analysis at its best; not an abandonment of critical training and specialist perspectives, but a fusion of institutional and personal understandings in a project that *taught* a generation of readers how to occupy with tolerant but 'positioned' analysis the sometimes uncomfortable interfaces between formal and informal learning, communal and mediated cultures, personal and impersonal knowledge, public and private life.

In recent years Richard Hoggart has been 'kicked upstairs' in critical writing even within the academic discipline of cultural studies that he helped to found. His name is invoked with respect, but his work isn't read all that much, and in

27

any case his reputation rests not on people's reading of it, but on academic lore; what has come to be accepted as his position by constant repetition in the textbooks. This is a pity, for even where his judgements are arguable, his project is still important. His Leavisite literary-critical training was by no means above criticism, and its legacy is criticized in this book. His elegiac description of working-class community has been, and you can see why, criticized as nostalgic, authenticist, humanist (among those for whom this is a boo-word) and atheoretical. His public service work, on government inquiries like Pilkington (a policy report on broadcasting), for NGOs like UNESCO, or in 'consultancy' work (in the High Court for Penguin Books), or managerial responsibility (as warden of Goldsmiths College) is less well remembered, even though the Tony Bennett branch of cultural studies has made the policy-wallah a familiar figure once again, at least in Australia. In any case, such worthy work has itself attracted criticism as merely reformist, in a period (especially the late 1960s and 1970s) when activists in academia were looking for 'structural change' rather than ad hoc 'papering over the cracks'. So trying to put Left activism into governmental or managerial action doesn't always go down well with the comrades.

But it isn't Hoggart's literary sensibility as such, nor his view of working-class culture as such, nor his practical, governmental and institutional work as such, that make him an important figure. Beyond his opinions, his allegiances and even his work, and beyond also those of his critics, is something that I have been trying to identify in this book as more important; namely teaching. Hoggart's teaching is not designed to inculcate this opinion or that policy, but to teach how to see, how 'I' see, how others see. He is reaching for access to the inner life of populations. To grasp a true sense of that yields answers to 'big' questions, including: 'Will they revolt?'; 'Will they be able to think as we do?'; 'What will they buy?'. These questions were of equal moment to those who wanted 'them' to revolt/think/buy, and those who feared revolutionary or indeed any change. But instead of addressing the fears, hopes and vested interests of onlookers, Hoggart's project was to teach his readers how to see 'them' (contemporary populations) as 'we' (fellow-readers); how to make seeing into knowledge; how to 'know' how others see. He made the relation between analyst and analysed convivial not conflictual. He addressed the common reader as a 'we' identity. For him the analysis of 'media and society' is not abstract sociological knowledge got by some formal(ist) method; it is an analysis of the relations between writer, reader and the culture both inhabit – striving to make that world inhabitable for both. Where in an earlier chapter I posited a three-way relation between television, television studies and readerships, here I am doing no more than applying Hoggart's model of a homologous relation between culture, writer and reader:

28

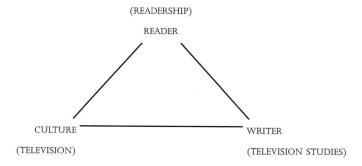

(READERSHIP)

READER

CULTURE

WRITER

(TELEVISION)

(TELEVISION STUDIES)

Hoggart lays out his method – to offer a personal setting followed by 'literary' analysis – in *Uses of Literacy*, he identifies his reader is 'the serious "common reader" or "intelligent layman" from any class'. He writes: 'The "intelligent layman" is an elusive figure, and popularization a dangerous undertaking: but it seems to me that those of us who feel that writing for him is an urgent necessity must go on trying to reach him' (Hoggart, 1958: ix).

TV STUDIES GOES TO UNIVERSITY

When looking back over the history of TV studies, it is the teachers rather than the more theoretical show-ponies who stand out for me. Figures like Terence Hawkes (who did for me personally what I am here making Hoggart do 'theoretically'), a teacher in the Hoggartian mould himself, John Fiske, a major recruiter of new students to cultural and media studies through his teaching, Horace Newcomb, Graeme Turner, and in the next generation Tara Brabazon, Catharine Lumby, Alan McKee, McKenzie Wark, thinkers who 'love to influence others' and who are thereby teachers 'in the best sense' (Hoggart, 1970: 55; see also his essay on his own mentor, 1970: 189–204).

This might also be the point – long overdue – where I acknowledge that television has attracted large numbers of writers whose wonderful teaching quality shows in their specialized research and scholarship: Robert C. Allen, William Boddy, Charlotte Brundson, Julie D'Acci, Peter Dahlgren, Herman Gray, Henry Jenkins, Noel King, Karal Ann Marling, Andy Medhurst, Patricia Mellencamp, Eric Michaels, Toby Miller, Meaghan Morris, Tom O'Regan, Ellen Seiter, Krishna Sen, Roger Silverstone, Lynn Spigel, John Tulloch, William Uricchio; all these and many more (see the references section) show that of course there is such a thing as TV studies, and that it boasts scholars, theorists, essayists, researchers and students of the highest calibre.

Indeed, now that television is getting old, and some of the fizz and pop of public controversy has subsided as moral entrepreneurs and techno-prophets move on to new technologies, new targets, it is becoming a calmer region for research in perhaps the way that cinema did once its own 'massness' had ebbed a little after the 1940s. In this context, the time is ripe for TV studies *as opposed to* media, film cultural, communication (etc.) studies; i.e. as a coherent field in its own right. It's my hunch that as the 'mass' audience subsides, it will be the influence of the (popular, unknowable) audience on television, not the influence of television on the (individual, vulnerable) audience, that will require explanation. Once popularity has gone, there will be style and design, history and archive, variety and comparison, cult and conversation; and of course the issues of production, text and audience will remain, as will 'anthropological' questions about the creation of meaning in everyday life. Certainly, there is plenty to be done now that TV itself is becoming 'historical', and plenty of international talent already doing it.

However, not despite but just because of this laudable development of TV studies into a professional academic subject area, the 'Hoggartian' project of 'popularization' for the purposes of teaching a 'lay' readership (the same people who are also 'the' TV audience, 'the' political public) is not easily taken up in the institutionalization of the subject. For obvious reasons the extension of the study of television ever-further into university education (where, one might wish to insist, its extension has been from the 'bottom' – from its earliest home in low-prestige polytechnics and colleges specializing in teaching rather than research, into older and more upscale universities later and sometimes rather grudgingly) requires ever-greater attention to the internal pedagogy of formal academia, and rather less time spent stalking the airwaves and opinion columns, journalistic criticism, the public committees and 'trade' books – the grandstand, if you like – of public culture. Indeed, there are those who caution intellectuals who work in universities against trying to achieve celebrity status beyond the academy, even if their motives are 'Hoggartian' – the training of critical literacy among the *general* public. Those who look 'out' to public stardom, not 'in' to their students, rightly attract a sceptical eye from their peers, as Joe Moran has pointed out:

> An academic star system can have a disabling effect on work undertaken within the academic field. Stuart Hall is one of many to suggest (1992: 290) that academics who see their work as part of an oppositional critique should concentrate, first and foremost, on an accessible and growing constituency – their students.
>
> (Moran, 1998: 76)

Point taken; but as Moran goes on to suggest, the realities of an academic career can actually militate against a proper concern with pedagogy. Academics who wish to make the most decisive and acclaimed contributions to the field may, these days, be the least likely to be *teaching* anyone:

> Pedagogy has long been a focal concern of cultural studies, one which can be traced back to its British origins in adult and workers' education. . . . This concern has been challenged, however, by an institutional apparatus

in which undergraduate teaching is seen as an irritating and unnecessary distraction from the real goal of publication and status, and the prize for being a star academic is to achieve remission from this distraction.

(Moran, 1998: 76)

Excellent though much published work in TV studies undoubtedly is, and 'useful' though that work may be for those who teach and learn within the academic context, there's still a gap between the 'knowledge professionals' and those – the general public of lay readers, TV audiences, ordinary citizens – about whom they know, even though many more of such people now attend universities and take courses in media studies as part of their general education.

'YIELDING PLACE TO NEW'

So what does Hoggart(ism) offer? He – it – offers **cross-demographic communication**; teaching people from 'they' communities how to operate successfully in institutions, from school to 'life', not of their own making. The trouble is, as Moran suggests above, this simple, desirable and valuable attribute has a very poor professional reputation nowadays. Teaching itself is at a low ebb socially; it's something you don't admit to being good at if you can claim some other talent, at least in higher education.

But even more importantly, perhaps, cross-demographic communication has itself suffered badly in the politics of identity, difference and subjectivity that has characterized cultural and media studies for two decades. There is a kind of default setting, saved to the operating programme when the cultural studies thinking-machine was first set up, that whenever cross-demographic communication is discovered, it needs to be assessed *critically* (meaning it has to be criticized), either as ideology or as populism:

1 If **Ideology**, then cross-demographic communication is seen as 'imperialism'; simply an attempt to take power over some actually or virtually colonized population.
2 If **Populism**, then it is seen as 'bad theory'; simply a failure to take into account the 'real' conditions of those involved, both communicator and the demographic group being addressed.

In each instance, cross-demographic communication is seen as subordinate to some other 'motor' of media processes. In the case of 'ideology', the motor or motivator is said to be *class*. Speak about 'communication' when the difference between the communicating parties is 'class', and you're in trouble. In the case of 'populism' the motor is *the economy*. Here it is not a case of communication, but of *capitalist* communication. Naturally, cross-demographic communication cannot take place outside the social structures in which people operate, including class and its transformations via 'the problem of the ampersand' to gender, ethnicity, etc., and it always occurs in historical circumstances that include specific modes of economic production. But nevertheless it does occur. TV studies can make a useful contribution to knowledge by investigating the way in which different populations with no necessary mutual affinity do produce and maintain knowledge about each other, communicate with each other, stay in touch. Naturally, since this is media communication on an industrial scale the communicative role taken by each party will not approximate the so-called 'dyad' (two-party) interaction of face-to-face speech. But it's quite a long step from that observation to the conclusion that audiences are subject to 'ideological abuse' by 'power-elites' who represent vested interests and repressive politics. Communication organized on a 'mass' scale and mediated through industrial-strength organizations is still communication. So what is it for?

What if cross-demographic communication is not 'populist ideology', but *teaching*? What if it is done by the likes of Rupert Murdoch as well as Richard Hoggart, and yet remains communication? Hoggart would doubtless part company with me here; he's not a fan of contemporary tabloid journalism. But it's horses for courses – I'm sure he'd allow Allen Lane, founder of Penguin Books, to be understood as a corporate 'teacher' by means of cross-demographic communication; why not the corporate 'teachers' of today? I don't ask him, or you, to love Rupert as you might an honoured teacher, but simply ask that the dismissive default setting be toggled off for a while, until there has been time to see whether cross-demographic communication can be recuperated as a positive rather than negative social activity, on the model of teaching, which itself needs to be recuperated in the same way.

In short, teaching is more important than correct theory, although the effort to theorize correctly is teaching; cross-demographic communication is more important than identity, although the effort to communicate respectfully and equitably is a recognition of identity and difference. Conversely, the intellectualist rhetoric of imperialism, ideology, populism and corporate conspiracy is much less explanatory of ordinary life, much less helpful in making ethical choices about possible action (both social and individual) than television is (the effort to make good television is however right up to speed on the pitfalls of populism, ideology and all that; in my observation producers can be as politically canny and intellectually literate as their academic critics, often more so). Indeed, it will come as no surprise to hear that I am proposing that the best model of cross-demographic communication currently to hand is television. It's not just a teacher but a good one; not just a teacher of ideology, false consciousness and bad habits but a 'teacher in the best sense'.

Richard Hoggart wrote of his favourite 'medium' – Literature – that 'if . . . music is the purest of the arts, then literature is the muddiest, up to its knees in the mud of life':

But, though there may be magic words and sacred words, no words are 'dirty' in themselves. A writer always wants to pick them up and make them fresh again, by the power of his love.

(Hoggart, 1970: 232)

If critical, educational and governmental rhetorics were more 'loving' in exactly this sense, if more ambition for popular media were inspired among both producers and audiences, then television, popular media, entertainment and even Rupert Murdoch would no longer be 'dirty words'. Certainly, writers for popular media (electronic, screen and print) are as keen as any literary author or educationalist to refresh the language. And if they're not, that's as much a failure of *teaching* as of their own imagination.

In his desire to teach what he calls *critical* literacy, Hoggart was keen not to be seen as nostalgic, self-indulgent or an apologist for commercial entertainment. He made sure he identified in working-class communities the less green patches of grass. In *Uses of Literacy* he pronounces: 'I shall be especially concerned with regrettable aspects of change' (p. 138), knowing that most readers − even those from working-class backgrounds such as himself − would know in advance and with certainty what is to be regretted. He shares with the 'common reader' their common sense of what constitutes opposing 'elements in the "mental climate"' (p. 138–9) of the period (Hoggart's preferred terms are on the left):

OLD	:	NEW
tolerance	:	freedom
group sense	:	democratic egalitarianism
need to live in the present	:	'progressivism'

Here, in my view, Hoggart fails his own project, and his readers. He wants to warn against what he sees as negative elements in popular culture, but associates these with the rhetoric of democratic modernity. The opposition is also:

English	:	American
industrial	:	suburban
lived	:	mediated

These oppositions are 'regrettable' for Hoggart, presumably because they weaken the common people's defences, causing changes he identifies as follows:

FROM	:	TO
tolerance	:	entertainers
scepticism/non-conformity	:	'tarnished ghosts of themselves'
''aving a good time while y'can'	:	soft mass hedonism

Hoggart wanted to protect 'freedom' from 'self-indulgence'; 'equality' from 'cynicism'; 'progress' from 'loss'. Fair enough, but the oppositions here take Hoggart perilously close to the rhetoric that I criticize in a later chapter; making *democracy* a *defeat*. Perhaps it is at this point that 'critical literacy' needs to do what it knows it must; 'yield place to the new'.

TV STUDIES AND THE READING PUBLIC

Engaging with 'the new' in conditions of what I've dubbed 'transmodern teaching' means doing more than using 'critical literacy' to 'read' TV as if it is literature. The 'triangular' relation between reader (audience), culture (television) and writer (television studies) is not the same as the traditional two-way relation between addresser and addressee in communications media. And because it is three-way, each perspective can be *triangulated*, that is, reality-checked from two other points. Instead of imagining the addresser/addressee relation as essentially two-way and thus open to undue influence (as in cult-brainwashing), a communication system which involves constant triangulation between three distinct positionalities can be investigated as a form of 'critical practice' in itself. Readers can constantly and independently 'check' TV against outside yardsticks. Now it is much more obviously a three-way 'conversation', with theory, reading and practice as facets of the same activity. Practice, in this context, means everything from full-scale involvement with popular media either as producer or critic, to the more interactive and participatory forms of literate consumption that are now available, from Dorling Kindersley 'action'-reading to computer software based on popular media shows, personalities and formats. For TV-literate people who are also theory-literate, the 'use' of television can easily be converted from reception to transmission; 'transmodern teaching' becoming a desire to influence others through TV.

Understanding TV now is not a technical, vocational or even philosophical undertaking, but a matter of integrated consciousness. Studying television is no longer a matter of being inoculated against its negative influences (for the brighter students) or being trained into technical orthodoxies (for the others). Knowledge-production in the context of the convergence between government, education and media (discussed in Chapter 1) means that critical consciousness for those who *produce* knowledge, the 'knowledge class', is a constant 'conversation' between different discursive domains that are no longer ideological adversaries, but merely generic choices in a repertoire of public teaching in which television may be a good choice for one purpose, a theory book a good choice for another.

This kind of integrated work is already being done by media scholars who are also media practitioners – I'm thinking of those like Catharine Lumby (1997) and McKenzie Wark (1994, 1997) in Australia (choose your own examples for your country). Both Wark and Lumby are columnists for leading Australian dailies, both are university lecturers, both are authors of scholarly articles on media topics, both have written books which have a scholarly 'provenance' but are released through 'trade' (as opposed to 'academic') marketing, such is their power to call into being a large 'popular' readership for a critical literacy explicitly based on cultural and media studies. Needless to say, both make regular appearances on TV, radio and the internet and, unsurprisingly though unilluminatingly, both get stick for populism and ideology from 'critical' colleagues.

Their work is 'cross-demographic' and pedagogic; but it is also dialogic and exploratory. It can perhaps be contrasted with a more authoritarian tradition of textbook-production in which received wisdom, specialist findings, disciplinary axioms or easily replicated research methods are dispensed in bite-sized nuggets with tests and exercises to ensure successful ingestion by the student whose only job is to imbibe, perhaps later to regurgitate. The very metaphors of exam-led learning, of taking in bland or processed food (like a child) and being required only to bring it up again later (like a cow), are reminiscent of what patronizing commentators think TV-pedagogy does too. But 'teaching' doesn't have to be 'schoolmasterly' (authoritarian) or 'pre-digested' (infantilized). Students are nowadays part of the 'we' community to which academics, writers and intellectuals also belong; 'teaching' is (or can be) truly a matter of 'life-long' or 'continuing' education, and the work done in formal institutions like universities can be part of a larger conversation beyond. 'The' public is, as it always has been, first and foremost a reading public; part of the republic of letters. While that virtual republic is still open to critical conversations conducted in print, it is now fully mediated by electronic 'letters' too – the reading public is also the TV audience.

Thus a book about television nowadays is as much about the readers as it is about 'television' as some sort of given object simply requiring to be described; TV studies now is a kind of participatory, cordializing philosophy of practice. Times have changed; students don't need to be warned about the colonizing conspiracies of media moguls; they need to be encouraged into confident research and information-seeking, inner purpose and understanding, and both professional and self-expression, in all available media. TV studies has moved, or has to move, from adversarial arguments whose purpose is to defend or detract, towards a 'conversational' mode whose social purpose is not power but teaching.

New technologies are rapidly changing the media landscape; broadcast television as the communal self-invention of nation-states is no longer the only option, though it is still there. It now competes with non-broadcast forms of TV, from satellite and cable to corporate communication and domestic camcorders. Television consumption has shifted from a 'universal' experience, where we all get the same three to five networks, the same low-def pictures, the same centrally-produced programming. Now there's 'class division' for consumers as some go for digital decoding, wide-screen formats, high-definition screens. Techno-junkies and 'early-adopters' can integrate video with computer applications, broadcasting with the net, consumption with participation, audiencehood with authorship. Times are shifting from ideologies to ideolects; from a society governed by central, corporate editorial functions to one characterized by more 'privatized' and personal choices. Semiosis has never been more pervasive, accessible, complex, easy; now technology can tread much more lightly, and the role of the teacher is more a matter of 'teaching how to see' than 'telling what to think'.

Of course, not everyone avails themselves of the full potential of media literacy. But perhaps if that is so it too is really a problem of teaching, rather than evidence of failure, either of the medium or of the population in question. The 'capacity' is there in the textual system and in the technology; it's just a matter of 'training what to do'.

But nowadays even 'training what to do' has changed; it is theoretically much more astute and self-reflexive than it used to be, and progressively 'out-sourced' by media organizations to universities who want to produce 'graduateness' in their students as well as 'employability'. The workplace is increasingly character-ized by 'work' rather than 'jobs' – casualized, temporary, freelance and project-based employment in a career which is itself a creative production of the individual, rather than a 'salaryman' job controlled by the employer.

In this context, the 'use' of TV studies is to nurture consciousness. It may take fifty years, since things always take longer than you expect, but consciousness must be nurtured if it is to grow, must start here and now and on a 'mass' scale for change to be democratic. If a vibrant, participatory visual culture and a demo-cratic political process are desirable outcomes, then positive teaching is the go, not critical lamentation. The much despised popular media don't *have* to ride roughshod over public good and private values, over cultural difference and diversity of identity; they can be used for whatever is wanted. The demand has to come from the populations whose media they are.

Already there are models of good practice, in which integration between demographic difference and national identity can be shown to work. In Australia it is possible to point to SBS-TV, a multi-cultural, multi-lingual TV service, supported by government grant and advertising, watched by ethnic communities whose mother-tongue is not English alongside monoglot Australians. It performs, on a shoestring, the integration of different peoples, and is an instance of the integration of government, education and media. In the UK, a similar and similarly radical form of 'teaching TV' can be found in the Welsh-language channel S4C – which broadcasts the lowest-brow shows (quizzes, sing-songs, chat) for the highest reasons of cultural policy (preservation of the *hen iaith*, the ancient language), and furthermore it does this to a minority audience (only 20 per cent of Wales's residents speak Welsh) at prime time. In the US, where things are both different and bigger, one might say that the comparable invention is network TV itself. For fifty years committed to 'Americanness' rather than 'dif-ference', but dedicated to it in such a way as to promote cordialization among people readily recognized as different (*Cosby*: see Gray, 1995: 79–80; soap-opera: see Allen, 1995), to provide a public sphere for media citizens to get to know each other (*Oprah*), to dramatize the integration of government and education (*Star Trek*), to teach 'naturally' antagonistic populations (e.g. inter-generational family members) how they can live together (*Moesha, Third Rock from the Sun*), and to use popular television forms to investigate topical problems while playing with the form and cultural politics of television itself (*The Simpsons*).

In such contexts, doing, thinking and seeing are integrated also – triangulating theory, pleasure and action for producers, consumers and the community alike. Television studies is no longer top–down; ideologically driven. It has learnt the politics of conversation, respect, mutual tolerance – these desirable, 'loving' virtues are now not just Hoggart's, but *television's*.

4

TELEVISION AS
TRANSMODERN TEACHING

This process to see other human beings as 'one of us' rather than as 'them' is a matter of detailed description of what unfamiliar people are like and of redescription of what we ourselves are like. This is the task not for theory but for genres such as ethnography, the journalist's report, the comic book, the docudrama, and . . . the novel. . . . The novel, the movie, and the TV program have, gradually but steadily, replaced the sermon and the treatise as the principal vehicles of moral change and progress.

(Richard Rorty, 1989: xiv)

PRE-MODERNITY, MODERNITY,
POSTMODERNITY, TRANSMODERNITY

I claim that television needs to be understood through the notion of transmodern teaching. It is therefore worthwhile to clarify my usage of terms associated with 'modern'. There are both temporal and categorical issues to think about. Temporally, it seems obvious that a sequence can be found from pre-modern to modern, modern to postmodern. Categorically, however, there are well-known distinctions between modern and postmodern phenomena that are simply not time based – the modern and postmodern can and do coexist in time – and, perhaps they always have, at least in relation to media. Indeed, it is the argument of this book that not only can 'postmodern' and 'modern' characteristics be found side by side in many media contexts, but also that the 'uses' of television continue social functions already present in pre-modern Europe (specifically, television is organizationally and socially a secularization of the medieval Catholic church, and also it connects with family and domestic contexts of sense-making that are largely oral and pre-modern). Hence I am anxious to characterize television as transmodern – partaking of pre-modern, modern and postmodern characteristics at once.

Modernity has been revitalized as an object of study in the period since postmodernity became a major debating topic in the humanities and social sciences; indeed, John Frow sees 'postmodernity' as a genre of theory-writing, rather than something which such writing describes in the world (see Frow, 1997: Chapter 1). Modernity can be understood approvingly as an era dedicated to founding knowledge on reason, truth, secularism and empirical or positive evidence; or disapprovingly as an era dominated by masculine knowledges, imperial powers and colonial exploitation. Similarly, postmodernity can be described approvingly as a retreat from myths of comprehensive, coherent truth, and a recognition of the need for self-reflexivity in the production of knowledge; or disapprovingly as an anything-goes relativism and the commodification of information, culture and communication.

It is not necessary for the cultural investigator to arbitrate such evaluative debates. Instead it is helpful to make some distinctions: moderniy is associated with specific historical developments.

- In **politics**, modernity began with the transfer of sovereignty from monarch to people; its inauguration can therefore appropriately be associated with the French Revolution.
- In **philosophy**, modernity began with the Enlightenment of the eighteenth century − again, centred on France.
- In **science**, modernity began with empiricism, positivism and pragmatism (the experimental method), associated with English writers like Francis Bacon and with the foundation of the Royal Society in the early seventeenth century.
- In **industrial** terms modernity is associated with the Industrial Revolution − again, centred on Britain in the late eighteenth and early nineteenth centuries.
- Meanwhile, what **historians** of Europe call the 'early modern' period began much earlier, some time after the introduction of technologies like the plough, gunpowder and printing between the 1200s and 1400s, the invention of capitalist banking in Italy in the 1400s and 1500s, the market economy growing up within feudal societies throughout Europe (in Britain during the 1500s), and the expansion of both geographical and mental horizons attendant upon the Reformation and the Renaissance (late 1400s to early 1600s).

In recent social and political theory, however, the multi-origined and historically contingent nature of modernity has been underplayed in favour of categorical discussions centred not on the *condition* or period of modernity, but on the *ideology* of modernism − the militant promotion of modernist ideas about truth, progress, science, reason. Hence, debates about postmodernity have also tended towards the categorical − postmodernity is calculated from its implied opposition to and apparent temporal sequence after modernity, leading to modernist fears that if postmodernity is not contested it will destroy the modernist project. Looked at historically, it can be shown however that many of the conditions thought of as postmodern are not post- but coterminous with the modern.

Hence it may be proper to assert that there's a difference between modernity and postmodernity (understood as conditions in society requiring explanation), and modernism and postmodernism (understood as ideologies held by contending factions of the knowledge class). Similarly, just as modernity can be shown to be multi-origined and calculated from various starting dates spanning nearly half a millennium, so postmodernity can be traced back to the very beginnings of modernity, indeed as the necessary twin to modernity, in conditions that were always there but only recently resolved into analytical coherence. Hence histories of modernist media (such as the press) now have to recognize the extent to which the press was 'postmodern' from the start: i.e. dedicated to the irrational and emotional as well as to reason and truth; to feminized, privatized, non-metropolitan knowledges as well as to public affairs; to questions of identity as well as power.

Modernist critics of 'postmodern' media like television, conversely, need to understand that TV is a part of the modern world not despite but because of its blivitousness, its emphasis on entertainment not information, on surface not structure, on celebrity not power, on distribution not production, on audience not reality, on semiosis not reality. These 'postmodern' features predate television in older media, and meanwhile television is also part of the modernist project of enlightenment, science, reason, progress, secularism, popular sovereignty, and the rest. And just as it follows that modernity was not a radical disruption of a pre-modern past to which it bore no resemblance (indeed there are those who think modernity has not yet occurred, certainly in its ideal form – see Frow, 1997: 1), so it follows that postmodernity is not a radical disrupture of modernity, but a part of the same world. Hence it is now possible to argue that media such as television, far from being hyper-present-tense and postmodern, share in some semiotic, social, political and cultural characteristics and functions that are present in both modern and pre-modern conditions – indeed that television is a transmodern medium.

Meanwhile, if it is the case that modernity is multi-origined, it is therefore likely that it has not reached certain spheres of life and is still an 'incomplete project'. The late twentieth century has seen an unusually intense modernization of information, communication, culture and semiosis. But this very process, coming after the great political and industrial modernizations of the nineteenth century, looks to some commentators like the very opposite of modernity, namely postmodernity, since the cultural sphere was routinely ignored or discounted in modernist maps of social progress. But the shift of critical attention from the rational, scientific, progress-seeking, industrial conditions of 'high' modernity to the cultural sphere of identity and semiosis does not mean that these things weren't there in previous times. Similarly, the very impressive monuments left to us by modernity in its most militant phase – from Manhattan and universal suffrage to the Soviet Union and science – don't obliterate previous realities entirely; whole areas of life, especially those connected with mothering and language-acquisition, are resistant to modernization and retain substantial pre-modern characteristics.

To summarize:

- Television is '**modern**' – it is organized as an advanced capitalist industry with divisions of labour and a commodified cultural form.

- Television is '**postmodern**' – its textuality is the ideal type of 'po-mo' style: 'the term refers to a broader cultural domain. . . . It is centred in the realm of the mass media rather than in high culture, and typically it refers to television (soap operas, advertisements, video clips, the "real world of postmodernism") and to phenomena of style and fashion' (Frow, 1997: 19).
- Television is '**pre-modern**' – its cultural use is prefigured by socio-semiotic aspects of the first mass medium, the medieval Catholic church, and its phenomenal form exploits pre-modern (oral) modes of communication based on family and a domestic setting.
- Television is '**transmodern**' – it spans, transcends and conjoins modern, pre- and postmodern aspects of contemporary life; specifically by using oral, domestic discourses to teach vast, unknowable 'lay' audiences modes of 'citizenship' and self-knowledge based on culture and identity within a virtualized community of unparalleled size and diversity.

IF TELEVISION IS TRANSMODERN

It would be provocative and self-aggrandizing for a professional educator to claim that the most popular mass medium the world has ever seen is a branch of the teaching profession. I'm not doing that. My own experience accords with those among the producers and audiences of popular media for whom one of the main attractions of TV is that it is not like formal education. The pleasure of media is that they can be taken outside of the institutional confines of scholastic compulsion, tedium, control and conformism. Proof of TV's distance from schooling is that many teachers and professors are irrationally prejudiced against it. But I am nevertheless arguing that teaching is what TV does; and that this is the use of television. This is a social, historical view of television and of usage, seeking to interpret, after the event, what has in fact been done with television in modern/postmodern societies, rather than pretending to describe the intentions of its producers or consumers, much less the ostensible purpose of TV companies and channels. Television is a social institution of teaching in a 'transmodern' (*longue durée*; see Braudel, 1958), anthropological perspective.

What constitutes the social function and practice of teaching? In pre-modern European society, a system lasting until the seventeenth century (at least in England and Wales), teaching was done by three social institutions: the family, the workplace and the church. There was no specific provision for social, political or civic education; persons were formed into *selves* by the family, into *roles* by apprenticeship into craft, professional or vocational mysteries – sometimes also performed within families, and into *souls* by the church. Obedience to apparently natural orders, themselves backed up by supernatural powers, was a high priority. Governance of the self was divided between family and church, each reinforcing the other's cosmological division of existence into hierarchies; obedience on the

41

basis of the resemblance between different orders – e.g. natural father, 'Father of the Nation' (monarch), 'Holy Father' (pope) and God the Father. Secular law helped the same process, without ever intervening in individual education. In cities, people in different vocations were organized into guilds with different clothes (liveries); more generally the 'vestimentary laws' ensured that people were what they appeared to be by forbidding anyone to dress outside their own rank and station. There were different legal systems for literate and non-literate people (clergy and laity); someone found guilty of a capital offence in secular law might save themselves from hanging if they could claim 'benefit of clergy'. Education in vocational skills was added to this mix both inside the family-system, for instance for women, craft workshops and rural workers, or in formal institutions outside the family, as in apprenticeships and military or religious training. It was only the military and religious training institutions – a small, specialist component of medieval teaching provision – that generated the formal school in the European context. The other functions of pre-modern teaching, the formation of *selves*, *souls* and most *roles*, were never included in formal school provision. They were catered for informally ('anthropologically' rather than 'institutionally' – culturally rather than sociologically), although none the less systematically and effectively for that (see Ariès, 1962: part two; Duby, 1988; Hunter, 1994).

It is my view that the private, informal, but systematic teaching of 'selfhood', belief-system ('soul') and social 'role' remains with families, but that the part played in the medieval period by the church has been taken over in the modern era by the media, culminating in television. In this model, TV is not an extension of school, though it may be a competitor for hearts, minds and methods; historically it is devoted to teaching other things than those for which schooling was invented and is best suited.

Some of the previously private and informal aspects of education were also taken over by the state, and adopted within the curriculum of formal schooling, making the competition for hearts and minds active and militant. Since the nineteenth century especially schools have taken on responsibility for more and more areas of life. The basic requirements of literacy, numeracy, discipline and obedience have been augmented by physical training, and by 'ideological' train-ing in moral, sexual, social and cultural matters.

Meanwhile, the pre-modern assumption that the state enjoys a monopoly in communications has taken nearly 500 years to erode (still by no means com-pletely), so the handover of functions from pre-modern family/church to mod-ern family/media has been accompanied by an unceasing stream of interventionist legislation, regulation and persuasion designed not only to poach from the informal to the formal educational sectors many of these more 'cultural' or 'anthropological' teachings, but also to discipline and control the media's own educative tendencies, dictating what can be said, to whom, at what times of day, in what quantity and for what purpose. This practice has been progressively abandoned in publishing, but remains militantly in force in broadcasting. So in postmodern media, a pre-modern monarchical monopoly (control or 'licensing' of communications) is joined by a modernist fear of 'private' life; the result is that there's now a rather too militantly drawn line between education and media, with KEEP OUT! signs all round formal schooling.

One of the reasons schooling exploded into a much more important social institution with the coming of modernity remains its number-one function to this day, namely the teaching of print-literacy. Conversely, the medieval institutions of family and church were almost entirely oral in their modes of communication. Television has inherited this non-literate tradition of teaching, using song, story, sight and talk rather than 'book-learning'. There are very good historical reasons, going back to the Reformation and Counter-reformation in the sixteenth century, for those engaged in teaching to become very passionate indeed about these alternative technologies. As has been well-documented, protestantism was a religion based on print-literacy and individual practice (reading the Bible), while the medieval Catholic church relied on orality and collective practice (going to church). Some of the hostility to oral/visual modes of teaching, especially the hostility inherited by those working in formal institutions of print-literacy like schools, is based on the lethal antagonism between protestants and papists going back to the Renaissance. In other words, teaching became a ground upon which rival belief-systems competed for souls. This is still the case in the inherited antagonism that print/school people unthinkingly reproduce when they castigate television (Ong, 1958).

If TV is teaching

Rethinking television as an object of study through the concept of teaching allows for a critical reformulation of some very well-established but not very satisfactory theories of television. For instance, if television is thought of in terms of teaching not power, then the idea that TV programming and TV pervasion is best explained by reference to such cold-war concepts as ideology, propaganda and surveillance – power over some group or population – can be reformulated into a much less coercive, sinister and negative version based on teaching; 'loving to influence others', in Richard Hoggart's throwaway phrase (Hoggart, 1970: 55).

- If TV is teaching, then accusations of 'populism' can be dealt with and the whole debate re-argued, for 'populism' and teaching are never entirely coterminous. One of the difficulties that has dogged those who write about television without critical pessimism is that this stance has too easily been dismissed as 'populism'. Populism is a 'boo-word' in social theory, for good reason. Many political atrocities have been committed 'in the name of the people', and politicians who veer from one position to another in order to follow popular opinion are universally derided. If cultural theory were to try to explain how society works by saying that whatever is popular is for that reason alone to be celebrated, then it would be wise to be cautious about the theory, for in certain circumstances crime, hanging and genocide have been 'popular'. Twentieth-century social and cultural theory has been powerfully influenced by émigrés from mid-century totalitarian regimes such as the Frankfurt School or Hannah Arendt, for whom 'the popular' is by definition populist and those who speak optimistically on behalf of the people are not democrats but demagogues; a reflex response has become standard in social studies of the media. Anyone who *likes* 'the popular', including television, is a populist and therefore to be criticized for depoliticizing culture and endangering freedom. But if television is seen as teaching, its institutional desire to influence its audiences doesn't have to be seen as populism, or demagoguery, or tending towards totalitarianism. Instead, television's love of influence can be interrogated along different lines; as a positive form of 'inter-generational' communication, perhaps, which is sometimes wonderful, sometimes woeful, but neither inspired by a desire to rule the world nor transforming its unsuspecting viewers into fodder for fascism.

- If TV is teaching, terms like 'market' and 'consumer' can be put into question; these do not describe the addresser/addressee relations of teacher/taught, nor do they fully explain the relationship between television and its audiences. It is true that TV audiences are understood as a market of consumers (increasingly so as TV moves towards non-broadcast forms that people pay for directly). But in relation to individual television shows or even whole channels in the broadcast network, the concept of the consumer market is quite misleading. People don't buy television shows, and those shows are not used up when they are 'consumed' by individual viewers. The only people who buy TV shows are TV stations, and TV stations' own customers are not their audiences but their advertisers (or regulatory authorities in the case of public TV). The market for television is therefore not the public but the industry; shows are not sold to the public; airtime is not sold to the public; the public doesn't buy anything from TV. If TV is understood as teaching, then the relations between TV and TV audiences can be rethought.

- If TV is teaching, it is integrated with the great twentieth-century institution of the three Ds – democracy, didactics and drama (Hartley, 1993); it is part of the convergent GEM-megalomerate (Government-Education-Media), each institutional component of which employs aspects of the other; government teaches via drama (politics as theatre); media govern by education (entertainment is both ideological and instructional); education dramatizes government (schooling instils (self)-discipline) – but it's all 'agoraphiliac' (Hartley, 1993); a love of public space, of 'the public' in the public sphere, teaching public virtues by means of dramatic entertainment. It's the place of ancient, classical citizenship.

- If TV is teaching, then arguments about quality are reformulated around the notion of democratization, not decline. Popular and elite/high culture are integrated into one system, of which they are differentiated parts. Here it is not a matter of some everlasting or absolute set of aesthetic standards to which whole media, populations or epochs approximate (or not, in the case of television and popular culture in the modern epoch), but of a system of semiotic and textual productivity encompassing societies as a whole, within which it might make more sense to say that 'high' culture is *a product of* popular culture – a necessary pole or antipode against which popular culture and media can set themselves in order to 'count' *as* popular. If TV is teaching, in other words, it is teaching audiences about cultural distinction, the expansion of difference, and the segmentation of both cultural productivity itself and of the audience for it.

- If TV is teaching, there needs to be some reformulation of the concept of teaching itself. Let me make clear that by *teaching* I never mean *schooling*. Of course teaching may take place in schools, but schools operate to a narrow, specialist and institutionalized notion of teaching, which I take to be a general human or 'anthropological' activity, taking place in societies that don't or didn't have schools, and in those societies that do have them, taking place in many contexts (such as the family, workplace and media) outside of school. Meanwhile, perhaps because of the associations with schooling, teaching-related concepts seem to enjoy rather low prestige ('pedantic', 'academic', 'sermonizing', 'didactic', 'school-marmish'). Professional teaching itself is undervalued both socially and in hierarchies of prestige. It is in stark contrast with philosophy, for instance, in the same way that TV is with the high arts – it is taken to be mere distribution or application, not creating original knowledge. School-teaching has of course both authoritarian and liberal internal philosophies and methods; it is both engineering and bricolage, profession and 'sitting with Nellie'. But while teaching in primary or secondary schools (a feminized and not wholly professionalized occupation) is undervalued, *theories* about the transfer of knowledge, culture, social structure and personal comportment are found at the very highest levels of educational prestige (departments of philosophy in ancient universities, or in social, political, cultural and anthropological theory). Some attention needs to be paid to the irony inherent in this; a rethinking of the importance of 'distribution' – feeling the 'width' of actual teacherly contact with people – and a less reverential attitude to the self-importance of 'philosophy', which is only a theory of teaching that has lost its practice. TV is all distribution and no theory as well, but an astute 'reading' of TV can yield important insights about how knowledge, beliefs, meanings and consciousness are actually communicated and transferred in the gigantic social systems of contemporary history.

- If TV is teaching, then concepts of entertainment, citizenship, life-long and distance learning, and domesticity need to be brought to bear on the understanding of teaching itself. Teaching and learning need to be seen as non-purposeful activities of a society, not outcome-oriented institutional practices.

- If TV is teaching, then we need to look at the producers of TV as part of the GEM 'knowledge class' – they too are teachers, and they are thus 'like us' (academics and critics) – converging with intellectuals and bringing popular culture and intellectual culture together.

- If TV is teaching, then we need to rethink the concept of the audience entirely – bringing together our understanding of TV audiences and that of students; where they are alike, where not. For instance, we do not formally examine TV audiences, nor do we knowingly entertain students. What is the use of TV for audiences; of school for students?

- If TV is teaching, then its international, commercial role can be rethought. Concepts such as 'public service' and 'education by stealth', even 'nation shall speak peace unto nation' (the motto of the BBC), apply equally to commercial, global screen entertainment (and of course vice versa – commercial and public service media are in historic convergence). The pathologization of commercial media and the equal but opposite reverence for BBC-style media needs historical revaluation. Here's where we might return to early modern pedagogical institutions, and the struggle between the medieval Catholic church and protestant printing. . . . The Reformation is still being fought in adversarial rhetoric; we need to rethink this in the light of the convergence of technologies of teaching in transmodern media.

- If TV is teaching we need to re-interrogate the concept of the text: textual features are not seeking power over audiences but they are trying to influence them ('loving to influence' rather than 'taking power over'). For instance, television violence is not a *behaviour* resulting from influence, but a *literacy* shared among users of the textual system – among the things that this literacy teaches is the differentiation of 'good' from 'bad' violence: the Gulf War from Ghaddafi; the cop from the villain; the justified defence from the unprovoked attack, etc. Similarly, television sex (see *Media International Australia*, 85, 1997, whole issue), bad-language (see Dening, 1992) and 'dirt' (see Hartley, 1992a) are not symptoms of the decline of civilization but the necessary and inevitable appeal of communication. What is important is whether they are used well or not in each case, each context. And that is a question of what we used to call aesthetics (perhaps allied with notions of tact, respect, recognition of difference); it is not a question of power.

- If TV is teaching, then the questions of what is being taught, to whom, with what outcomes, are interesting to investigate. It is the argument of this book that television, via cross-demographic communication, visual culture, talk and narrative ('per sona' in fact), teaches the formation of identity and citizenship in a society characterized by the unknowability of its nevertheless sovereign populations. The outcome is both literacy in audio-visuality and citizenship of media (which I argue in later chapters has evolved from 'cultural citizenship' to 'DIY citizenship' or 'semiotic self-determination'), to be used who knows how, by populations whose purposes and actions are outside of the pedagogic relations used by TV.

- If TV is teaching, then it is a part of and 'witness to' the transmodern, transnational democratization of culture.

5

TEACHING NOT POWER

Ideological atrocities and improper questions

After you're dead, as it were, when you've gone away,
you can't keep your hands on things.

(Richard Hoggart, 1998: 19)

POWER AND READERSHIP

Reading through academic journals and books, it often seems impossible to avoid the conclusion that there are two tribes of commentators ranging the terrain of cultural studies; those who analyze power and those who experience pleasure. This binary opposition is part of a large and elaborate system of binaries operating in critical rhetoric; one that is partly disciplinary, dividing social scientists (power) from textualists (pleasure), and partly ideological, separating the critical pessimists from the postmodern optimists, the realists from the 'virtualists'. I want to assert that such divisions are in no sense warranted by the object of study. Power and pleasure go hand in hand in the media, and to analyze them social scientists and textualists need each other like never before. Critical scepticism (reason, argument, truth-seeking) and postmodern relativism (an understanding of the *textualization* of modernity and the capitalization of *language*) are not incompatible; the virtual is real; the social is textual — and one look at a tabloid newspaper or glossy magazine will confirm all this, whether you write up the results of your observations for social scientific Sage or radically relativist Routledge.

There is, however, a methodological gulf between the social science faculty, which favours sampling statistical frequencies in populations that are taken to pre-exist the act of investigation and are capable of being described in neutral if not transparent language, and the humanities faculty, which favours critical readings of texts and discourses, chosen variously for their aesthetic and ideological qualities, and analyzed in language which foregrounds its writerly and self-reflexive (if not self-presenting) status. But post-disciplinary cultural studies, it transpires, can leap this chasm at a single bound, and now thrives in both faculties, to the mutual bemusement of its practitioners. You can be a realist-modernist-scientist or a textualist-postmodernist-theorist, and be doing the 'same' thing.

What is that thing? It is a dialogue about popular media and culture that is being conducted between two analytical communities whose languages are not mutually translatable and whose practices are asymmetric to each other, bearing in mind that untranslatable asymmetry is a precondition for communication, according to Yuri Lotman (1990). To summarize the dialogue I've outlined so far in this chapter:

POWER	:	PLEASURE
SOCIAL SCIENCE	:	HUMANITIES
CAUSAL ANALYSIS	:	TEXTUAL ANALYSIS
CRITICAL PESSIMISM (DEPLORE)	:	CRITICAL OPTIMISM (EXPLORE)
MODERN	:	POSTMODERN
REALIST	:	VIRTUALIST
SCEPTICISM	:	RELATIVISM
SAGE	:	ROUTLEDGE
STATISTICAL SAMPLING	:	CRITICAL READING
INDEPENDENTLY EXISITING POPULATIONS	:	AESTHETIC/IDEOLOGICAL TEXTS/DISCOURSES
NEUTRAL LANGUAGE	:	WRITERLY SELF-REFLEXIVITY

Since the advent of cross-border talks between social science and textual analysis, power and pleasure, evidence and criticism, 'that thing' – what we do – has shown a tendency in some cases to produce not dialogue and communicative efforts towards mutual understanding between two different analytical languages, but rather a standardized discourse in which 'power' and 'pleasure' (like other such pairs above) appear as taken-for-granted terms. The result has been to produce not turn-taking conversation but paradigmatic repetition, or Kuhnian 'normal science' (Kuhn, 1970). Despite sometimes radical differences in the way that our post-disciplinary truths are sought and taught, it does seem, to some observers at least, that cultural studies has begun to churn out one particular brand of truth with the predictability and blandness of margarine. The film theorist Robert B. Ray, for instance, in *The Avant Garde Finds Andy Hardy*, describes 'a particular way of doing business' since 1970 that has:

> constructed an enormously powerful theoretical machine for exposing the ideological abuse hidden by the apparently natural stories and images of popular culture. That machine, however, now runs on automatic pilot, producing predictable essays and books on individual cases.
>
> (Ray, 1995: 7)

For him then, the question of method is not that it doesn't yield results, but that it works too well, and always says the same thing. The 'exposure of ideological abuse' in popular culture is, for Ray, repetitiously redundant – it was all done in Barthes's *S/Z* (Barthes, 1975) – and we are seemingly condemned to endless re-runs of that original show. He describes modern communications technologies themselves, such as the camera, typewriter, phonograph and the movies, as 'repetition machines' (Ray, 1995: 11), and this is indeed the aspect of popular media which has preoccupied ideological analysis. But in his view cultural studies has become a 'repetition machine' too – a player in the game it seeks to adjudicate. He cites Robert Benayoun's 1970 quip that those for whom the 'structuralist/semiotic/ideological/psychoanalytic/feminist approaches' are 'the coin of the realm' may be identified as '*les enfants du paradigme*'.

Or, as Meaghan Morris has put it in a famous passage from her essay called 'Banality in Cultural Studies':

> Sometimes, reading magazines like *New Socialist* or *Marxism Today* from the last couple of years [she was writing in 1988], flipping through *Cultural Studies*, or scanning the pop-theory pile in the bookshop, I get the feeling that somewhere in some English publisher's vault there is a master-disk from which thousands of versions of the same article about pleasure, resistance and the politics of consumption are being run off under different names with minor variations. Americans and Australians are recycling this basic pop-theory article too.
>
> (Morris, 1990: 15)

We may as well name names – the 'English publisher' was Routledge, and since Morris's article was (partly) about John Fiske, one of the 'minor variations' must surely have been me. Be that as it may, for Morris the problem is that the issue of power/pleasure is reduced to 'resistance'. Clearly both writers are right to call attention to unthinking repetition where it results in 'basic pop-theory' running on 'automatic pilot'. However, it should be noticed that their impatience with cultural studies is also a refusal to get involved in the *popularization* of theory and method. But ironically, one result of such avant-garde squeamishness about popularization is that theory and method get stuck; as writers like Ray and Morris disengage from the conversation, so the conversation stops at the very moment when the means to broadcast it to a much wider audience is switched on.

For in fact, 'thousands of versions of the same' is theory in its quotidian, everyday aspect, in short, theory as *teaching*. 'Thousands of sames' are only possible if avant-garde writers such as Ray and Morris are accompanied by postgraduate researchers, classroom tutors and undergraduate readers, whose interest in the theory of the *quotidienne*, of the everyday (see Lefebvre, 1988: 78–80), is itself ordinary and repetitious. Diffusion or popularization of the field of study is not necessarily a bad thing. Indeed, cultural studies remains interesting because of the tensions and interaction – the dialogue – between research and teaching, the theoretical and the banal, avant garde and everyday. Certainly there's no gain in choosing between them, plumping for one or the other, just as it remains important to hold on to both sides of the 'power/pleasure' and other disciplinary oppositions mentioned earlier if anything meaningful is to be said.

TEACHING READING

As a developing field of study, cultural studies does not obey the same rules as more established disciplinary domains, where it is relatively easy to identify the most important work as the refereed monograph on an original and specialized topic. After that might come the refereed article and the book chapter (like this one), and at the bottom of the heap is the textbook. But in a new field, conversely, it is often the textbook (a repetition machine par excellence) that is the first arrival, the most important or original initiative, in the sense that it *gathers new readers* around a new approach, method or object of study. As I've already pointed out above, semiotics is founded on a textbook, and cultural and media studies has become the elaborated, institutionalized and widespread thing it is today very largely through the proliferation of textbooks, in a phenomenon that I have called the Routledgification of the world (Hartley, 1992b: 464). Because of this *gathering of populations* of students, postgraduates and researchers, and their conversion into the *readership* for a new field of study, I would argue that textbooks and teaching, the repetitions of the theoretical machine, the minor variation on the same theme, can be original, even *avant garde*. They are also, in line with the utopian ideals of the best attempts to popularize knowledge by theoretical repetition, from Allen Lane's Pelican Books to Terence Hawkes's New Accents, empirical-historical evidence of a desire for democratization in and of the domain of knowledge. Extension, repetition, ordinariness, standardization – *teaching* – are here not the derivative and normalizing rearguard, but a seriously intended and potentially subversive innovation in the very institution that functions to produce theory, originality and the intellectually avant garde (that 'institution' being a strategic partnership between higher education, intellectual culture and commercial publishers). As Ray himself observes: 'while artists don't have to explain, teachers do' (Ray, 1995: 17).

So I wouldn't be happy if the 'proper' response to Morris's and Ray's observation of a machine element in cultural studies was that we should abandon repetition (teaching), and wander off into the urban cool, discussing the latest theoretical enthusiasm. However, I am at one with both of them in wishing to avoid the mechanical application of some supposedly explanatory template to any and every aspect of social and cultural life in order to 'expose' another example of the 'same' 'ideological abuse'. What's needed is a teacherly (quotidian, ordinary, population-gathering, readership-producing, user-friendly, interesting, imaginative) embrace of each new area of study or of thought, to create a new readership for newly observed phenomena, new ways of thinking.

Before *teaching* the media, it strikes me that the very first necessity is caution about finding ideological atrocity, and the second is caution about abandoning a 'teacherly' approach in favour of a supposedly avant-garde theoreticism. So here is a tension between two positions, between an avant-gardist resistance to standardization and a need to extend to a wide readership the important (that is, the avant-garde) insights of a field of inquiry that seeks not only to retain but to popularize its radical, non-standard credentials. This is in fact a tension that the news media, along with popular media in general, themselves have to handle, since they too, like intellectual institutions, have to balance innovation and creativity with familiarity and popular address. Indeed, historically there is an increasing convergence between academic and popular *discourses*; partly as a result of a measure of democratization of higher education, and partly because the popular media produce ideas as well as popularizing them.

There is therefore an increasing convergence between academic and popular *readerships*; since higher education is now just as 'mass' as are the media, the 'audience' that cultural studies investigates is none other than the 'student' who reads the results of the investigation. It is here that the routine exposure of ideological atrocity, the reduction of pleasure to power, and power to an unending tussle between the would-be perpetrators of these atrocities ('the media') and the heroic resistance conducted on the living-room couch by 'the audience', can be seen as ill-advised. To teach those for whom popular media are popular that all the time they are dupes of ideology is to alienate people from their own semiotic practices. Better advised, perhaps, would be to explain how readerships and audiences are formed; how alike they are; how conversations between avant-garde theory and popular address can be productive of new knowledge.

Such a conversation might want to start by recognizing how 'ideological' critical habits are, never mind the popular media. For instance, notice how in 'critical' discourse many of the terms that seem to go together so readily to describe critical and audience activity respectively turn out to be paired oppositions, each a transformation of the others, so that it comes to seem self-evident that the relationship between analyst and audience, intellectual and media, is *adversarial*:

READERSHIP	:	AUDIENCE
INTELLECTUAL	:	POPULAR
CRITICISM	:	COMMODITY
PRODUCTION	:	CONSUMPTION
AVANT GARDE	:	EVERYDAY
ORIGINAL	:	REPETITIOUS
OBJECTIVE	:	SUBJECTIVE
POWER	:	PLEASURE

If you're schooled in these oppositions, it would be quite proper to assume that '*intellectuals read critical, original, avant-garde knowledge about the objective workings of power*', while it would be equally proper to assume, conversely, that '*popular audiences consume everyday repetitious commodities for subjective pleasure*'. I think this is 'two-tribism', however, and it serves only to mask the underlying (dialogic) connections between apparently adversarial positions – connections between the intellectual critic and the popular reader, for instance, or between avant-garde and everyday knowledges, between thinking and teaching, and between the camps devoted to power and pleasure respectively.

A simple 'method' that seems to recommend itself to cultural studies from noticing this would be to adopt an 'in-between' or perhaps 'go-between', dialogic position, or what I call in the Post-script (below) one of 'not-quiteness'. Trying to understand media textuality from such an 'improper' position has resulted in a model of the semiotic universe elaborated in my book *Popular Reality*, a study of the history of popular readerships constructed by the textual system of journalism (Hartley, 1996). From this perspective, the most important questions are not about the atrocities and abuses of journalism, but the system itself. The greatest creation of modern journalism is not this story or that, but its *readership* – the 'public' of modernity. Historically, 'the public' is not an extension of 'the public sphere', but of 'the reading public' – it is a differentiated part of 'the audience'. It includes knowledge-creating professionals (both in the popular media themselves and in institutions of higher learning) as well as the 'mass' of consumers of images and stories. Furthermore, a history of both journalism and modernity since 1789 has been a history of repetition, distribution, extension, as something that Ernesto Laclau and Chantal Mouffe (1985: 154–5) describe as the 'logic of democratic equivalence' has both quickly and slowly rippled its way throughout the 'semiosphere' (Lotman, 1990) via the 'media-sphere' (Hartley, 1996), taking popular sovereignty from its earliest site – adult, urban males – eventually to classes of people hardly regarded as human at that time, never mind citizens, starting with women, and moving on from there through the ethnic and colonial populations until it came to children, where it is still stuck fast. In fact it seems to have flowed right past them and is now lapping up against the coastline of the animal kingdom: 'Astonishingly, nobody knows exactly how many children are victims [of child abuse] because there are no official records. Yet the SSPCA [Scottish RSPCA; the peak animal protection organization] can tell us how many ANIMALS were abused last year' (*Scottish Daily Record and Sunday Mail International*, 4–10 March 1996). Certainly animal rights and needs are more debated in the media and in parliament than those of children (see Franklin and Franklin, 1996).

The ripples of the logic of democratic equivalence do not stop with citizenship, but extend democratization through the semiosphere of culture, taste and text, bringing the energies of freedom and comfort to fiction, furniture and fashion, song, story and sight. Journalism is the medium of these energies too, translating knowledges to and from different sectors of an overall cultural universe which is united only in its textual technologies (readerships). Here it is all the more important to hold on to the dialogic tensions elaborated above; power and pleasure are close confidantes in the context of freedom and comfort; and as well as the familiar 'critical' reading there is what has been called an erotics of reading (Barthes, 1975: xi–xii), a *jouissance* in journalism.

Ray proposes that the rhetoric of scientific realism may not any longer be the appropriate form of writing for the postmodern but still Habermasian project of 'critique and rational understanding' (Ray, 1995: 9). He prefers the Barthesian essay, not least because such a form is frankly being *made* by the writer, not simply *reported* from supposedly self-evident facts. The indeterminacy of knowledge (knowledge as 'bricolage' rather than engineering), the form of the essay, become 'method' – bearing in mind that 'essay' means 'to try' and is fundamentally a teacherly genre even in the hands of intellectually advanced and ideologically astute writers. (Barthes's S/Z is itself a book arising out of a seminar taught by Barthes in 1968–9 at the Ecole Pratique des Hautes Etudes in Paris.) So here's more dialogic asymmetry at the methodological level; and again, the method is to keep these differences in productive tension, not to choose between them:

RESEARCH : TEACH
ENGINEERING : BRICOLAGE
FUNDED STUDY : FOUND OBJECTS
REPORT THE FACTS : WRITE THE ESSAY

The facts that I shall 'try' forensically (Hartley, 1993) in this essayist mode are about readership, not ideology; attraction, not abuse. Looking at popular media in the context of a critical history that finds it easy to reduce television to a form of social child abuse, but forbidding oneself the methodological convenience of uncovering yet another example of it, allows 'improper', in-between questions to arise. Mine are these:

- Is television a transmodern teacher?
- What has been the effect of the audience upon television?
- How has television been affected by the attacks on it from critics, intellectuals and from TV studies?
- Has television promoted the formation of new kinds of citizenship – cultural and DIY citizenship?
- Is television better thought of via 'Hoggartian' notions of teaching, population-gathering and cross-demographic communication than via 'Birminghamite' notions of power, hegemony and ideology?

6

KNOWLEDGE, TELEVISION AND THE 'TEXTUAL TRADITION'

O Freunde, nicht diese Töne!
Sondern laßt uns angenehmere anstimmen, und freudenvollere!

O friends, not these sounds! Rather let us sing something more pleasant and joyful!

(Ludwig van Beethoven)

In this chapter I consider television in its historical context and argue that the history of television is best explained not by 'internal factors' like the invention of television technology, but by 'external factors' which determined what impact that technology would have and what people would think (or at least say) about it. While there are many other possible ways of looking at the history of television, and indeed many have already been published (see for instance Boddy, 1990; Attallah, 1991; Curthoys, 1991; Hartley, 1992a: Chapter 14; Spigel, 1992; Hartley, 1993: 100–16; Marling, 1994; O'Regan, 1995), my purpose here is to show how television was *taught* to its first generation of planners, producers and viewers, and how as a result television came to be *used*.

To do this, I am concentrating on what I'm calling throughout this chapter the 'textual tradition' – that is, the tradition of intellectual thought, writing and knowledge that has been applied to texts, whether these are oratorical (as in pre-modern ancient Greece), religious (as in pre-modern medieval Europe), literary (as in modern education), or the more complex texts of audio-visual media culture (as in postmodern cultural studies). It is my contention that the *use* of television was *taught* to its first public by a textual tradition stretching back to antiquity.

THE GENERATION OF TELEVISION

The 'generation' of television refers equally to three different but related phenomena:

1   television's own genesis as a medium in history;
2   programmes generated by the TV industry;

3   the generation of people called into audience-ship by TV.

Historically, television as a medium was generated before its programmes generated a TV generation; there was a time lag between each stage – technological invention, cultural form, social impact. Of course, the time sequence of these three stages is exactly the reverse of their importance and interest – television's social impact is more important than its cultural form, which is more important than its technological possibility. So it is not necessarily a good idea for the researcher to treat television history in a sequence suggested by time: in what might be called, with all due respect to learned spectacles, a 'four I-ed' approach:

1   Invention
2   Implementation
3   Institutionalization
4   Impact

If you really want to explain and trace TV's social impact it might in fact seem rather pointless to begin at the beginning, ferreting around in some grotty laboratory to see how the thermionic valve and the cathode ray tube were brought into being. They are not the determinants of what television was to become; not the reason why you would be investigating it in the first place; not the acorn from which the rather extensive oaktree of contemporary television grew.

Instead of looking at scientific invention to account for television's socio-cultural form, it might be better to look for evidence of what social impact television was *able* to have, what was expected (and what feared) of it, what situation it found itself in when it was still a fledgeling medium. Were its cultural form and social impact something new or had these functions been performed by some other cultural institution before TV? What discourses were in place at the outset with which to make sense of TV; both to control and to encourage it? What forms of presentation and programming, reception and 'reading', were available to producers and audiences? The history of television, seen this way, is a history of how it was *generated* as a socio-culturally meaningful phenomenon; it's a history of the discourses and practices which surrounded, shaped, permeated, disciplined, enabled and frustrated its development. In short, more important than television's invention and technical potential was how it was *taught* to its first public; a public that knew nothing of it, that had to be *tutored* as to what its implementation, institutionalization and impact might be. That first TV public was not an undifferentiated mass of potential consumers, but included interested parties like the government as regulator of communications, commercial and other industry bodies (such as existing broadcasters like the BBC), political parties with views on the popularization of culture and democratization of communication, and critics with views on how the future should be captured and fixed, never mind new technology.

Even though television technology was scientifically feasible in the nineteenth century (pre-dating cinematography), it was not a practical proposition until the 1920s and 1930s. But effectively, what separated the 'generation of television' from the 'television generation' was the Second World War and the Atlantic Ocean. Regular broadcast TV began in Britain in the mid-1930s, although the technology had been known for much longer and numerous TV set-ups had been demonstrated to the public in Britain, Germany, the US and elsewhere. But first-generation television would remain meaningless without *broadcasting*, and the BBC took the honours there, transmitting the first regular broadcast television service starting on 2 November 1936. Nevertheless, the first 'TV generation' was decidedly American, following the establishment of network television in the 1940s and the post-war boom during which American economic supremacy and wartime military success made its cultural values (comfort and freedom) unusually attractive to the whole western world. Although Britain and other European powers developed their own national television systems along with their own nuclear bombs, it was American television (perhaps not unconnected with American bombs) that counted in the end, especially among viewers themselves. The first 'television generation' was *culturally* American, no matter which country counted as home. In one of those technological truths that show how impact (effect) is much more significant than invention (cause) in the world of culture if not science, the American system NTSC (known disparagingly to European technicians as 'Never Twice the Same Colour') was technically inferior to the European system PAL. No matter, it was American programming, and the American *use* of TV to promote domestic consumerism, and the American discourse of private, commercial, apolitical entertainment for TV that was successfully *taught* to the succeeding generations.

But it was not easy to foresee any of this in the afternoon gloom of an imperial London November in 1936. The world's first broadcast television service was not a fat, healthy child. The BBC transmitted programmes for an hour or two each afternoon (plus the test pattern in the mornings) to a few hundred viewers within reach of its single transmitter in North London. Considering what television was to become over the next sixty years or so the opening was not an especially auspicious occasion. In 1936 the dominant communications and entertainment media were radio, where the BBC reigned supreme in Britain, and cinema, already dominated by Hollywood. Movies were audio-visually far superior to television and cinema was just beginning to enjoy its most popular decade ever, after the introduction of talkies at the end of the 1920s.

As for the audience, they were already 'trained' to take their visual pleasures in cinemas, which during this period were treated in a way which is much closer to the way *television* eventually came to be watched than to the way we now watch cinema. In the 1930s and 1940s, people went to cinemas in their own neighbourhoods and suburbs, three or four times a week, casually. They didn't necessarily know what was on in advance, nor did they queue up for a particular start time. Instead, people would drop in at any time (like switching on the TV to see what's on) and sit through a repertoire programme until the point where they began watching was repeated, when they could either leave or see it again. The cinemas were demographically indifferent, unlike today's highly segmented cinema audience, and the shows were a hybrid mixture of newsreel, comedy, action serials, cartoons, advertisements and features, with a series of one- or two-reelers (10- or 20-minutes) and a full-length B-movie on offer as well as the main feature film. Although viewers were highly tutored in the star system and would be familiar with movie gossip, scandal, news and publicity, there was little formal film reviewing of the sort associated with theatre and literature. Differences between the 'regime of viewing' of early popular cinema and later popular television should not be overstated. Certainly cinema-watching was public and TV domestic; cinema was high definition and TV was not. But at the same time the casual, indiscriminate (hybrid), neighbourhood character of cinema audience practices was exactly the same, and when TV first started people would darken their living rooms and invite the neighbours round to make the difference even less marked. Given that there were programmes on television from an early date which were familiar from cinema – especially Disney cartoons – it is arguable that as far as *popular* viewing was concerned, the similarities were more important than the differences; TV was *treated* like cinema. This was important in the opening few years, for of course TV was no match for its highly capitalized neighbour. Cinema was in its most popular phase ever, while TV receivers were expensive, hard to watch for any length of time, and very low definition. And if you wanted home entertainment – comedy, music, news, talks and drama – there was always the wireless. Why bother with TV?

This was certainly the view of the BBC, which had television foisted on it by the government, and never considered its potential as a mass medium until it too was 'educated' by American TV with the arrival of the American form of TV (i.e. the commercial ITV network) into Britain on 21 October 1955, having had it to themselves for twenty years without doing much more than making sure it remained subservient to radio. To begin with the BBC handed TV over to junior staff, forbade it to collect or broadcast its own news, and housed it in an outer metropolitan suburb at the Alexandra Palace (the 'Ally Pally') rather than in the beautiful, West-End, award-winning, custom-built Broadcasting House itself.

At the very beginning the top brass had not even decided on its technical specifications, so for the first few months every programme was broadcast twice – in the EMI electronic format using cathode ray tubes, and in Logie Baird's mechanical system using a revolving wheel with holes in it which digitized light, transforming a film-frame into thirty-three lines which could be transmitted (a similarly revolving wheel in the receiver then projected those lines on to the (very) small screen). With hindsight it seems obvious that the EMI cathode ray tube system should have won this contest (despite Baird retaining the credit for 'inventing' television), although in some ways Baird's curious system was a precursor of the CD, which also works with digitized light. What really scuppered his system, however, was its dangerous and immobile camera, which shot film, processed it in internal tanks, and then televised the resulting footage fifty-six seconds later. Ingenious, but cumbersome, and disliked by camera-operators who took a dim view of lethal chemicals, including cyanide, sloshing around their legs. The bizarre colours of make-up that presenters had to wear in order to look 'natural' for the EMI system (blue and russet faces scanned better than pinkish ones) seemed a smaller price to pay.

The first programmes were based on existing performance styles, available talent and familiar media – the opening shows took newsreel from cinema, singing and comedy acts from radio, and variety acts from the stage, pantomime and the circus. These very early programmes were broadcast live and few have survived in the archives (and then only if they were filmed at the time), but in any case they were not necessarily indicative of how programming was to develop into its characteristic style. They were experimental only in the sense that the first producers and performers had to make it all up as they went along. What they made it up *with* was *existing knowledge* – generic, commercial, cultural.

THE 'TEXTUAL TRADITION' IS 2,500 YEARS OLDER THAN TELEVISION

Where did that 'existing knowledge' come from? And can we reconstruct what it was?

In early 1997, just before the general election propelled New Labour, New Britain into history, the Chief Inspector of Schools for England and Wales, Chris Woodhead, denounced television. Focusing especially on the situation comedy *Only Fools and Horses*, which had just scored the biggest rating ever for such a show with its Christmas special, Her Majesty's Inspector received wide press and radio coverage for his belief that such sympathetic portrayals of working-class characters had a bad effect on the standards of speech and literacy of the nation, encouraging young people to admire the wide-boy antics of the disreputable-but-lovable main character Del-Boy (played by David Jason) rather than admiring great literature. What's interesting about this opinion is less its accuracy than its longevity, and the fact that it is held by such a senior official in the apparatus of governmental regulation of education (a man who, to the surprise of media-onlookers for whom such 'elitist' views were understood to be congenial to Tories but not to their more egalitarian Labour opponents, kept his job after the election). How did television come to be identified as the cause of failures in the education system, and why is 'great literature' placed not only as the *antithesis* of popular culture but as its *antidote*; the serum of culture with which 'we' ought to be inoculating our children so they don't catch bad thoughts, habits, speech-patterns from television?

This chapter is about the 'textual tradition' in TV studies, so it's concerned not with television, but with *ways of understanding* television; how television was *taught*. Such ways of understanding are themselves 'traditional' – we become habituated with their use, to the point where, like driving a car, we can do it without knowing we're doing it — that is, we can make sense of a given phenomenon, using a specific way of understanding, without consciously manipulating the controls of the mechanism we're using. The difference between driving a car and driving a discourse, however, is that most people can remember a time before they knew how to drive a car, and remember also the process of learning how to do it before it became 'second nature.' This is not the case with ways of under-standing; these are used first unself-consciously in the practical activity of every-day life, and only afterwards, with further training, is it possible to learn how we learnt them, or begin to understand how they work. With sense-making practices, it is almost always the case that we experience the whole first, and only later learn to distinguish the constituent parts, and how they fit together, and which bits make other bits work.

Whenever we look at TV critically or analytically, rather than just watching it routinely, we're driving a 'tradition' of explanation and understanding some of whose elements are over 2,500 years old. But they are also driving us. Perhaps this is not so different from driving a motor vehicle after all, since the individual skill and the local experience of driving *this* car along *this* highway *today* are all contingent upon the prior existence of a network of roads together with their infrastructure (from fuel stops to traffic police), and upon the major capital investment made by countries and companies in the road-transport industries, as well as the socio-political and cultural processes that caused motoring to develop as an individual, private, 'mass' activity with high social acceptability despite its well-known environmental diseconomics. These socio-economic, tech-nological, cultural and political conditions have to be in place for us 'simply' to get from 'a' to 'b' — and to experience that movement as an act of our individual volition. So it is with the social, historical and institutionalized work of thinking. All understanding is 'traditional', not 'personal' — the work of human thinking is done collectively and impersonally, not by 'you and me' as individual persons, but by semiotic systems which are both widespread (synchronic) and long-lasting (diachronic). As the cultural semiotician Yuri Lotman has put it, in a fundamental insight:

> The individual human intellect does not have a monopoly in the work of thinking. Semiotic systems, both separately and together in the integrated unity of the semiosphere, both synchronically and in all the depths of historical memory, carry out intellectual operations, preserve, rework and increase the store of information.
>
> (Lotman, 1990: 273)

Within what Lotman calls the 'semiosphere' — that is, the whole 'universe' of human sense-making taken as a whole, on the model of the notion of the 'biosphere' — there are regions and specialisms of semiotic activity, including national cultures (based on speech communities sharing the same language), but also including transnational communities which maintain semiotic relationships that cut across the boundaries of national culture. Two such 'virtual' communities are *popular culture*, and *intellectual culture*. Each of these has its own semiotic systems, and its own appropriate ways of making sense, which, like the semiosphere to which they belong, are both extensive (synchronic) and customary (diachronic), and which can also be in intense dialogue with each other. Since these are 'virtual' communities, they are not as strongly bounded as others, and 'membership' is not necessarily a lifetime experience; everyone belongs to the virtual community of 'popular culture' when they're pursuing the activities and making the meanings proper to that system. The same is true for intellectual culture, which is encountered by much larger populations than those few who are, as it were, professional intellectuals. Everyone in what Lotman calls 'the integrated unity of the semiosphere' is a participant in, and product of, the collective work of thinking, of information and knowledge-production, which goes to make up human 'thought'.

Nevertheless, it is also the case that this general human effort is itself organized, gathered into historically evolving intellectual institutions and discursive activities, some of which last for centuries, in which the 'individual human intellect' is subsumed into the larger process of thinking. Just as has occurred in other spheres of human activity in modernity, intellectual operations have been subjected to a division of labour and specialization, to intense capital investment, and to concentration in those areas when the greatest economic returns may be hoped for. Equally, because modern societies are both very complex and also full of tiny details which need attending to if things are going to work, a good deal of 'thought' needs to be invested in control, administrative and organizational functions, and here too intellectual effort has become specialized. Caught up in these processes, of specialization, control, investment and concentration, traditional intellectual work inevitably changes even as it continues, in 'dialogue' with the forces and energies which surround it in the semiosphere. Such energies include those of popular culture.

In order to trace the tradition of understanding which has become established to account for television, it is necessary to go back in time well before the invention of television itself, and talk mostly about things other than television. This is because the ways of understanding television don't arise from television itself (whatever that is – something yet to be discussed), but from other discursive regimes, institutions and genres which are already established and which themselves already have a history of advances and arguments of their own.

In the case of the '*textual* tradition' it can be argued that this history is very long indeed, because it draws, first, on the traditions of textual exegesis as elaborated in literary studies, which have their own origins in biblical exegesis going back to the early Middle Ages in Europe with the founding of monastic orders and the work of literate clerics, and second, on the traditions of western philosophy going back to Aristotle's aesthetic theories and to Plato's socio-political theories, which have remained the coins of the realm in the exchanges of intellectual and critical thinking ever since.

The 'textual tradition in TV studies' can be traced back to the groves and gardens of fifth-century BC Athens, one of which, the grove belonging to some-one called Academus, was where Plato taught, hence 'academy', while Aristotle taught in the Lyceum gardens, a name which is still used for universities and colleges in France and Italy (lycée and liceo), while in Britain and America the name lyceum has become attached to learned societies, libraries and lecture halls, and thence to not a few cinemas. It can also be traced back to the windy promontories of medieval monasticism, where textualism, empiricism, nomin-alism and many other schools of thought have their origins. I have suggested in my book *The Politics of Pictures* that the philosophical and political pre-conditions necessary for the invention of television as a social institution (rather than merely as a technology) were thought through by the early-modern political philosopher Thomas Hobbes in 1651 (Hartley, 1993: Chapter 5).

This short romp through the seedbeds of our semiosphere is important, to feel the weight of the 'dead generations' (weighing like a nightmare on the brains of the living, as Karl Marx famously put it) in these 'textual traditions'. They have their own history, not only of advances and arguments in the discursive con-versation which takes place between the players and pages involved, but also of material institutionalization in academies, buildings, libraries, books, professions (and so on . . .), of investment of capital resources and people's lifetime energies, and of power struggles, contested for years and sometimes centuries, over how best to arrive at what kind of truth on whose behalf and for what purposes. Without feeling the weight of these 'traditions', it is not easy to comprehend why or how television came to be 'taught' in the ways that it has been.

How did television come into the world? Was it a pure entity, gift-wrapped and shiny-new? Did the first astonished beholders undo the bows, rip off the pack-aging and then gather round in a huddle, stroking their chins as they observed the peculiar infant medium? Did they explain and understand it by an act of deductive reasoning *after* they were confronted by the new invention? Of course not. Television came into a world which was already intensely and complicatedly semiotic, seething with discourses, 'traditions' of understanding, semiotic regimes and really venerable institutions of knowledge. All this caused television to mean something specific at every point and in every detail of its invention, throughout the process and subsequently as it became established as a cultural form.

Furthermore, what these sense-making strategies 'made' of television does not necessarily tell us anything at all about television. It's *there* right enough, but because 'it' is a mixed phenomenon, and has no essence, no pure properties of its own, what is known about it depends on the conditions and traditions of knowing, not on the thing 'itself'. What we know about television, in short, depends very largely, and first, on what we've been taught to see in it.

EXTERNAL FACTORS

Given the history of semiosis, which is both long and pervasive, and given that elements of our thinking survive from extremely ancient times, the question of where to begin an account of the textual tradition in television studies must in the end be dictated by external factors – the disciplinary orientation of the analyst, the length and purpose of the study, the intended readership. In the case of this chapter, the external conditions include an intellectual-critical tradition which is frequently accused of ignoring external factors altogether, namely literary criticism. Sometimes literary criticism is rightly castigated for ignoring factors external to a given text, but more positively a single-minded attention to textuality can be accepted as a necessary division of labour within the overall study of human culture; as a specialism which is devoted to isolating what constitutes 'the textual' in both formal terms and in terms of the cultural impact of textuality.

One 'external factor' which television studies certainly does neglect is the 'textual tradition' which has established itself in the television production industry itself. For those who work in the industry – producers, directors, actors, critics, regulators, advertisers and all the other professionals both creative and managerial – there is an internally shared 'textual tradition' which is an informal but quite powerful history of particular shows, series, personalities and genres, marked by anecdotes about famous triumphs and disasters, notable figures and notorious scandals. Such a 'textual tradition' performs some useful functions for the industry; it provides an occupational ideology to cement and cohere the profession (whose personnel move freely between different TV channels and production companies), and it offers those in the know a shorthand system by means of which new people and products can quickly (and surprisingly accurately) be placed and judged – generically, aesthetically and commercially. 'What's it like?' is the first question asked of a new venture. The answer can determine whether it gets commissioned, scheduled and promoted, or whether a new face or format gets to be seen.

However, the inside story of TV textuality is not very significant to TV studies, since the 'textual tradition' in TV studies comes not from TV itself, but from a combination of *external forces*, concentrated in several very influential discourse-producing *institutions of knowledge*:

1   formal **educational institutions** with their apparatus of research, conferences and publication and, of courses, lecturers, textbooks and exam questions;
2   **governmental institutions** with their apparatus of policy-formation, democratic will-formation (lobbying) and regulation/policing;
3   **critical institutions** within intellectual culture, including political organizations, unattached intellectuals, journalists and media commentators.

The interesting thing about these institutional forms of knowledge-production is that they may have a great deal to say about television without knowing anything about it from the inside; critics from universities, the government and the intelligentsia may hold very strong views about television's textuality without ever having watched TV.

It is worrying to discover that a 'textual tradition' can claim to speak authoritatively and – as we shall see – damningly about a new textual domain without first undertaking dispassionate detailed *textual* investigation, for the 'textual tradition's' own *reputation* among other academic disciplines is that of a mode of inquiry which neglects everything else except such textual details. For those who don't do it, textual analysis of television is often said to be inadequate because it fails to give due emphasis to *external factors* such as:

1   the **ownership and control** of television corporations;
2   the **political economy** of the industry;
3   the class, gender, ethnic or other **power structure** of society;
4   the psycho-social **impact** of the medium on members of the public;
5   the forms of community, identity and subjectivity which characterize different **audience** segments.

Even within textual analysis itself, 'external factors' are always at issue, although it is by no means safe to assume that they can be 'traced' or 'illustrated' in the textual features of a given text, whether that's a TV show or a Shakespeare play (sometimes of course these are the same thing). However, textual analysis has variously, and with varying success, been used to think about *external factors* such as:

1   the **intentions**, upbringing or psychology of the author/producer/director/star; ditto the critic or analyst (don't try this one at home);
2   the **historical and national context** in which a given text circulates and/or is analyzed;
3   the **social and cultural context** of production, distribution and readership;
4   the **general semiotic structure** of the discursive and linguistic systems which permit texts to be generated in the first place.

The suspicion directed at the 'textual tradition' by those in other areas is itself intensified by the addition of three other currents flowing through the discourses engaged in this dialogue:

1   **Causation** – the problem of science. Textualists are not scientists, because semiotic systems don't yield to scientific methods of analysis. They cannot 'prove' what they say about texts in general, or any given text, by reference to some demonstrable, verifiable chain of causation, using a method which can be repeated by others to give the same result and which provides empirical evidence in support of a hypothesis which is nevertheless falsifiable.
2   **Theory** – the allegiance to an 'ism'. Textualists (like most other academic researchers) are prone to analyzing texts according to the dictates of the

theoretical paradigm from which – consciously or unwittingly – flow their ideas and prejudices, their purposes and desires. Their 'readings' may turn out to be mere side-products of their theoretical allegiance, be that stated or implicit, liberal-individualist or Marxist, patriarchal or feminist, realist or postmodernist, imperial or postcolonial, straight or queer.

3   **Disciplinarity** – the institutionalized idiom, method and culture of knowledge-production. Disciplinarity can of course be useful where it promotes a recognition of the specialist methodologies and finding of different fields and thereby facilitates due allowance being made for other knowledge. But inter-disciplinary colloquy is not always characterized by such generosity or tolerance. It is not unknown for textualists working in cultural and media studies to be accused of not knowing and doing what sociology, political economy, history, statistics and demography, philosophy, anthropology (to name but a few) know and do. They are criticized from one branch of the knowledge-institution for not sharing the methods, personnel, common sense and truths of another.

Even the most formal and abstract types of textual analysis are trying to do and to prove something beyond analyzing the text. For instance, they may be trying to demonstrate the power, adequacy or limits of the formalist method itself, especially in relation to other textual methods which have become compromised with unwarranted claims (e.g. those literary studies which purported to know what a writer 'really meant' by referring to psychological concepts). Or they may be trying to test a theory, by showing how it is possible to make claims based on textual evidence (e.g. is it possible to say how good an aesthetic text may be without reference to its provenance, or what a text means without reference to its own 'biography' in the world?). Or they may wish to answer an empirical question, in particular the very difficult problem of how, if external factors are important, they manifest themselves in a text in such a way as to cause that text to have the individual or cultural effect claimed for it. Perhaps most importantly, the textual tradition's earliest and most sustained interest in television was based on what was feared to be the new medium's negative impact on 'external factors'. TV was confidently expected to result in the decline of everything other than and outside of television that the textualists held dear; culture, taste, order, decency, modesty. So, the most notoriously 'textual' parts of the textual tradition are the very places which are most militantly engaged in struggles about 'external factors'.

Hence, the 'textual tradition' was not interested in television's own textuality at all, but in its effect on others. We seem to have reached a point where a tradition of intellectual inquiry, analytical method and aesthetic classification and judgement going back several millennia is not interested in anything outside the text, but equally, not interested in anything inside television's textuality. This seems to require some explanation; which is that the 'textual tradition' entered the field of television studies (before television was invented), not as a neutral academic subject but as the moral centre of the school curriculum.

TEXTUAL TRADITIONS

The textual tradition in TV studies began when people trained in literary theory and 'practical criticism' turned their attention to popular culture. Unfortunately for the cause of television analysis, such training tended to emphasize strong hostility to popular cultural aesthetics and fear of the cultural impact of new entertainment media. So whereas many traditions of study in the general area of the arts have presumed some pleasurable investment by the student in the object of study, the textual tradition in television studies set out with the avowed intention of denouncing television and all its works. People who specialize in the textual study of forms like literature, the visual arts, photography or even cinema are presumed either to *like* their chosen form, or to have some talent in their textual *creation*. But the opposite was true of TV studies when it entered the academy; the successful student was the one who could catalogue most extensively the supposed evils associated with television, although of course these evils only affected *other* people, possibly because the students were not encouraged to watch TV themselves, only to opine haughtily about it. This powerful rhetoric of denunciation was in place, complete with a full repertoire of concepts, theories, even phrases, ready to be applied to television before it was invented, since the small screen was simply assumed to be an extension (perhaps even more pernicious) of previously despised popular media from newspapers to Hollywood; a threat to the traditions of culture. I.A. Richards, 'inventor' of the influential literary analytical method of 'practical criticism', explicitly linked these fears about a threat to cultural 'standards' with an equal fear of democratization:

> With the increase in population, the problem presented by the gulf between what is preferred by the majority and what is accepted as excellent by the most qualified opinion has become infinitely more serious, and appears likely to become threatening in the near future. For many reasons, standards are much more in need of defence now, than they used to be.
>
> (Richards, 1924: 36)

Television was not even on the public horizon when Richards expressed this need to defend 'qualified opinion' from 'what is preferred by the majority' in 1924. It follows that the critical onslaught which television has faced throughout its existence has its roots not in the medium itself, but in a pre-existing discourse of anxiety about popularization and modernity; a quite straightforward fear of and hostility to the democratization of taste. In this context 'what is accepted as excellent by the most qualified opinion' is 'the textual tradition' of literary culture and criticism, which Richards believed to be 'much more in need of defence' than in a period before 'the increase in population' associated with the Industrial Revolution.

Richards was not a lone voice, but part of a class action, as it were. Perhaps the best-known advocates of the 'textual tradition' are T.S. Eliot and F.R. Leavis, who elaborated, during the period when television was being invented, institutiona-lized and popularized (principally the 1930s to the 1950s), a 'way of under-standing' literature which was to prove enormously influential over the thinking of educators, policy-makers and commentators in schools, government depart-ments and in the middlebrow press, from those days to these. Their idea of 'tradition' was to say that 'Literature' (with a capital L; the received literary canon) was not something an author, much less a reader, could add or respond to on a case-by-case basis, but was an 'organic' whole, a 'tradition' which must be grasped imaginatively *as* an organic whole by those who would seek to understand or to contribute to it. And so Leavis and Eliot took the previously descriptive notion of 'the great tradition' – a succession of named 'texts' by 'great' authors – and upgraded it into a full-blown ideology of 'culture'. This ideology, which caught on among educators through the remarkable success of Leavis's journal *Scrutiny*, which spread its judgmental, finger-wagging certainties through the college seminar rooms and school staffrooms of middle England, was that 'the great tradition' provided the *antidote* to modern life, industrialization and what Leavis called 'machine-applied power.' In a famous passage, Leavis and his collaborator Denys Thompson set out what they were *against*:

> The great agent of change, and from our point of view, destruction, has of course been machine-applied power. The machine has brought us many advantages, but it has destroyed the old ways of life, the old forms, and by reason of the continual rapid change it involves, prevented the growth of the new. Moreover, the advantage it brings us in mass production has turned out to involve standardization, and levelling-down outside the realm of mere material goods. Those who in schools are offered (per-haps) the beginnings of education in taste are exposed, out of school, to the competing exploitation of the cheapest emotional responses; films, newspapers, publicity in all its forms, commercially-catered fiction – all offer satisfaction at the lowest level, and inculcate the choosing of the most immediate pleasures, got with the least effort.
>
> (Leavis and Thompson, 1933: 3)

This pessimistic snobbishness so wants to sneer at cultural forms which are 'cheap' (at point of sale only of course; films, newspapers, and the rest are far from cheap at the points of production and distribution) that it cannot entertain for a moment the idea that standardization might produce *good* products, or that 'choosing immediate pleasures' might be OK (it's what art-lovers do), or that 'rapid change' *is* (rather than '*prevents*') the growth of new forms, or that the 'old ways of life' were abandoned, by those whose lives they were, just as soon as modernity allowed, or that 'education in taste' suffered from 'competition' out-side school because it was not really what Leavis thought it was – an absolute standard of objective quality – but actually a prejudicial ideology of supremacism based not on the 'perfection' of the 'great tradition' but on the fact that the 'taste' in question was a projection of a rather narrow, sectional cultural hierarchy on to the entire semiosphere. For those born of industrialization and urbanization, the growth of 'mass' society was not experienced as a cultural calamity but as life, and mass communication, whether physical (transport and tourism) or virtual (popular media and entertainment), was not a 'competing exploitation' to which innocent victims were 'exposed', but an intrinsic component of a socialized mode of living.

What accounts for the astonishing success of the Leavisite ideology of 'the great tradition' of 'texts' is not its internal coherence, nor the stability of its judgements, nor even that it was an heroic attempt to do something impossible but valuable in the face of massification. Leavisite textualism took hold for two more prosaic reasons – it was suited to classes and classrooms. First, it was suited to the class position, life-outlook and professional skills of a particular group – middle-class, college-educated schoolteachers, bureaucrats and administrative workers, products of neither of the 'fundamental' classes of 'capital' and 'labour', whose only means to take power in the world was to textualize it, and thence to manipulate the texts into orders which *could* be controlled and managed. Second, Leavisism offered a coherent and principled stance which was radical without being political (i.e. it was militant, but not Marxist) and which seemed to be able to make sense of modernity without being part of it. In other words, it offered its adherents a sense of personal exemption from the rigours of historical change ('decline'), and put in place a system of what it claimed were timeless values – ideology posing as objective truth. It was thus perfectly suited to adoption in the classroom as the moral successor to religious faith in a secular, modern world. It quickly became what it most wanted to be – the moral centre of the school curriculum:

> The school-training of literary taste does indeed look a forlorn enterprise. Yet if one is to believe in education at all, one must believe that something worth doing can be done. And if one is to believe in anything, one must believe in education. We cannot, as we might in a healthy state of culture, leave the citizen to be formed unconsciously by his environment; if anything like a worthy idea of satisfactory living is to be saved, he must be trained to discriminate and resist.
>
> (Leavis and Thompson, 1933: 3–4)

And so literary contempt for modernity in its commercial and popular aspects did not remain confined to professors of English who didn't like mass culture, but infiltrated the schools as part of an agenda for *resistance* by the radical Right; an agenda which is still vigorously pursued by even the most senior apparatchiks in the schools system (such as the Chief Inspector of Schools in England and Wales, as mentioned above). While officially 'political' propaganda was forbidden in schools, Leavisite 'training in resistance' was officially encouraged. Ironically, having become the unarguable common sense of schooling, it was largely taught by and to those who were the products of modernity, beneficiaries of democratization and audiences of popular media. Here's the *Report of the Consultative Committee on Secondary Education* of 1938 (the Spens Report):

> Teachers are . . . not to be envied their struggle against the natural conservatism of childhood [i.e. resistance to learning standard English speech] allied to the popularization of the infectious accents of Hollywood. The pervading influence of the hoarding, the cinema, and a large section of the public press, are (in this respect as in others) subtly corrupting the taste and habits of the rising generation.
>
> (quoted in Goulden and Hartley, 1982: 14)

This 'struggle' against childhood and Hollywood was conducted with *texts* – 'culture' – and it was waged against industrialization. Here's another government report, this time the Symonds Report on *The Education of the Adolescent*, published in 1926, the year of the General Strike, which was itself the most public and theatrical manifestation of the 'dangers' of industrialization in the period leading up to television:

> Industrialization has its grave effects on national life. It demands, only too often, a narrow specialization of faculty: it produces, only too readily, a patterned uniformity of work and behaviour; it may, unless it is corrected, infect the minds of men with the genius of its own life. Education can correct industrialization by giving to the mind the breadth and the fresh vitality of new interests, as it can also make industry more effective.
>
> (quoted in Goulden and Hartley, 1982: 14)

It transpires, then, that 'culture' is the antidote to the 'infections' of industry, the genius of whose own life included not only standardization and uniformity, but also class antagonism and, in 1926, political resistance. Ever since Matthew Arnold theorized a political connection between culture and modernity (1869), the belief among 'university-men' and schools inspectors was that culture would tame the Englishman's propensity to use his freedom to riot. The 'textual tradition', then, is for the textualization of cultural value (and its 'inculcation' in schools); it is *against* the 'infections' of popular culture, but its underlying agenda is the control and management not of the culture so much as the population. It's a species of counter-revolutionary ideology in a period of 'mass' politics, 'mass' production, 'mass media'.

In this context, television's reputation was established before it ever went on air. The 'textual tradition' couldn't see television outside of the terms I've just outlined – Leavis and his followers had written the script of what has since become the standard line of criticism. Television's 'pervading influence' would be the same as the rest of popular culture; apt to 'corrupt the taste and habits of the rising generation' – before that generation was born. It was into this intellectual environment that television itself was launched. What that process seemed to *mean* at the time, and how television's own *textuality* began to establish itself into what has since become its obvious forms, is the subject of the next chapters.

7

BRIEF ENCOUNTERS, KHAKI SHORTS AND WILFUL BLINDNESS

Television without television

And here the first crude television image was created from the Farnsworth system when a photograph of a young woman was transmitted in the San Francisco Green Street Laboratory on 7 September 1927.

(Newcomb, 1997: 595)

IN THE BEGINNING WAS (NOT) THE BBC

The BBC's first regular broadcast television service, begun on 2 November 1936, was by no means the world's first television. As a technical possibility it had been invented in the nineteenth century (before cinematography). It was demonstrated experimentally in the 1920s, in Britain by John Logie Baird in 1922.

Indeed, by 1927, it was well-enough known to become the subject of an article in a Boy's Annual by one William J. Brittain (1927: 13–14). It had already entered the realms of primary-level teaching discourse. Brittain describes the electronic and mechanical systems, and reports on developments in Hungary

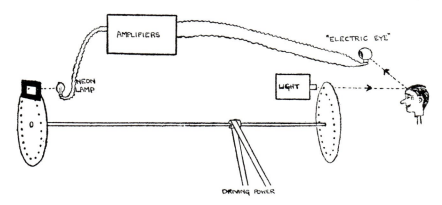

Figure 7.1 'A possible method of achieving television', 1927
Source: *Young Australia*, 1927

71

and Berlin (Denes von Mihaly), Munich (Max Dieckmann), Paris (M. Belin, who has a machine with 'wagging mirrors') and America (no details). The American equivalent to these pioneers would have been one Philo T. Farnsworth, a private inventor who eventually sold his patents to RCA (CBS) in 1939 (Spigel, 1992: 196; see also Newcomb, 1997: 595). Saying that 'television promises exciting things for boys', Brittain predicts that 'now we believe we are approaching the stage where the handy boy will be able to make his television set at home and operate it, just as he exercises his handiwork on his radio set'. After all, Baird himself used homely DIY materials: 'The lenses were from bicycle lamps; and other parts of his apparatus were biscuit tins and sealing wax and string' (making TV sound like a cross between Heath Robinson and Lewis Carroll), and with 'these materials, made up in his attic, he was able to show eminent scientists the winking, blinking face of somebody in the next room' (Brittain, 1927: 13).

Describing how 'Professor Max Dieckmann, another famous experimenter' was 'working with his young assistants, in an open-neck shirt and khaki cotton shorts' (making TV sound like a cross between Baden Powell and the Hitler Youth), Brittain introduces the principle which was eventually to prevail — that of the cathode ray tube:

> Electrons Professor Dieckmann hopes to use. They are tiny particles of electricity which fly across inside your wireless valve, and they are given off whenever you have two plates attached to high tension current inside a vacuum tube. Streams of these electrons have already been made to zig-zag over a screen in a television receiver, and Dieckmann hopes that by similarly zig-zagging them he will be able to use them at the sending end. The great value of electrons is that they have hardly any weight and can travel almost as quickly as a wink across a room.
>
> (Brittain, 1927: 14)

If 'real television' can be achieved, Brittain predicts, with real insight as to the demand for what TV might do (as opposed to his rather sketchy notions of how it might do it), a boy could 'sit at home and watch the Cup Final, or the Derby, or a boxing match in New York'. Rounding off his study with some advice for the boy who wants 'to join the famous group of television inventors by planning your own machine', Brittain suggests that 'the most promising method to start with is that chiefly used in America', but although he adds a helpful diagram showing how the thing ought to work (Figure 7.1), he concludes:

> I have been purposely vague in my details, for as yet no man in the world can say which is the best way. If a boy, using his ingenuity, happens to hit some new and simple way of achieving the necessary point by point exploration he will make his fame and fortune.
>
> (Brittain, 1927: 14)

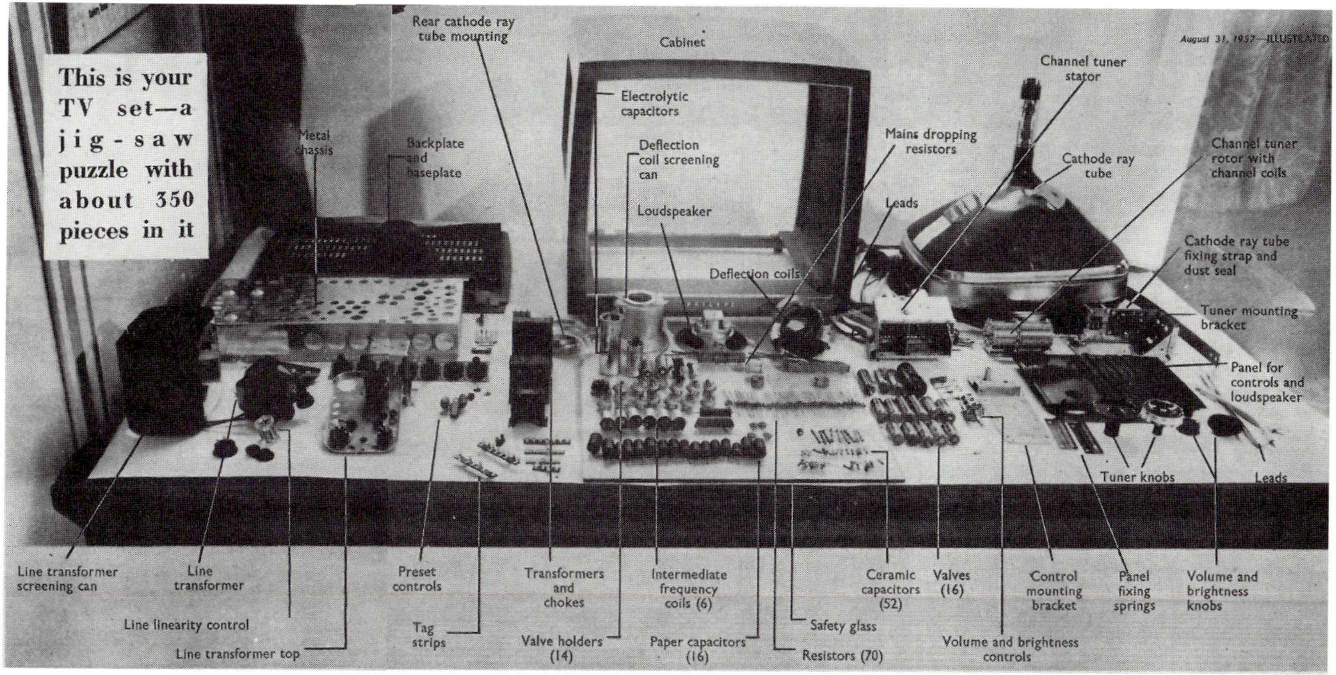
August 31, 1957—ILLUSTRATED
This is your TV set—a jig-saw puzzle with about 350 pieces in it
Metal chassis
Backplate and baseplate
Rear cathode ray tube mounting
Cabinet
Electrolytic capacitors
Deflection coil screening can
Loudspeaker
Deflection coils
Mains dropping resistors
Leads
Channel tuner stator
Cathode ray tube
Channel tuner rotor with channel coils
Cathode ray tube fixing strap and dust seal
Tuner mounting bracket
Panel for controls and loudspeaker
Tuner knobs
Leads
Line transformer screening can
Line transformer
Line linearity control
Line transformer top
Preset controls
Tag strips
Transformers and chokes
Valve holders (14)
Intermediate frequency coils (6)
Paper capacitors (16)
Safety glass
Resistors (70)
Ceramic capacitors (52)
Valves (16)
Volume and brightness controls
Control mounting bracket
Panel fixing springs
Volume and brightness knobs

Figure 7.2 'This is your TV set', 1957
Source: *Illustrated*, 31 August 1957

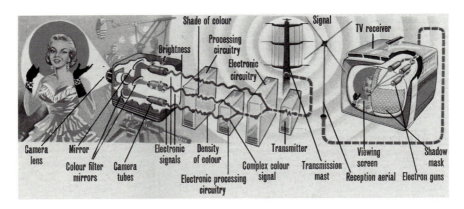

The labels in the figure read:

Shade of colour · Signal · TV receiver · Brightness · Processing circuitry · Electronic circuitry

Camera lens · Mirror · Electronic signals · Density of colour · Transmitter · Viewing screen · Shadow mask

Colour filter mirrors · Camera tubes · Complex colour signal · Transmission mast · Reception aerial · Electron guns

Electronic processing circuitry

Figure 7.3 'How colour TV is made', 1957
Source: *Illustrated*, 31 August 1957

In the event, that 'boy' turned out to be the electrical manufacturer EMI (Electrical and Musical Industries); their cathode-ray tube system was adopted by the BBC after competitive trials with Baird's system. But more to the point, William Brittain's short disquisition on television in 1927 ensured that boys throughout the Empire were offered the beginnings of home-tutored demand for whatever it was that the EMI-BBC-GPO cartel eventually came up with.

Numerous public systems were up and running by the 1930s, notably in America, where television was an attraction at various exhibitions, taverns and department stores, developed for public/theatrical exhibition along the lines of cinema, and in Germany, which broadcast the Berlin Olympic Games in the summer of 1936, making these the first-ever television Olympics. Even in Britain, television had been seen by quite a large public prior to its official 'beginning' in November, during various exhibitions such as 'RadiOlympia' at Earl's Court in mid-1936 (see Spigel, 1992: 32; *Die Olympischen-Spiele*, 1936, 162–3; Hartley, 1992a: Chapters 11 and 14).

In fact, the difference between these spectacular one-offs and the BBC's first regular television was not only that the latter was a continuing service, but also, interestingly, that far more people would have seen the exhibition version of television than ever watched the early regular broadcast. People flocked in their masses to huge purpose-built halls at Olympia and Earl's Court to see annual exhibitions ranging from the Ideal Home Exhibition to the Boat Show. Such shows mixed technical advances with consumer-fever, corporate marketing with national advancement, private pleasure-seeking with mass-congregation, sales with sensationalism. It was in this superheated context that British television was first publicized, with live pictures being sent from a transmitter at the Alexandra Palace in north London to thrill the watching crowds in central London.

The BBC's regular television service, by contrast, broadcast to a tiny audience made up mostly of electrical retailers and some affluent consumers of the type which has since become known as 'early adopters' – people interested in the technology, the medium itself, and in being as up-to-date as possible with modern innovation, rather than those who simply want to purchase an already-familiar entertainment service. The early broadcasts were 'regular' because they occurred every day, but only for a couple of hours in the afternoon and early evening – timed to help retailers demonstrate the newfangled and expensive device. Clearly this pioneering experiment was no match for the much more popular and massively capitalized BBC radio service, nor could it compete with cinema, which was aesthetically at its zenith and close to its all-time highest worldwide ticket sales (which it reached in the early 1940s) during this period. Anyone on the look-out for semiotic intensity in November 1936 had only to step out to the local picture palace to see Eleanor Powell in Cole Porter's brilliant musical *Born to Dance*, or Charlie Chaplin's anti-fascist comedy *Modern Times*, or Fritz Lang's lynch-mob melodrama *Fury*, while BBC television's first viewers were treated to Pogo the Pantomime Horse and a re-run of last week's *British Movietone News*.

BRIEF ENCOUNTERS WITH POSSIBLE HISTORIES

Television was first seen by the public as a collective, one-off spectacle, typified in the twin Olympiads of Berlin (the Games) and London (the Radio Show) in the summer of 1936. Television as an individuated, private, regular experience for affluent consumers to enjoy in their homes was not first on the scene, and was not exactly a smash hit when it got there. It was in America that these two strands, of public spectacle and private consumption, eventually came together, in the 1939 New York World's Fair and, decisively, in the development of the commercial network television industry during the 1940s. But before we get to that, it is worth pausing to notice just how different from what has since become familiar television was when it was seen by its first audience.

First, it was a popular attraction associated with crowds, spectacle, urban activity, technology and modernization at venues in Berlin, New York and London which carried a massive ideological charge over and above their ostensible purpose. In their different ways, the crowd-pulling events where TV got its first popular airing – the Olympic Games, World's Fair and the Radio Show – all celebrated the mid-century passion for spectacular national self-aggrandizement, for the politics of mass-mankind and for the public display of industrial innovation as the aesthetic of the age. The form taken by the politics of mass-industrial-modernization was of course decisively different in different countries, as each system vied with the others to prove both its popular appeal and its capacity for planned but unlimited growth. Germany (Nazism), America (the New Deal), the Soviet Union (socialism) and the British Empire (free trade) were, however, competitors in the same race, in which totalitarian, democratic and imperial systems of governmental organization were all pursuing the same goal – the completion of modernity, whatever that might turn out to mean.

It was in this live, collective, exhibitionary, urban, competitive, nationalistic and modernizing context that television was encountered by its first audience. This was its textuality; never mind the 'text' on screen at any given moment. For those who first watched it, television was something out-of-the-ordinary in the most literal sense, and it required the mobilization of the resources of modern life even to get to it. People would have to leave home, catch a train, bus or tram to get to a huge venue – a stadium, exhibition hall or purpose-built park – in or near a giant metropolis, in which thousands of other similar but unknown people would be congregating, milling around the places where the euphoria of inten-sively capitalized modernity could be experienced directly through rides, shows, displays and spectacular one-off events. Such experiences were of the cheek-by-jowl, jostling variety, where wonderment at the new technology could be shared and multiplied among the crowd, whose skills in collective oohing and aahing, in looking and listening, in the expression of mutuality by laughter, applause, banter, repartee, singing and even catcalling, had been rehearsed and honed by decades of music-hall and variety, not to mention fairs and markets going back to time immemorial. These audiences were attracted by novelty and held by celeb-rity, for which non-material 'goods' they were willing to spend quite substantial amounts of time and money – a whole day out and the price of entrance-plus-extras (substantial expenditure in the still-hungry 1930s). Once confronted by the big, public television apparatus, they were guided and encouraged in their reactions by popular figures from radio, stage and screen appearing live, and by the blandishments of the public address system, as the organizers attempted to marshal uniform responses from the ever-changing and easily distracted throng, whose attention was not only fixed on the show, but also on the children darting about threatening to get lost, on the backchat and jocular remarks emanating from wiseacres among the crowd, and on the pressing need to visit as many attractions, stalls and rides as time allowed, keeping an eye out for the location of food and toilets.

These were the same people who took their routine visual pleasures from visiting the cinema an average of three or four times a week, watching a repertoire of newsreels, documentaries, cartoons, comedy shorts and cliff-hanger serials as well as two feature-length narrative films. It was possible for people to fit 'the flicks' into the rhythms of modern, urban work-life by going into a small local theatre on the way home or in a break, watching the continuous programme through to the point where they came in, then carrying on their way. You can get a sense of this way of experiencing cinema from watching the opening sequences of Noel Coward and David Lean's 1942 film about inconstancy and its attractive dangers, *Brief Encounter*, where strangers meet and lives are entangled in the anonymous but intimate spaces of the fast-food cafeteria, railway station and cinema. A young married-but-independent woman becomes detached from her home and family life, pursuing her most private desires and doubts in the

Figure 7.4 *Brief Encounter*, 1942: Inconstancy, mobility, modernity . . . danger
Source: Kobal Collection. Courtesy of National Film Archive/Stills Library

dislocations of public mobility, beginning a clandestine liaison among – even because of – the metallic gleaming machinery of industrialized eating, timetabled travel and capital-intensive entertainment, falling in love with someone from the anonymous crowd after repeated chance encounters in public places, their relationship nurtured in the safe-but-dangerous darkness of the local picture-house, paced by laughter and enjoyment, first of Donald Duck and jungle adventure, then of each other.

Mobility, anonymity, organized city life and the special, pleasurable but always dangerous disruptions of *routinely* being out in public, away from home, a citizen of a country whose official culture was doing its best to convince you that it was the most comfortable, fashionable, forward-looking, fastest-growing nation among all those striving to distribute to its populace the benefits of modern associated living; these were the 'influences' on television's first audience, as it gathered, dispersed and assembled again in the big, collective, spectacular spaces of the great metropolis, seeing TV as one of those modern marvels, wonders of technology, alongside the automobile and the aeroplane, mixed in with the contradictory promises of mass production and mass propaganda, the contrary pulls of democracy and the demagogue, popular sovereignty and populist hegemony, planning and totalitarianism.

An audience trained in collective reception, travelling into Town from far and wide to encounter television at a spectacular venue as a one-off novelty, is clearly going to *see* something very different from an audience made up of people sitting in their own homes, viewing regular programmes within the ordinary rhythms of everyday family life, on an apparatus they privately own, even if the audience is made up of the same people, watching the very same 'text'. People were used to listening to radio at home in their millions, but travel, a public venue and novelty were the stock-in-trade of live shows or the movies, not of broadcasting. If the new medium bore any resemblance to radio (beyond being produced by the BBC), it was more like the experience of being present at the 'live recording' of a new show, than like that of receiving it as a scheduled broadcast. In other words, it is important not only to realize how very different television could have been, compared with what we have become used to after more than sixty years, but also to recall how it actually *was* very different. Its 'textuality' at this and any moment includes the context of viewing, the knowledges, skills and habits of its viewers, and the familiarity or otherwise of neighbouring media, which in this case included, beyond the obvious 'mass' media of cinema and radio, other urban forms ranging from vaudeville and variety theatre to sporting events up to and including Olympic Games, and modernist spectacles, exhibitions and shows which promoted industrial production, private consumption, political philosophies and national competitiveness.

ABDICATING 'NOWNESS' – WILFUL BLINDNESS

In this context, it is interesting to note that the fledgling medium was embarked on a career of historical development which had no foregone conclusion, no obvious direction, no pre-ordained form. The television technology developed in Germany for the Berlin Games was, naturally, understood at the time as part of German technological supremacism, and was in fact much more advanced and sophisticated than either the Baird system in Britain or the American system. Beyond this, of course, German television was developed within the context of a country which was rapidly moving towards totalitarianism throughout its industrial, communications and public sectors; a fate television could not help but share. It was celebrated in the Berlin Olympics, then, not as a branch of the private consumer industry, but of public spectacle; a means of propagation for the cause of national socialism, which was at this stage promoting 'strength through joy' for its preferred community of future-orientated healthy young Aryans (like the 'Volkswagen' launched in 1934), before moving to the exterminatory ideology of 'work makes free' for excluded and subjected populations (see Bleuel, 1973: 119–21, 128–9). From such beginnings, television could – and did – develop as an instrument of mass communication for state propaganda, to be enjoyed as a matter of national pride and collective will-formation, not as a means of suburban relaxation for the office-worker class.

Figure 7.5 TV camera at the 1936 Olympic Games. The caption reads 'The TV camera
  seems like the barrel of a giant cannon'
Source: From *Die Olympischen-Spiele 1936*. Published by Cigaretten-Bilderdienst Altona-Bahrenfeld, 1936;
  vol. 2, p. 162–3

Figure 7.6 TV as mass spectacle (artist's impression of the closing ceremony)
Source: From *Die Olympischen-Spiele 1936*. Published by Cigaretten-Bilderdienst Altona-Bahrenfeld, 1936;
  vol. 2, p. 160

Figure 7.7 Mass spectacle as national self-aggrandisement (artist's impression of the airship
    Hindenburg over the stadium)
Source: From *Die Olympischen-Spiele* 1936. Published by Cigaretten-Bilderdienst Altona-Bahrenfeld, 1936;
    vol. 2, p. 16

As we've seen, Britain launched another variant of mass/spectacle television in the depoliticized form of the exhibitionist's gadget designed to thrill the idle crowd for a day. But the form in which television was to become familiar, that of a commercial leisure entertainment medium for individuals living private lives in family homes in suburbia, did not grow out of the earliest versions of the new medium; not even the 'regular' service launched by the BBC in November 1936. Although this service continued broadcasting for three years, during which it trialled new ideas, including the first outside broadcasts (for instance the 1937 Derby horse-race and the Oxford v. Cambridge Boat Race – just as the *Young Australia* Boy's Annual had predicted a decade earlier), and various genres of programming which have since become standard, from single-play drama to variety shows, it was not in Britain at all that the 'cultural form' of television began to take definitive shape. British television was cancelled for the duration of the Second World War, returning only in 1946 (with a re-run of the same Mickey Mouse cartoon which had been playing when the plugs were unceremoniously pulled in September 1939). By this time, commercial network television was in full swing in the USA, and although the British government did not allow commercial TV for another decade, the American form of television was eventually re-imported to both Britain and Germany, and everywhere else. After the war had given way to the cold war, the menace of national socialism to the spectre of communism, and the British Empire and German Reich had both given way to the newly ascendant American hegemony, it was the American version of television which finally conquered the world.

One of the reasons that Britain did not invent the cultural form of television even though it was in at the outset of its technological invention is that the circumstances were not right for this kind of development. Not only did the managers running the BBC see television literally as a sideshow, but they actively and deliberately downgraded it as a broadcasting priority. On no account was it to compete or even interfere with what they saw as their main business, which was the creation of a national cultural institution in the form of BBC radio, and a national community in the form of popular radio audiences. The bigwigs at the BBC were actually quite hostile to television, refusing it resources, personnel, premises and even entire genres of output – the BBC television service was not allowed to make its own news programmes at all, having to make do with cinema newsreel and 'soft' feature material for fear of undermining the authority of the radio news. Thus, it so happened that one of the most important political news stories of the century broke exactly one month after broadcast television opened, but TV had nothing to do with it. The constitutional crisis of 1–10 December 1936, which culminated in Edward VIII's abdication, was not permitted to be a 'television event'. However, the departing king's *radio* broadcast to the Empire was an intrinsic part of the unfolding story at the time and even now it is regularly recalled and revived (often on TV); we can still hear the *tone of voice* of that individual tragedy in which the young king chose his American divorcee over his imperial duties, but we can't see its face.

Figure 7.8 Announcer Elizabeth Cowell, 1936, 'in one of the first photographs ever taken from a television set'
Source: Illustrated, 31 August 1957

Figure 7.9 The Six Princes Girls dancing for TV in 1937
Source: Illustrated, 31 August 1957

82

Figure 7.10 The domestication of television: Germany, September 1939. 'Fernsehen − nah gesehen' (far-seeing [i.e. television] − seen close). The captions read:
1   'I liked the earlier method better; you didn't have to look elsewhere!'
2   'Made it myself from a TV set and a dummy − yesterday I danced a rumba with La Jana − geez, hot babe.'
3   − 'Can't you switch it on, the TV?'
    − 'Can't − my wife locked it. 'Bout this time there's ususally a show on: "1,000 Red Lips in Hawaii".'
4   'Now kids, be nice and do what the auntie says . . .'
Source: Münchner Illustrierte Presse, 14 September 1939

There are other faces that can't be seen – or see. They come from a series of ads for forthcoming TV, radio and photography hardware in wartime *Picture Post* just before victory. These are very peculiar ads, first of all because they are advertising something that cannot be bought. Radio sets and TV sets were not just rationed in the Second World War, they were unobtainable, and television was closed down altogether. However, manufacturers like GEC, Marconi and Mullard wanted consumer-demand to build up a head of steam in readiness for the post-war release of consumer goods; they wanted potential consumers to remember their own brand name; and they wanted to associate the values and virtues of war with their products (see Figures 7.11–7.16). This wasn't difficult for high-tech machinery and electronics firms whose productive apparatus had been given over wholesale to the war effort. Hence these peculiar ads; associating the unattainable with the unseeable. The images in the ads are of blindness, death, isolation and precision-hardware. What do they presage? Certainly not a future full of consumer euphoria. Death of the future? Of Empire (see Taylor, 1991)? They do seem poignantly honest images of British expectations about its televisual future – high-tech, certainly; heroic, possibly; lost, unable to see where it's going and doomed, definitely. As with so much else in 1945, from global spy networks and the jet engine to the burden of world leadership, so in consumer-television – the British Empire simply handed the whole lot over to the Americans. BBC television broadcasting re-commenced in 1946. When it eventually allowed itself to carry news of the day (as opposed to soft-feature newsreels, to which the BBC

Figure 7.11 Ekco Television
Source: Picture Post, April 1945

84

Figure 7.12 GEC Radio and Television
Source: *Picture Post*, April 1945

Figure 7.13 Mullard '1912'
Source: Picture Post, April 1945

restricted the television service until the later 1940s), it was just as blind; news had to be read from the radio news department's scripts with absurdly restricted visuals. This and other rules of presentation were explicitly designed to prevent the new medium developing its own style, its own literacy, its own autonomy.

There were of course at the time voices of those who were keen to point out the one thing TV had that cinema didn't – *nowness*. Here, for example, is Maurice Gorham, a former head of the BBC television service, writing in 1950 in favour of the then seemingly doubtful proposition that television is a medium in its own right:

> The ability to transmit images of things that are actually happening, whether or not they are enacted specially, is the hall-mark of television

Figure 7.14 Mullard 'Deeds not words!'
Source: Picture Post, April 1945

as compared with films. . . . The appeal is simplest and most unmistak-
able when it is a question of real events in which people are interested,
and not events created by the effort of writers, actors, and producers,
and in this sense television has given new meaning to the world
'topical.' In films this applies to anything that has happened recently;
in television, to things that are happening now.

(Gorham, 1951: 137)

Gorham goes on to suggest that public events (like election results or the
coronation of 1937), sporting events (the boat race and cup finals) and news
are the forms most appropriate to television's immediacy. But, as he notes, British
television was in fact obliged to develop without news at all. The reason was not

Figure 7.15 Ilford film
Source: Picture Post, May 1945

because the BBC failed to recognize the primacy of nowness, but – on the contrary – they *did* recognize that TV's liveness, immediacy and hybridity of inputs made it the 'ideal vehicle for the radio newspaper'; and precisely for this reason they were determined not to let it 'invade the sacred precincts' of their authoritative radio news:

> But television can handle real news. . . . British television has not often entered this field, but that is probably due to the conservatism of the B.B.C., which sets great store on the 'news policy' that it has built up for sound radio and hesitates to let the television men invade the sacred precincts. American stations, less reverent, have been doing news

Figure 7.16 Electricity
Source: Picture Post, April 1945

programmes bad and good for years, and I suspect that behind its impenetrable curtain Russian television is doing the same. It is surely obvious that the television medium, with its power to combine actuality pick-ups and prepared illustrations, radio news, films, diagrams, and live speakers in the studio, is the ideal vehicle for the radio newspaper that will undoubtedly come in time, even here.

(Gorham, 1951: 143)

Thus, having inaugurated its broadcast form, the BBC at managerial levels tried quite hard to starve it, if not to death, then at least to the point where it posed no

It's hard to choose between
rival attractions, but we sort
out guinea-winning letters

WOMAN TO WOMAN

Figure 7.17 The birth of the 'choice-oisie': the week ITV was launched, October 1955
Source: *Woman*, 16 October 1955

threat to radio. As is well known, the two events which finally provided the incentive to make television in Britain into a popular cultural form came from the audience and the government respectively, not from the BBC at all; they were the coronation of the young Queen Elizabeth II in June 1953 and the launch of ITV (commercial television) two years later, in October 1955. Only then did the BBC look to its laurels, responding to popular and legislative demand, and begin competing for a popular audience in earnest. With the launch of what became known as the 'duopoly' (BBC-TV as the monopoly national public-service broad-caster, plus the ITV commercial monopoly, where a dozen or so regionally-based companies competed with the BBC, but not with each other), British television finally became 'television proper', as it were, formally and culturally, and the form was American. Not only did both ITV and the BBC import many American shows, but they copied American formats, from soap opera to sitcom, up to and including news presentation – the ITV news provider, ITN, borrowed the format and even the studio decor of Ed Morrow's respected American show *See It Now*, and eventually the BBC copied ITN.

It is a matter of historical record that British television did not garner the huge popular audiences that made US TV so powerful so quickly (only 0.2 per cent of US homes had TV in 1946, and 2.3 per cent in 1949; installations jumped to 9 per cent in 1950, rising to 65 per cent in 1955 and 85 per cent in 1959; (see Attallah, 1991: 72). But perhaps there is more to this fact than merely the short-sightedness (or different priorities) of BBC management. Perhaps the problem was in the audience itself. It may well be that in Britain at least, as in Germany, the conditions were not right culturally and socially for the development of a giant popular following for television, and hence for the programming and textual offerings associated with its beginnings in Europe. Perhaps, in short, the *problem* with television's early textuality lay not with *television* but with *housing*.

Before it could become a domestic medium, there had to be houses for TV to occupy; before it could entrance its family audience in the privacy of their own homes they had to *have* their own homes. And in 1935–6, when television was being invented in both its spectacular and its domestic forms in Britain, there were simply not enough of the right kind of homes for it to occupy. The reason for this can plainly be seen in – is the subject matter of – *Housing Problems*.

8

HOUSING TELEVISION
A film, a fridge and social democracy

O welche Lust, in freier Luft
Den Atem leicht zu heben!
Nur hier, nur hier ist Leben!
O what joy to breathe freely in the open air! Up here alone is life!

(Ludwig van Beethoven)

In 1935, one year before the official 'first' television broadcast in Britain, a short film called *Housing Problems* was released, made by Edgar Anstey and Arthur Elton for the Gas Council; a film which has since become very famous, being a staple on courses in film and cinema studies (at least in the United Kingdom), where it is used as an example of the tradition of documentary filmmaking established by John Grierson. As a result of this critical and historical attention, the film is still available for viewing, unlike early television, little if any of which survives. Despite being made for cinema, *Housing Problems* makes a very good 'opening' text for television studies, because it shows what screen semiosis *looked* like at the very outset of the new medium. *Housing Problems* articulates together the two themes of public spectacle and domestic life outlined in the previous chapter; it shows urban modernism mixed with the private lives of working people, public policy applied to family circumstances, and for the audience, the sensation of being *away* from home (at the cinema) to *think* about home (as a 'problem'). Just as television itself was launched in both spectacular and domestic forms, so *Housing Problems* is an essay in bringing public semiosis to the aid of private distress; publicity to the aid of privation.

The film is very short at fifteen minutes, and comprises two main sequences. The first sets up the 'problems' of the title, showing slum housing in London's East End, with a commentary by a local councillor and a succession of working-class tenants speaking for themselves, telling the viewer about the lack of light, water, clean air and cooking facilities, and illustrating with vivid unscripted anecdotes the dilapidation, vermin and noxiousness, the want of privacy, sound-proofing and amenity, of their tiny flats and rooms. The second section produces what are clearly meant to be seen as ideal solutions to these problems, introduced by an unseen and unidentified 'expert' voiceover, with a professional, male authoritativeness. We see a series of models of steel-framed and concrete housing blocks, and although the point is not pressed, it transpires that the room-

Figure 8.1 *Housing Problems*
Source: Courtesy of the BFI

heaters, hot water systems and cookers are all powered by gas. The film's sponsors, the British Commercial Gas Association, are buying PR rather than advertising; they're not attempting to sell gas installations or contracts to cinema-goers (the film is not an advertisement); rather they are trying to associate themselves with positive values, which are seen in the film as modernization, urban renewal, planning, hygiene, mass production using modern materials and scientific methods; a clean break with the unhealthy, unplanned, exploitative and inhumane conditions of the past.

Housing Problems was regarded from the moment of its first release as a radical film, and its enduring reputation rests upon its importance in the history of semiosis. Here's Roger Manvell's classic statement of its importance, written in 1944:

> *Housing Problems* took the camera and microphone to Stepney and recorded the slum-dwellers' views on the slums: spot interviews, unrehearsed and unscripted, are the feature of the first part of the film, supplemented by remarkably revealing shots of slum property for comfortably-housed citizens to contemplate on the screen.
>
> (Manvell, 1944: 102)

93

Figure 8.2 Housing Problems
Source: Courtesy of the BFI

Manvell's view of the film is clearly organized around its effect on viewers – its potential to cause a change in the knowledge if not the actions of 'comfortably-housed citizens' – and by implication this produces the momentum to achieve social change too. Here then is a proto-televisual text whose immediacy (unrehearsed and unscripted) and visuality (remarkably revealing) is put at the heart of the relation between social problems and citizens, with a suggestion that social change is made possible by such exposure. This is among the founding ideologies of the positive potential of popular visual media, especially among documentary filmmakers and actuality reporters.

Its most radical innovations are the very aspects that are now most easily overlooked, for the simple reason that what was surprising and never-before-tried in 1935 has since impressed enough producers and filmmakers to have become the bedrock of standard practice. *Housing Problems* uses real people, not actors. They are named in the film, which lets them speak in their own words in their own houses, not to a verbally tidied-up, editorially vetted and visually shaped script. It treats a mundane subject seriously, ordinary life with respect, and working-class people without patronization. Even the voice of 'authority' – a Labour councillor from the East End of London – speaks in tolerant tones of 'taking people as you find them'. In today's television parlance, the film is an 'actuality segment' in a 'current affairs' slot using 'vox pops' together with the viewpoints of authoritative and expert figures. Like any such segment in the early-evening news shows, the compelling quality of the film comes from the use of authentic eyewitnesses in real locations, its 'show and tell' simplicity. It has the logic of the glance, rather than that of formal argument; viewers can tell at a glance not only that this is obviously a 'problem', but also that this is clearly what must be done about it (a false progression from premise ('if this') to conclusion ('then that') which in formal logic is called a solecism). Expertise is distinguished from actuality formally in Housing Problems just as it has been on current affairs television segments ever since. The experts don't appear as themselves, but as an author-itative male voiceover. Expertise is not brought into the narrative until the problem has been so well illustrated that there's a strong narrative demand for resolution. Instead of the messy domesticity of the workers at home, we see the technological purity of plans, models, science.

On reflection, the 'logic' of Housing Problems is far from compelling, especially in the harsh light of hindsight, for the cure proposed was in some places to prove worse than the disease. With sincere conviction and militant self-con-fidence, the film wants to clear away slum conditions. But the shots it uses to demonstrate how uncomfortable and intolerable such life is for tenement dwellers – shots of women sweeping and beating the dust out of rugs in the back alleys, while the children play and muck around (see Figures 8.1 and 8.2) – these are the very scenes which the next generation claim as illustrations of the solidarity, community and supportive mutuality of working-class life. They show in fact the kind of unselfconscious communality of working-class life which Richard Hoggart is famously elegiac about, just as it was passing out of history (Hoggart, 1958: see especially the sections 'There's no place like home', pp. 20–6 and 'The neighbourhood', pp. 41–52). Hoggart was brought up in Leeds, in the very kind of poor neighbourhoods to which Housing Problems is so opposed. He is quite firm that housing is at the centre of what he valued about working-class culture:

> The more we look at working-class life, the more we try to reach the core of working-class attitudes, the more surely does it appear that the core is a sense of the personal, the concrete, the local: it is embodied in the idea of, first, the family and, second, the neighbour-hood. This remains, though much works against it, and partly because so much works against it.
>
> (Hoggart, 1958: 20)

In fact, the slum clearances which began in the early 1930s, and which were continued after the war into the 1950s and 1960s, struck at the physical heart of 'family' and 'neighbourhood'. It was only later that commentators started blaming 'the media' – television especially – for the dislocated culture, 'broken' families and hostile neighbourhoods of some working-class life.

Meanwhile, *Housing Problems* is passionate for working families to live in high-rise concrete blocks of flats, and in giant housing developments like Quarry Hill in Leeds itself. Again, the irony of history is that these 'solutions' to the 'housing problems' of the inter-war years in turn became major social, architectural and political problems after the Second World War. Quarry Hill itself, a model of which is presented in *Housing Problems* as the last word in light, airy, healthy, clean, convenient and pleasant living, was indeed built, but it was eventually demolished as an eyesore unfit for human habitation, taking a good deal of blame as the cause of individual isolation, family breakdown, juvenile disaffection, petty crime and social disintegration; a form of mass housing so brutal that it managed to produce the same human desolation it was designed by the experts to replace.

But in *Housing Problems*, the *semiotic* imperative is oblivious to such – or indeed any – consequences. The film is driven not by the needs of the people so memorably interviewed, but by its own need for narrative closure. *Housing Problems* has the political intention of improving conditions for working families, but it has the semiotic effect of producing not *solutions* to *problems*, but *victims* for *experts*. It is this move which has become traditional in television reporting ever since, as Brian Winston has argued: 'Given that the victim was to become a staple of the realist documentary, especially on television, the significance of *Housing Problems* cannot be overstated' (Winston, 1995: 45). News and actuality stories routinely adopt the same 'grammar' as *Housing Problems*:

- **subject**: visualization of what Winston calls the 'problem moment', together with vox pops of victims;
- **verb**: action by experts who also represent corporations, whether commercial or governmental;
- **predicate**: happy consumers commenting enthusiastically on the measurable improvements they've experienced.

In these narrative terms, then, it's an 'opening' text of televisuality, establishing the conventions by which reality was to be recognized, before the medium itself was invented.

One test of just how televisual it is is to look at those elements which now seem peculiar or even slightly ludicrous, to show how, in the history of looking, some things do change, while others have remained remarkably stable for over sixty years. For instance, the interview shots (as opposed to the location shots) look very odd to a TV-literate eye. The framing is too wide, the lighting too perfect, the composition very formal, the camera too static, the take too long. The whole thing is too cinematic, classic, in its composition, causing the action to occur in front of the coolly observant camera, rather than taking the camera into the action. Paradoxically, Anstey himself thought it was precisely this detached, disciplined immobility which gave the film over to its subjects. He later explained the effect he was trying for:

Nobody had thought of the idea which we had of letting slum dwellers simply talk for themselves, make their own film . . . we felt that the camera must remain sort of four feet above the ground and dead on, because it wasn't our film.

(quoted in Sussex, 1975: 62)

Housing Problems glimpses television's intimacy and involvement by going into the homes of ordinary people, but it retains a cinematically-trained vision of what such intimacy ought to look like.

Similarly, the interviews, which are its main claim to fame, are very peculiar to the TV-tuned ear. It is perhaps quite hard to recover a sense of how innovative they were at the time. In 1935, ordinary people did not participate in public culture without a script. Every interviewee on BBC radio, for example, had to follow a script, even if they were engaged in what was intended to sound like an impromptu or improvised conversation. Ordinary people, speaking for themselves, were almost unknown in mainstream cinema, which was in its spectacular, commercial, American heyday at this time. The idea of putting real people on the screen, without the mediating 'help' of a seen interviewer, to articulate in their own words the truth of their circumstances, was indeed an innovation, but of course it has since become standard practice. What's odd about these scenes to the post-television viewer is exactly that part of them which did not take hold as a routine semiotic practice. For instance, the interviewees are mostly standing, looking directly into the eye of the viewer, looking very formal and posed. Their stories are constructed out of the anecdotal traditions of working-class speech, which makes them sound rambling and repetitive to the ear trained in the sound-bite and, far from sounding 'natural' or as though it was 'their film', their delivery sounds stilted.

Housing Problems manifests organizational as well as semiotic attributes of television. As a socially campaigning film which was nonetheless sponsored by a commercial interest, it provides an exact model of the commercial form of 'public service broadcasting' that is still in place today. It managed to show, seemingly quite naturally, out of the realities of the situation, that the commercial interest of the gas industry (to lobby for public investment in apartment blocks which would use gas for heating, cooking and hot water) was also the national or public interest (better housing for 'the people'). The film's public service agenda – of investigating problems in the organization of modern society, focusing on improving the everyday, prioritizing the needs of ordinary people in central government planning, and of almost mystical belief in the ability of (capital intensive) technological inventions to solve social problems – these are still central doctrines in TV journalism and current affairs. Housing Problems is in many ways a straightforwardly commercial film; it was funded by commercial investment and made by a production team which commercially charged for its services, it was shown in commercial cinemas as part of a visual experience which consumers paid for. All this was seen as quite compatible with innovative semiotic and social ideas that were publicized by a production team in the name of non-commercial public interests. This shows that the 'mixed economy' of public semiosis and private enterprise which has been a feature of television ever since was fully in place before TV was born.

Housing Problems was revolutionary in the same way that Bolshevism was revolutionary – it favoured centralized planning and the imposition of expert knowledge to implement modernizations whose form was governed by experts, not by the people whose problems they were expected to solve. This revolutionary modernism extended to the use of film itself – the most advanced and the most popular information medium of the day to propagandize these changes in people's lives. *Housing Problems* proposes the destruction of entire neighbourhoods and their replacement with hitherto untried schemes whose novelty is only matched by their breathtaking scale. The housing projects it promotes are 'sold' on the basis of positive values like hygiene, convenience, privacy and affordability, but none of the experts who designed them is ever seen on screen, or asked to defend their schemes to the viewer, or discuss them face to face with the 'victims' of the slums who will be moved into them. Here then is the beginning of the use of the media – and television is still the most important site for this – for the *hegemony* of the modernizing knowledge-class expert to be popularized, in the name of the needs of the ordinary working population (see Frow, 1995, for the concept of the knowledge class). Such 'popularization' is a top–down process which capitalizes on the one productive force which knowledge-class professionals can command (information), by turning it from merely instrumental power ('know-how') into real social power (the management of populations and of social change).

Meanwhile, of course, the eyewitness-victim, who plays no part in the decision-making process which results in a nice new tower block to live in, is wheeled back in at the end to comment, invariably favourably, on the improvements they've been 'given' by the experts. So it is in *Housing Problems*. The gratitude of the woman in her bright and breezy flat is palpable and touching (and achieved by *good lighting*), as is the urgent need of the man who's already 'lost' two of his children to the lethal conditions of the slums. But the truth of their emotion is no guarantee of the thing it most powerfully underpins, namely the ideology of expertise, which semiotically preys upon the condition of the working class in England to take power over the means of material and social reproduction in their name. This is the power of *Housing Problems*, and of television after it – a power to cause change as well as to record it, by naturalizing *as* public opinion the passions of the knowledge class, and thence, in due course, swaying government policies and public resources towards its own mediated image of the desire of publics.

THE FRIDGE

Now people no longer have opinions; they have refrigerators.

('German critic' cited in Marling, 1994: 267)

Notwithstanding its semiotic difficulties, Housing Problems certainly alerts us to a real 'problem'; in 1935, a year before television's inaugural regular broadcasts, the population was clearly short of decent housing in which to put a TV set. What was needed, before television could be invented as a domestic medium, was 'the home'. TV was a lounge-room medium, but many working people didn't have a lounge. Philip Gibbs estimated in a book published in 1935 that 'sixty families in a thousand were living more than three to a room' in East End districts like Shoreditch and Hoxton that year, an extreme of overcrowding that so memorably features in Housing Problems (Gibbs, 1935: 62). And this is to say nothing of the thousands of homeless who roamed the streets of the 'monstrous city' by day, taking shelter in the crypt of St Martin's in the Field at night, or in a Salvation Army hotel, or in one of the men's hostels – like Rowton House in Hammersmith, which had 1,500 beds (Gibbs, 1935: 27–63). Of course, the standard of living of the majority of families, even working-class families, was higher than these extremes, but at the same time, even where they did enjoy more than one room, working-class families did not use them for prolonged entertainment, and the dwellings themselves were not designed for leisure.

Television was invented not as a 'mass' medium, but a *domestic* one. Its economic platform and cultural form were developed in the USA in the 1940s to provide programming as entertainment, rather than individualized two-way communication like telephone or video. Programming was supplied by centralized agencies (networks) to private consumers. In New Deal America, in a process which accelerated throughout the 1940s and 1950s, 'mass' housing was perfected, in suburbs and high-rises, as the necessary precondition for television, which in turn became the advertising medium of choice for promoting the values of domesticity and the products and services by means of which that ideology could most visibly be espoused (see Attallah, 1991; Spigel, 1992). For TV to 'happen', the consumers had to be at home. To be at home, they needed two things:

1 **capital investment** in the home to *sustain* their activities there;
2 an **'ideology of domesticity'** which would *maintain* their pleasures there, rather than in the street, pub, cinema, music-hall . . . or even in brothels or communism.

For the above conditions to be met in practice, every home had to have a refrigerator.

Without the fridge, there would be no television

Although not the first nor the most fundamental item of home technology, since it was preceded by the gas-cooker, laundry-copper, heating and lighting, the refrigerator was a pivotal item of capitalization in the home, transforming it from a place of dispersed and independent *productivity*, producing food, cleanliness and recuperation, into an end-point in a long, industrialized chain of *consumption* – it turned local 'produce' into 'agribusiness'. The point is Paul Attallah's, who says:

> The home refrigerator, one of the earliest household technologies and markers of the value of the private sphere, is not unlike broadcasting in that it provides a clear illustration of the option of the split between centralized production and distribution and private home consumption.
>
> (Attallah, 1991: 86)

In other words, the choice to invest in homes as sites of privatized consumption, the very cultural effect so often claimed for television, was already made before television was invented.

The fridge was indeed 'not unlike broadcasting', and like broadcasting it allowed for mutually interdependent changes in both production (entire industries were transformed) and consumption (people changed their uses of time, space, food and semiosis). The fridge allowed people (housewives) to go to food markets once a week instead of once a day. It allowed different kinds of foods to be stored – uncooked, leftover and 'convenience' foods – and the freezer compartment stimulated dietary changes with 'fresh' meats and non-seasonal or foreign vegetables, and exotic foods like ice cream. It was a technology accessible to all ages in the family, requiring little parental surveillance or manual skill (though there were occasional suffocations of toddlers who had shut themselves inside), and thereby encouraging juvenile decision-making in food choices. With this capital investment, family habits could change. Weekly shopping was different in kind from daily shopping. It encouraged shoppers not only to buy in bulk but also to buy different things, including impulse-buys and specials. Like the fridge itself, weekly shopping was often a family affair, increasing men's and children's choices in purchasing decisions, and supermarkets used 'loss-leaders' and shelving layout to entice them further. Concentrated shopping (meat, groceries and bakers in one store), bought in bulk, means that non-food products can be sold alongside the perishables, including all those things needed in wet areas, magical cleaning agents for house, body and baby, inside and out, floors and furniture, hair and skin, dishes and cars, liver and teeth. Increasing amounts of entertainment products (toys, records), hardware (for improving the home) and convenience foods displayed at the same store suggest that staying at home is a pleasurable option. Such bulk shopping soon required a car. Weekly shopping entailed different kinds of retailing – a change from cornerstore and daily-market to supermarkets. In supermarkets, people were widely believed to be prone to

Figure 8.3 Without the fridge there would be no television – 1952 ad for GEC
Source: Lilliput

distraction and bemusement, so they needed strong branding to remind them of what they wanted. Supermarkets needed TV advertising, where people at home would be reminded every day (hour) of what they were going to buy in the weekly trip to the supermarket, and also to familiarize consumers with the surprising range, surprising novelty and surprisingly low prices of the products available.

TV advertising was, and remains, obsessively *orificial* and *alimentary* – concentrating on what people put into their mouths, and with the cleanest and most efficient way of getting it through their alimentary canals and then out of the house. Everything edible was constantly harassed throughout its domestic career by cleansing. Besides this image of endless eating and evacuation, assisted by consumer-chemicals from toothpaste and antacid pills to toilet cleaners and deodorizers, from airwaves to peristaltic waves, TV programming supplied a virtualized image of the urban life and community involvement which people were foregoing by staying at home and watching TV. They may not have spoken to many neighbours in suburbia or in the high-rise, or talked to fellow-shoppers in the supermarket-aisle, but they were kept in touch with the talk and tactility of the back-alley and the street by soap opera (set in these very neighbourhoods), magazine programmes and advertising itself. Because it was both orificial and clean – handsomest of the 'white goods' – the fridge itself became a central icon in both TV ads and in daytime TV shows, which got going in the USA in the period 1950–5. Daytime shows and ads centred on convenience-food preparation, and on the wonders of products which could clean, and keep clean, the house and kitchen in which these foods were stored and prepared. This TV was explicitly educational – teaching women at home the ideology of domesticity, and incidentally how to watch TV as part of that. Food preparation was the most important part of it, followed by home and body hygiene. The fridge was the centre of both of these aspects of the ideology of domesticity – it became the point of intersection between food (sustenance) and cleanliness (maintenance).

Once that intersection was achieved, it focused (responded to and facilitated) some very large-scale economic changes. Weekly shopping meant supermarkets; supermarkets meant cars. Branded retailing with TV mass marketing meant a reorganization of the industries which supplied retail groceries, eventually giving rise to the vertical integration and internationalization of food-production (agribusiness), standardizing of produce and transfer of market power from producers to distributors – farmers to General Foods, GF to retail giants. It all had to be sustained, all the time and in all possible countries, by the development and ongoing capitalization of private homes, and by the maintenance of home-life as a positive choice of lifestyle by families, especially in their childbearing years.

This sort of thing was not as inevitable as it might seem in retrospect. If you look at pre-TV homes, they are not very promising sites for domesticity, leisure, capitalized consumption or even food storage. The 'slum-dwellers' of *Housing Problems* had to cook on a gas-ring in the same room they slept in, and could not store food overnight because it would either go off with the combined bad breath of five (sometimes more) people sleeping, or it would be subject to vermin attack (both of these points are made by interviewees in *Housing Problems*). Cooking, washing and keeping these places clean was difficult with communal water taps out in the yard or landing, and doing clothes- or laundry-washing was impossible. So working-class people tended to spend as much time as possible outside their homes, they kept the children outside as long as possible for their health, they ate in cafes and sent or took their washing to laundries. Talk and play were available in the back-alleys.

The technology which transformed all this was centred on the kitchen, not the lounge. The cooker and 'copper', or clothes-washing boiler, came first, of course, and the car was increasingly necessary, but the fridge was decisive, for it allowed the woman as *producer* to become, simultaneously, the woman as *consumer*. Without the fridge, there'd be no TV dinners. . . . But once you'd got started, there was every reason to continue the capitalization of the home, in order to maintain its ideological and economic value. So after the kitchen was kitted out, capitalization spilled out into the other wet areas – laundry, toilet – and to the lounge, where, after the radiogram, the TV-set would be the most expensive item. With all this equipment in the house, and all this time spent enjoying it, there was an equal demand for cultural sustenance (raiding the fridge) and cultural maintenance (watching TV).

HOUSING TELEVISION

This material history of the invention, capitalization and popularization of domesticity, of homes and ideology, technology and time, is a way of addressing some issues of television's reputation, especially the widespread but negative commonsensical assumptions about TV's social impact as a mass medium. I want to show that TV in general, and its textuality in particular, involve much larger cultural developments, so much so that its supposed 'behavioural effects' actually precede its adoption by large populations. The downside of the domestic scenario, according to the critics, was the supposed anomie and isolation of living in nuclear families without neighbourhood or community contacts; the supposed decline of public civilization and national culture in the wake of the mass media; and the supposed evils of unabashed consumerism, which was criticized on the Left for being a capitalist plot and on the Right for debasing the taste and authority of the nation.

From the very start television attracted attention as a potential evil – it brought sex, violence, bad language and excessive or unthrifty habits into the home, and it caused vulnerable people to behave badly. Vulnerable people usually turned out to be everyone except adult men and social psychologists – women, children, adolescents, ethnic minorities, the working class, people in the third world – all were expected, and indeed shown, to be suffering from watching TV, and the symptoms of their disease were both individual and social, including aggression, passivity, narcotization, desensitization, susceptibility to persuasion, manipulation, ideological control by communists, capitalists, advertisers, libertines, moral decline, atheism, propensity to escape control by parents, subversion of orthodox political/religious/cultural institutions and beliefs, anorexia, rotting teeth and bad posture.

This pathologization of everyday life (achieved by treating social technologies as bodily symptoms) proceeds from two things:

1   a **fear of democratization**, fear of a popular culture which is perceived as beyond the control of established agencies of surveillance and discipline;
2   the **ascendancy of psycho-sciences**, from clinical psychology to mass media research science, whose function and professional purpose it is to pathologize others – all others, from individuals (clients) to populations (TV audiences).

There has been very little to counteract the dominance of this anti-democratic pathologization, especially in the media themselves, where stories about the effect of TV are still both commonplace and the explanation-of-choice in reports of serial murder, shopping-mall massacres, rape and violence, especially the 'mindless' variety. So although the mass media have found their defenders among cultural theorists, there's still a systematic prejudice against them in the public domain, and against mass consumption, mass persuasion, mass entertainment, etc., a 'popular' prejudice against the media, curiously enough fostered among the people themselves by the media themselves. . . . This results in the unsatisfactory cultural situation where there is no easily available or widely distributed discourse or framework of positive explanation for watching TV among the very people – i.e. the majority of the population – for whom it is still, after all these years, the top leisure pastime. The gap between doing TV-watching and denigrating it is a measure of the knowledge class's fear of the popular classes. The extent to which television is still not routinely made sense of in terms of culture and politics – and is instead accepted as a 'mass' technology with 'behavioural' effects on 'other' populations – is a measure of the knowledge class's success in 'popularizing' its own fears.

In such a climate, an attempt to understand what the social impact of TV might actually be, both historically and at the present time, is hard to contemplate beyond the terms of the bad reputation enjoyed by TV among its many critics. This is where the fridge comes in. As far as I know there's no climate of cultural criticism directed at the fridge. Beyond its physical effect on the environment after its use-by date, which is a manufacturing rather than a cultural problem, and the occasional toddlercide by pre-magnetic doors, the fridge has no negative reputation. It is not a pathologized other in the eyes of the psycho-professionals, and it's not seen as a cause of cultural or political decline by social commentators in the media, government or academy.

As far as I know, the fridge has not been accused of impeding democracy, but it may well take some credit for spreading and stabilizing it (for the minor role the refrigerator played in the cold war, see Marling, 1994: Chapter 7). Without it, TV would be impossible, for there would not be enough homes in which to put the TV to sustain it as a mass medium, not enough families staying at home to watch it; not enough goods to advertise on it (goods both to go in it and in the home environment it sustains), and no domestic culture within which its entertainments could appeal to audiences. TV, fridges, motor cars and homes are all 'machines' to sustain a production system based on centralized production and privatized consumption. The fridge's centrality to domestic and TV history has not often been recognized, but there is one instance which gives credit where it's due – an episode of the American animatronic sitcom series *Dinosaurs* called *Fridge Day* – where the wonders bestowed by the fridge are celebrated in Dinosaurland by a national holiday. Both housing and the ideology of domesticity were items of major social policy in Europe and America from the nineteenth century, although the pace picked up after the Second World War, at which point – the late 1940s in the USA, the mid-1950s in the UK and Australia – housing and domesticity, fridges and television developed together in mutual reinforcement, along with the motor car, so much so that they're all inexplicable without the others.

What I'm describing is a long-term movement from 'dwellings' to 'homes'. A dwelling is a domestic habitation of any kind, from shanty-town to slum, tenement to high-rise, city to suburb. But a home is a much more particular place. It was invented as a single family unit, cut off by physical boundaries – walls at least, but ideally space in the form of garden or yard – from its neighbours. It was designed to accommodate just one family, ideally a married couple and their children, with some minor variations, like grannies in the back bedroom. The internal topography 'produced' family functions, with special emphasis on separating sex, hygiene and living – heterosexually conjugal parents in one bedroom, out of sight of their asexual children, who were ideally in single rooms each, or at least sorted by gender into pink and blue areas. Cleaning (surfaces, clothes and bodies) was separated from social living, wet areas from dry, as was cooking and food preparation, although many families contradicted planners by living in the workroom – i.e. sitting in the kitchen. So the classic home was born – and it fitted equally well into urban high-rise, suburban sprawl or even rural and provincial cottages.

What was it for? It was initially a fantasy in the minds of social planners and engineers; Victorian philanthropists who were equally motivated by the 'plight' and the 'threat' of the uncontrolled urban working poor. It was thus a solution to the problems of urbanization, industrialization and population explosion in modernizing societies in the nineteenth century (see Donzelot, 1980). The problem was an uncontrolled and ever-increasing urban working class. Instead of controlling such a beast from the outside, with repressive state apparatuses like the law, government, armed forces, prisons, police and, eventually, psychologists, it was thought by some to be better to create the conditions for self-control and self-administration by the populace; a regime in which their wilder tendencies would be governed by themselves. In this campaign, the principal recruits were women. If women could get men off the streets, cause men to govern their unbridled lusts – for alcohol, night-life and seditious assembly – then there'd be no need for direct coercion. Women became the focus for a number of campaigns to achieve social docility, chief among which were temperance, hygiene and domesticity. A mother and wife offers alternative attractions to those of the city street; the home is a technology invented to amplify, secure and separate this alternative attraction. Comfort, cleanliness, cooking, security and regular if regulated monogamous sex were on offer.

This was the ideology of domesticity – a campaign, both political and commercial, which took up existing aspects of respectable life – religion, femininity, thrift, shame, privacy, self-help, property. These were centred then on the home rather than on their earlier sites – the soul, as in Bunyan, or the workshop, as in traditional artisanship. The home became more than a dwelling, more than a refuge – it became a lifestyle in itself and in the activities it was expected to sustain. The proletarianization of individual dwellings occurred in the first half of the twentieth century, and it extended both upwards, with high-rise and high-density social housing in urban centres, and outwards, as suburbia went from the bourgeois exclusiveness of the Victorian period to mass-housing developments on uniform, speculatively-built housing estates. Housing was democratized after the Second World War, and television made its domestic appearance as an essential part of that process.

Television was called, among other things, a 'machine for advertising' following and exploiting the architect Le Corbusier's notion of the home as a 'machine for living in' (Attallah, 1991: 61). Le Corbusier's language was applied to the work of making housework efficient rather than drudgery, and especially to the provision of technologies which were at once affordable by ordinary people and designed to be 'labour saving' – the classic 'white goods' being chief among them. The 'machine for living in' was explicitly connected to those other wonders of the Machine Age, the 'machines in which to make things' (so named in the 'Plan for Britain' issue of Picture Post, 4 January 1941) – better known as factories. The factory system became the model for the productivity of housework (see Figure 7.16, p. 89), but in order for housewives to be efficient producers, they had also to become efficient consumers of the products of factories . . . they must see the consumption of goods, both durables and consumables, as productive, of domesticity, happiness, healthy contented families, etc. The fridge allowed women as producers to become women as consumers, and the TV – the 'machine for selling' – trained them in this role. Thereafter, the fridge enabled all family members to participate in orificial and alimentary gratification on an as-you-please basis. Where the television set has been pathologized as a 'bad influence' – an elder brother or unruly father leading paedocratized viewers astray – the fridge has held its place in discourse as a surrogate 'good mother'. And in soap opera, such as the long-running Australian serial Home and Away, for instance, the fridge has become a significant item on set: young people especially gather round it in multiple-occupancy homes; each one helps to delineate the 'character' of the household in its design and decoration (with Greenpeace stickers, for example); and at a significant moment in a story-line a character will go to it for a bit of business while talking through a personal dilemma with a visitor or family-member (see Turnbull and Bowles, 1995 for an excellent analysis of Australian soapies' sets). All this suggests that the fridge has attained the status of visual 'motherliness' in television drama. But the division of the maternal function and its mechanization into domestic technology was not calculated simply to give mum time to put her feet up. If the fridge did some mothering, it was because mothers were busy doing economics. They were the bearers of the domestic ideology, and this in turn sustained what Hugh Stretton has called the 'domestic economy'. This is not only the 'home economics' of cooking, cleaning and childrearing, though these aspects of it were capitalized (via consumer/advertising) and mechanized (home economics and domestic science were educational subjects in the 1950s and 1960s); but it is also something much larger, more anthropological, in scale. The domestic as opposed to the commercial economy is that sector of culture (unwaged work) which reproduces *human life* rather than *material goods* (Stretton, 1974).

The commercial, social and political policies which focused on the development of mass housing and mass media were international but, rightly or wrongly, the 'ideology of domesticity' itself is associated with post-war America, where it was developed in its most spectacular form and was espoused most enthusiastically by promoters, producers and not a few people. Thenceforth television was associated with the company it kept – personal experience, private life, suburbia, consumption, ordinariness, heterosexual family-building, hygiene, the 'feminization' of family governance. Indeed, these things have become so ineradicably a part of the general description of TV's 'textuality' that by looking at the historical conditions of its earliest context-of-use, we have arrived at a recognizable description of the 'textual tradition' in TV without looking at a single programme.

HOUSING PROBLEMS – TAKE TWO

Whether *Housing Problems* is thought of as being revolutionary in a positive way (it takes workers seriously, wants modernity to benefit ordinary people and wants films to engage critically with public policy-making as advocates of the ordinary), or revolutionary in a negative way (it centralizes semiotic and social power on vanguardist experts, and makes ordinary people into victims), it was not all that revolutionary in its own time. It was located in a complex web of media (film, journalism, literary documentary) and redevelopment (both commercial and state-sponsored); a web of meanings and practices which places *Housing Problems* as part of what amounted to a *craze* for slum clearance and 'doing something for the distressed areas' after the depression, unemployment and war had dampened the spirits of workers and intellectuals alike for the previous few years. While it may be a significant film in the history of screen semiosis, then, *Housing Problems* was by no means unique in its views on the housing situation. Most important was the National Government's programme of slum clearance and house-building, but this project was accompanied by a running commentary in the popular media, not only arguing the need for slum clearance but reporting its progress. Brian Winston, for instance, has pointed out that 'it is clear that the entire range of documentary film subjects was heard on the radio and was heard earlier' in BBC talks programmes on 'the condition of England'; a list of topics that 'included the slums, in programmes such as *Other People's Houses*' (Winston, 1995: 44). Much of what was done on the radio was itself borrowed from writing and journalism that was earlier still. Philip Gibbs, for instance, wrote in 1935 about just such a radio programme:

> I had a voice test at the B.B.C. The director of talks – what a man of responsibility! – was anxious for me to speak over the microphone once a week or so, about the progress in slum clearance and other social work on behalf of the distressed areas. The Prince of Wales was going to lead off, and I was keen to do it.
>
> (Gibbs, 1935: 124. In the event, the BBC did not use Gibbs for this series.)

Gibbs's book itself shows that the filmic 'innovation' of letting ordinary people speak for themselves, in the service of public enlightenment about the state of the nation, was by no means confined to *Housing Problems*; the full title of *England Speaks* speaking volumes about the tenor of the times:

ENGLAND SPEAKS

By PHILIP GIBBS

Being Talks with

ROAD-SWEEPERS, BARBERS, STATESMEN, LORDS AND LADIES, BEGGARS, FARMING FOLK,

ACTORS, ARTISTS, LITERARY GENTLEMEN, TRAMPS, DOWN-AND-OUTS, MINERS,

STEEL-WORKERS, BLACKSMITHS, THE-MAN-IN-THE-STREET, HIGH-BROWS, LOW-BROWS,

AND ALL MANNER OF FOLK OF HUMBLE AND EXALTED RANK

WITH A PANORAMA OF THE ENGLISH SCENE

IN THIS YEAR OF GRACE

1935

This too is an echo (all the more conscious since Gibbs had already written a book called *European Journey*) of J.B. Priestley's celebrated *English Journey* (Priestley, 1977), published in 1934, whose own title was clearly on Gibbs's mind the following year:

ENGLISH JOURNEY

BEING A RAMBLING BUT TRUTHFUL ACCOUNT

OF WHAT ONE MAN SAW AND HEARD AND FELT AND THOUGHT

DURING A JOURNEY THROUGH ENGLAND

DURING THE AUTUMN OF THE YEAR

1933

Both Gibbs's and Priestley's books were published by William Heinemann, and of course Priestley was to become the most famous radio broadcaster of his generation. In short, the encounter with ordinariness that so startles in *Housing Problems* was as much a writers' craze of the time as it was a cinematic innovation. Stuart Hall has commented:

> Many writers, journalists and reporters took to the road, in that period, as the muckrakers and naturalists in the United States were also doing, to try to capture in descriptive prose a 'reality' which seemed to outrun literature in its traditional sense (as documentary, in Grierson's eyes, 'outran' the cinema as an 'art form').
>
> (Hall, 1972: 101)

In the epilogue to his English 'panorama' (itself to become a familiar word in English television actuality), Gibbs weighs up the pluses and minuses: 'It would be good to write that all's well with England. Not all is well when there are thousands of homeless men and boys on the streets of London every night', but on the other hand, 'the National Government is advertising its service to the country. There are a million less unemployed. A million houses have been built. Good!' (Gibbs, 1935: 457–8). In other words, the slum clearance advocated in *Housing Problems* was well under way, and plenty of commentators were interested in the results; its 'magical resolution' to the housing problems it discovered was by no means original – it had been rehearsed already, at least a million times.

The craze for exposing housing problems was not confined to literary and cinematic documentary, but extended into news itself. An unusually significant example of the genre, published in the year before *Housing Problems* was released, is a double-page story in the *Weekly Illustrated* (17 November 1934), under the headline 'Pull Down the Slums!' (reproduced in *Creative Camera*, 1982: 586). Pictures by Kurt Hutton show overcrowded tenements in East London, and compare them with the light and airy pleasantness of new developments and new suburbs: exactly the strategy used in the later film.

The story accompanying the photographs reports on the 'great National scheme of slum clearance' that was launched in March 1933. It points out that publicity has made slum clearance into everyone's business, not just that of the slum-dwellers themselves:

Now, at last, pictures, films, books and articles – above all the statistics and opinions of health-workers and scientists – have brought home to every one of us the need for complete, immediate clearance of the slums.

(*Weekly Illustrated*, 17 November 1934)

But it is the photographs that do the work. They are juxtaposed and captioned to present a stark, binary choice:

HOW HUMAN BEINGS LIVE . . . A row of old houses in a slum quarter of London.
Life here is one long struggle to keep the home clean and tolerable
. . . AND HOW THEY OUGHT TO LIVE . . .
A big block of modern flats for workers in St. Pancras.

A CONTRAST IN HOMES – THE GRATING 'FRONT WINDOW' OF A BASEMENT,
AND THE FRESH AIR OF A GARDEN SUBURB.

The sub-caption to the first of these pictures gives the grim facts: 'Down below that grating is a window. Behind that window is a room. Inside that single room there live five people – three of them children.' The contrasting sub-caption gives the bright hope: 'What does it mean to boys and girls to be removed from the filth of the slums and set down where there is sunshine, air, trees, rabbits

Figure 8.4 'Pull down the slums!'
Source: *Weekly Illustrated*, 17 November 1934

[rabbits?], and green fields?' Naturally, the caption-writer cannot wait long enough to answer his own question, but the answer doesn't matter anyway, for all the ideological work is done by the pictures – they make it seem *self-evident* that 'removal' to a greenfield site in the middle of nowhere is better than a grating in the middle of town.

The scene was set. Radical reformists could and did use visual culture and the latest media technologies, from photojournalism to television, to promote new solutions to old problems. *Housing Problems* and 'Pull Down the Slums!' were joined later on by such notable interventions as *Cathy Come Home*. This celebrated television 'docudrama' was Jeremy Sandford's 1960s update of the homelessness theme, this time with the issue of one-parent families and teenage mothers to provide an added twist to the vicious circle. *Cathy Come Home*, *Up the Junction*, and *Boys from the Blackstuff* were all dramatizations of urban working-class deprivation 'from below', as it were, while other shows, from the very early *Coronation Street* of 1960–1, via Michael Apted's *Seven-Up* series, to sitcoms such as *Till Death Us Do Part* and *Whatever Happened to the Likely Lads*, where working-class family life in crisis was explored 'from the inside' – these were television's meditation on the 'housing problems' of its own core audience. Questions were tabled in another kind of house – the House of Commons – and the Labour government of the day discussed *Cathy Come Home* in cabinet. Television itself had come home, as it were, taking its place in public politics as well as in private culture as an instrument of public education and governmental policy-making; but the terms had been set in the 1930s.

9

DEMOCRACY AS DEFEAT

The social eye of cultural studies

Even the Catholic Church of the Middle Ages was tolerant by modern standards. Part of the reason for this was that in the past no government had the power to keep its citizens under constant surveillance. The invention of print, however, made it easier to manipulate public opinion, and the film and the radio carried the process further. With the development of television . . . private life came to an end.

(George Orwell, 1954: 165)

It is historically interesting to discover the *Weekly Illustrated*'s treatment of 'housing problems', not least because although it predates the film, it uses exactly the same 'arguments' as *Housing Problems*, and even hints at a bit of a media 'feeding frenzy' on the issue of slum-clearance during 1933–4. However, *Weekly Illustrated* is of historic importance in its own right. 'Pull Down the Slums!' is just as important to the tradition of photojournalism as *Housing Problems* is to the tradition of documentary filmmaking. The creative force behind *Weekly Illustrated* was its editor Stefan Lorant, who went on to found *Picture Post*, and *Picture Post*'s editor during its legendary, wartime years was Tom Hopkinson, associate editor and caption-writer for *Weekly Illustrated*. The photographer responsible for the slum story in *Weekly Illustrated* was the German Kurt Hutton, who went on to become one of *Picture Post*'s most celebrated staff photographers. Just as *Housing Problems* occupies a pioneering place in the history of screen semiosis and in film studies, so the much less well-known *Weekly Illustrated* story marks a pioneering moment in British photojournalism (Hopkinson, 1982), for it is the vision – the punchy radicalism of the *photo that shows* and the *caption that tells* – that is carried through to fruition in the great days of *Picture Post*.

THE 'DEATH THREAT TO THE COLLECTIVE'

Taking *Picture Post*, working-class housing and the traditions of British photojournalism as its starting point, this chapter considers the other side of an argument presented in earlier chapters. I have suggested that television was 'housed' inside the discourses prepared for it by its critics so effectively that its own semiosis can be accounted for by attending to these discourses. However, I don't want to leave the impression that the 'textual tradition' in TV studies is just a matter of conservative critics and reactionary literacy politics. In this chapter, I show that the very same tendencies characterize even the most radical and highly theorized approaches to television. Television itself was invented and first established in a socio-cultural field that can best be described as 'ordinary' – middle-ground, suburban, modern, politically unaligned. For many observers at that time, such 'ordinariness' was a problem, both culturally and politically. Critics on the Left as well as the Right lamented the perceived lack in the English of revolutionary fervour and metropolitan taste. They were scornful about the propensity of the British to accept (or to have foisted upon them) pragmatic politics and a Betjemanian 'Metroland' culture (see Medhurst, 1997: 241–2). What they were looking for was popular resistance, not middle-class and middlebrow ordinariness. And they wanted television to nurture (teach) popular radicalism and social criticism, not *The Good Life*.

So here's an irony: social reformers wanted to pull down the slums and remove the inner-city working-class population to places where they might live better lives, but the actually-existing model of such a refuge was suburbia. When the copy-writer of *Weekly Illustrated* (almost certainly Tom Hopkinson) had asked in 1934, 'What does it mean to boys and girls to be removed from the filth of the slums and set down where there is sunshine, air, trees, rabbits, and green fields?' (*Weekly Illustrated*, 17 November 1934), there was really only one answer: it means moving to the suburbs. The irony – the problem – was that many of the most vocal and influential of the social reformers (like George Orwell) seemed to hate the suburbs culturally even more than they hated poverty politically. So ordinariness was and has remained ever since a difficult problem for the intelligentsia. Not for them the easy American democratic acceptance of a suburbia that 'stayed home, happier on the smaller, domestic screen, finding a snug, congenial niche amid television's abiding concern with what the American television playwright Paddy Chayefsky once called "this marvellous world of the ordinary"' (Medhurst, 1997: 251). And despite Raymond Williams's recognition, long since, that 'there are essentially no "ordinary" activities if by "ordinary" we mean the absence of creative interpretation and effort' (Williams, 1961: 54), the message did not get through to his intellectual allies and successors in cultural studies. 'Ordinariness' was not understood as a creative part of a Williamsite 'long revolution' when it came to television, because television was regarded, along with the suburbia it both symbolized and served, as irredeemable. As the American historian Gary Cross has pointed out, 'modernist intellectuals and architects combined an aesthetic snobbery, self-interest, and a lack of understanding of popular aspirations in a many-sided attack on the popular suburb in the interwar years' (Cross, 1997: 110).

The problem here is that a need is recognized for popular media (time) and popular housing (space), but that the cure is understood to be worse than the disease. Vicky Lebeau, in an essay on punk music and suburbia, describes how for some working-class families who actually experienced the move to the suburbs, television is welcomed (in the absence of other community infrastructure) as 'a member of the family, a friend' – an outcome that is seen by critical observers as 'the overwhelming presence of that so-called death threat to the collective: television' (Lebeau, 1997: 292–3). Significantly, Lebeau starts her analysis (as I do below) with an account of the work of Phil Cohen, the first writer in contemporary cultural studies to argue for a relationship between housing and subculture, suggesting that the spectacular youth subcultures of the post-war era could be read back to the policies of post-war slum clearance. His arguments rely on a pathologization of popular housing. How did it come to this?

As part of a long tradition in British political journalism, the links established in the previous chapter between *Weekly Illustrated* and *Picture Post* are significant beyond the biographies of the creative personnel. The urge to 'Pull Down the Slums!' represented a strong strand of modernist-reformist thought in British public life that lasted for more than a generation. It was in fact a three-ply strand, spun together from three different enthusiasms of the modernizing 'knowledge class' of the mid-century:

1 popular-pedagogic visual journalism (both print and film);
2 concern for the material conditions of working-class people (a concern articulated by knowledge-class professionals);
3 radical politics, both revolutionary (or Marxist) and reformist (or Fabian).

It wasn't just the slums that had to come down, according to this radical strand of British intellectual thinking; it was the whole edifice that allowed for slums, an edifice apparently founded upon three pillars – capital, class and country. Big business, middle- or ruling-class hegemony, and a governmental apparatus that seemed to render the sectional interests of capitalism and class-supremacism into the national interests of the country; these were the real targets. Television and popular journalism, in so far as they raised consciousness of such structural matters, or stirred up popular action against the dominant forces, were useful. But if popular media satisfied themselves with merely entertaining their audiences by showing and sharing this ordinary life, no matter how accurately or imaginatively it was done, then they were understood to be part of the problem.

This three-ply strand ran through the Second World War and the subsequent period of the 'affluent society', right through to the beginning of another, much more recent tradition, this time an intellectual one, which has come down to the present day in the form of cultural studies. Interestingly, there's a direct textual marker of the link between the elements I've been discussing (*Weekly Illustrated* and *Picture Post*) and the theoretical-analytical work of contemporary cultural studies. It so happens that photographs of slums published in 1938–9 in *Picture Post*, themselves visual echoes of the earlier ones published in *Weekly Illustrated* and screened in *Housing Problems*, were taken up again after thirty-odd years, to be republished as the frontispiece of British cultural studies' founding journal, *Working Papers in Cultural Studies* (WPCS). In WPCS 2, published in spring 1972,

Stuart Hall analyzed 'The Social Eye of *Picture Post*', while Phil Cohen, in an equally celebrated article, wrote about 'Subcultural Conflict and Working Class Community'. Indeed, Cohen located that conflict in the very housing estates in London that *Housing Problems* had wished upon the population:

> The pattern of social integration that had traditionally characterised the East End began, dramatically, to break down. . . . This breakdown coincided with the wholesale redevelopment of the area, and the process of chain reactions which this triggered. . . . No-one is denying that redevelopment brought an improvement in material conditions for those fortunate enough to be rehoused. . . . But while this removed the tangible evidence of poverty, it did nothing to improve the real economic situation of many families. . . . But to this was added a new poverty – the impoverishment of working class culture.
>
> (Cohen, 1972: 14–16)

Among other cultural effects, Cohen suggests that the physical redevelopment of East End slums produced a new reliance on consumerism, on media-defined needs, arising from a new form of social organization which isolated people into families, and families into homes: the neighbourhood and extended kinship networks were no longer accessible to young mothers in high-rises. While 'only market research and advertising executives imagine that the housebound mother sublimates everything in her G-Plan furniture, her washing machine or non-stick frying pans', the alternative is pathologized to such an extent that even violent child abuse is seen as reasonable – and somehow *caused by* television images of comfort: 'feeling herself cooped up with the kids, cut off from the outside world, it wouldn't be surprising if she occasionally took out her frustration on those nearest and dearest!' (Cohen, 1972: 17).

The result, suggests Cohen, was the development of subcultures like Mods and skinheads, whose dress (see), music (hear), speech (say) and ritual (do) formed the original *subject* of cultural studies itself: a three-level strategy of analysis:

1 **'historical analysis'** (meaning class analysis);
2 **'structural or semiotic analysis'** of the subsystems; the way they are articulated together and how they change;
3 **'phenomenological analysis'** (which became better known as audience ethnography) (Cohen, 1972: 22–3).

This is a new beginning for the 'textual tradition' in cultural and therefore in TV studies; a recognition on the one hand that 'semiotic' (textual) analysis of meaning systems (seeing, hearing, saying, doing) is required in order to understand socio-structural change, and on the other that such analysis must be set in the context of history and life.

TEXTUAL TRADITIONS – TAKE TWO

It is significant that the Centre for Contemporary Cultural Studies (CCCS), the most influential recent British powerhouse of theorizing about 'culture' (and thence television), should have taken its cues from *Picture Post*, from the condition of the working class in England, and from mid-century radicalism. The CCCS had been founded in the mid-1960s by Richard Hoggart, after the success of *The Uses of Literacy* had attracted widespread debate and a grant from Penguin's founder Allen Lane. It was under the directorship of Stuart Hall (from 1970), and with a collective 'speaking position' which was Marxist, that the CCCS began to work systematically towards an analysis of culture which was class-based, theorized from (Marxist) first principles, and intended not to describe culture but to change it (and a lot more about Britain besides). In short, the CCCS became a radical think-tank, and as a result it was interested not in tradition at all, but in radical ruptures – 'conjunctures' in history in which intellectual movements may coincide with popular discontents to produce new challenges to 'traditional' power structures.

The effect of this agenda on Stuart Hall's reading of *Picture Post* is instructive. He obviously *likes* it and, in a long article (fifty pages) where he analyses it from several points of view (historically, semiotically and politically – though not 'phenomenologically' as required by Phil Cohen in the same issue of *WPCS*), he is both astute and complimentary about its achievements. But *Picture Post* was a commercial undertaking, not a political one, and its success beyond its own covers was *democratic*; it did not represent a 'sharp break with the past', and its politics was based on reform, not resistance:

> *Picture Post*, in photographs and text, registered with remarkable veracity the substance and quality of ordinary life. Its mode of 'telling' was direct. It was strongest in capturing the native strengths of English life 'under pressure'. Its 'social eye' was a clear lens. But its 'political' eye was far less decisive. It pinpointed exploitation, misery and social abuse, but always in a language which defined these as 'problems' to be tackled and remedied with energy and goodwill: it was instinctively *reformist* – in both a good (humanist) and bad sense. It never found a way . . . of relating the surface images of these problems to their structural foundations. In this dimension, we can see a clear continuity between *Picture Post* and the 'social problem' area of television documentary in a later period.
>
> (Hall, 1972: 109)

It was, in short, like *Housing Problems* before it and like television afterwards, 'strongest' in capturing what Hall identifies as the 'native strengths of English life'. It has to be noted at this point that in fact *Picture Post* was hardly 'native' at all. On the contrary, it was the creation of Stefan Lorant, a Hungarian Jew who was an émigré from Nazi Germany where he had worked on pioneering photojournal-ism magazines in the 1920s, and it used émigré German photographers Kurt Hutton, Felix Man and Tim Gidal among others. Bill Brandt, another legendary *Picture Post* photographer, was brought up in Germany. Indeed, as Gidal himself has written:

> It should be stated here that *Picture Post*'s photojournalism, and this means to a very great extent British photojournalism, was imported into London by three reporters ('three bloody foreigners') who were emigrants from Germany and immigrants to England.
>
> (Gidal, 1982: 572–9)

But as well as linking *Picture Post* forwards to television documentary, Hall links it back to *Housing Problems*: 'The British documentary impulse was rooted in the Thirties: without it, *Picture Post* could never have happened' (Hall, 1972: 96). So Hall was wrong here, despite the convenience of his assertion for the lineage I too am trying to trace; it was not *British documentary* but *German photojournalism* of the 1920s without which *Picture Post* 'could never have happened'. It is perhaps a footnote to history, but nevertheless here is an irony that ought not to be forgotten: Hall saw *Picture Post* at its 'strongest in capturing the native strengths of English life "under pressure"', but the editor and photographers who played the most creative part in capturing those 'native' strengths were German or German-trained, during a period when the 'pressure' mentioned by Hall is a total war against Germany. Despite his own sensitivity to ethnic issues of 'English-ness' (a Jamaican, Hall arrived in Britain as a Rhodes Scholar to Oxford in the 1950s), Hall does not pursue this poignant story of how British 'native' strengths were best communicated by those who were at the time about as far from 'native' as could be imagined. I think this is a pity, because I believe it leads Hall to under-rate *Picture Post*'s communicative (cultural, journalistic, visual) achievement, in his pursuit of political objectives.

So what were Hall's *political* objections to *Picture Post*?:

> The grey half-tones were a perfect visual equivalent for the mood of emergency which prevailed on the home front. The brisk, activist, resiliently *cheerful* note in the magazine, inscribed everywhere in its pages, paralleled the stubborn cheerfulness, the underplayed heroism, the wartime quips and repartee, the shelter-humour and the Blitz folk-lore which were authentic manifestations of a collective popular spirit; in essence, a 'culture' of the Home Front.
>
> (Hall, 1972: 103)

So far, so good; but in Hall's analysis, cheerfulness, authenticity and 'perfect equivalence' with the 'collective popular spirit' are by no means good enough:

117

There is a highlighting in a *Picture Post* photograph – of the Blitz, of unemployment, of people's everyday pursuits: an accenting of the essentially *human* and the essentially *ordinary* qualities of experience. There is a rhetoric of change and improvement there, of people capable of resilience and courage: but there isn't anywhere a language of dissent, opposition or revolt. . . . *Picture Post*, as Orwell saw, could retain its authenticity only because it was constantly and resolutely in touch with a movement for change which had surpassed 'party labels' and 'the old distinction between Right and Left', and because it spoke straight to 'multitudes of unlabelled people who have grasped . . . that something is wrong'. But *what* was wrong *Picture Post* had no language for.

(Hall, 1972: 109)

The effort to create the 'language' for 'what was wrong' was in fact the project of CCCS in the disputatious 1970s; in such a context, the textual tradition of *Picture Post* – cheerfulness, ordinariness, talking straight and voting Labour (Hall, 1972: 95) – was a *defeat*. As far as Hall is concerned, and Orwell is his key witness (indeed his only one), the chances for an 'English Revolution' had come and gone somewhere between 1941 and 1944. In the early part of the war, Orwell wrote, in what Hall signals as a 'crucial' passage:

Progress and reaction are ceasing to have anything to do with party labels. If one wishes to name a particular moment, one can say that the old distinctions between Right and Left broke down when *Picture Post* was first published. What are the politics of *Picture Post*? Or of *Cavalcade*, or Priestley's broadcasts, or the leading articles in the *Evening Standard*? None of the old classifications will fit them. They merely point to the existence of multitudes of unlabelled people who have grasped within the last year or two that something is wrong. But since a classless, ownerless society is generally spoken of as Socialism, we can give that name to the society towards which we are now moving. The war and the revolution are inseparable.

(George Orwell, quoted in Hall, 1972: 105)

Later, Orwell recanted – he called the passage above a 'very great error', for 'after all we have not lost the war . . . and we have not introduced socialism' (Orwell, in Hall, 1972: 107). Hall comments that the war drew the classes together, rather than polarizing them, but this democratizing tide was an impediment to 'structural change':

Orwell was right, then, to remark that the conditions were there for an 'English Revolution' of a quite new and remarkable kind, and that such conjunctures would be few and far between: what he did not see . . .

was how quickly a popular movement, without benefit of conscious radical leadership and articulation, would crest and find its limits. . . . The radical version of social democracy, which attained its peak in the early days of the 1945 Labour Government, was as much as that popular drift to the Left could manage unaided. And *Picture Post* represented the high water-mark of the tide of social democracy as a legitimated 'structure of feeling.'

(Hall, 1972: 108)

The analytical rhetoric which makes *democracy* a *defeat* is highly characteristic of the British Left, Old and New, and it has entered the 'textual tradition of television studies' in interesting ways, not least through the work of one of the New Left's most important writers, Raymond Williams, whose phrase 'structure of feeling' (which is sometimes revived as a kind of 'definition' of culture) Hall borrows here to signify the moment when all was lost, from the revolutionary point of view.

There is a characteristic trace of this *anti-democratic* leftism in the 'textual tradition in TV studies' to this day; a pessimism about the political potential of the popular media, and a habit of reducing 'popularity' to 'populism', democracy to defeat. But in fact the new popular media were taken up at the time as being the very place where the old distinctions between Left and Right, working class and capitalist class were least relevant, least sustainable. Rather than insisting upon them, popular media ignored them, gathering their audiences and topics from both sides of the class and political divides. Before television was invented, radio broadcasting was attracting attention as the place where cultural change could be heard and felt by everyone, as Philip Gibbs observed when he met Sir John Reith, founding Director General of the BBC:

There is a never-ending conflict between the high-brows and the low-brows, who try to tear him down, because the first accuse him of pandering to the lowest tastes and the others accuse him of intellectual snobbery. The Die-Hard mind charges him with using the air as an instrument of subversive propaganda. The Left Wing mind asserts that he is the paid agent of Toryism. Every owner of a wireless set paying ten shillings for his licence feels himself entitled to abusive criticism because when he switches on he hears something which is displeasing to his soul. . . . It is all very difficult for Sir John Reith. But the B.B.C. has entered the life of England with immense and irresistible influence.

(Gibbs, 1935: 129)

Since 1935 the idea that if it is upsetting 'both sides' it must be getting things about right has become a self-serving cliché of the BBC, but the point remains that broadcasting *gathers* different populations, politics and tastes, rather than choosing between them, and it is precisely this – the fact that everyone is exposed to points of view they don't hold and cultural material they don't like – that critics from both Left and Right have disliked about television's textuality. Philip Gibbs, quoted above, was on the Right of the political spectrum; Orwell, who also commented on the failure of 'the old classifications', was on the Left. Somewhere between them was J.B. Priestley. At the end of his *English Journey*, published in 1934 (two years before the start of British television), Priestley reflected on three different Englands that he had observed in his journey. They were, in my terms, **transmodern**:

1 **Traditional** England, centred on the county (**pre-modern**, in my terms);
2 **Industrial** England, centred on the nineteenth-century city and the factory (**modern**, in my terms);
3 **Modern** England, centred on the suburb (**postmodern**, in my terms; see Hartley, 1997).

Of 'modern' (i.e. postmodern) England, Priestley has this to say:

> America, I supposed, was its real birthplace. This is the England of arterial and by-pass roads, of filling stations and factories that look like giant exhibition buildings, of giant cinemas and dance-halls and cafes, bunga-lows with tiny garages, cocktail bars, Woolworth's, motor-coaches, wire-less, hiking, factory girls looking like actresses, greyhound racing and dirt tracks, swimming pools, and everything given away for cigarette coupons. . . . This England [was] all around me at that northern entrance to London, where the smooth wide road passes between miles of semi-detached bungalows, all with their little garages, their wireless sets, their periodicals about film stars, their swimming costumes and tennis rackets and dancing shoes.
>
> (Priestley, 1977: 375)

What did Priestley make of this post-political landscape; ripe, though it has not yet been invented, for the television system which will eventually replace Wool-worth's as its icon?

> It is, of course, essentially democratic. After a social revolution there would, with any luck, be more and not less of it. You need money in this England, but you do not need much money. It is a large-scale, mass-production job, with cut prices. . . . Notice how the very modern things, like the films and wireless and sixpenny stories, are absolutely democratic, making no distinction whatever between their patrons: if you are in a position to accept what they give – and very few are not in that position – then you get neither more nor less than what anybody else gets, just as in popular restaurants there are no special helpings for favoured patrons but mathematical portions for everybody.
>
> (Priestley, 1977: 376)

Naturally, Priestley had his reservations about this society which was as 'near to a classless society as we have got yet':

> Too much of this life is being stamped on from outside, probably by astute financial gentlemen, backed by the Press and their publicity services. You feel that too many of the people in this new England are doing not what they like but what they have been told they would like. (Here is the American influence at work.)
>
> (Priestley, 1977: 377)

Priestley worries that this new England is too bland, too cheap, too apolitical (though he tells himself off for doubting it). However, his description of the more affluent developments of English suburbia – the very places recommended by *Housing Problems* and *Weekly Illustrated* alike as the antidote to the slums, is not only physically but also culturally the place where television, television culture and democratic post-binary politics alike could take root and flourish.

While it is interesting to note the similarities in the descriptions of – and the doubts about – the new England expressed by literary writers from Priestley and Gibbs, via Orwell, to Williams, Hall and contemporary cultural studies, it is also worth stressing that something was lost along the way. The radicals of the Left disliked democracy, suburbia and the post-political consciousness of the ordinary suburban population as much as did the radicals of the Right. They didn't like popular visual culture's cheerful ordinariness. Hall's comment on *Picture Post*'s optimism is exactly mirrored in Paul Attallah's later criticism of the regime of 'fun' in American television:

> Entertainment regulates pleasures and proposes a range of commodities and behaviour patterns. In short, entertainment constitutes audiences so they can have fun – the broad range of consumer goods and associated behaviour patterns which defines wealth, progress, and happiness for us today. Unlike happiness, however, which describes a state of being, fun describes a state of ownership – it is something one has. TV, as the main advertising medium and central disseminator of information and entertainment is also the site of the struggle for fun. Procedures of systems management and quality control are applied not only to the technology of TV but also to the audience of TV: fun is the extreme limit of the audience's position.
>
> (Attallah, 1991: 95)

The American declaration of independence, which protects the 'pursuit of happiness' as a political right, is cashed in as 'fun' in the democratic vistas of network television, which limits the pursuit to *The Beverly Hillbillies*. Such bathos is more than TV critics can bear – but more to the point it is a rhetoric which is turned against democracy, for stupidly remaining cheerful, having fun, when there is *structural change* to be done. Raymond Williams has this mood too, as the book of his TV criticism makes clear; the editor, Alan O'Connor, explains at one stage:

> Against most predictions the Conservatives under Edward Heath won the June 1970 general election, defeating Harold Wilson's second Labour government. The radical May Day Manifesto movement, in which Williams played a key role, wished to break the Labour-Conservative hegemony over national politics but itself collapsed over the issue of whether or not to run its own candidates in the election. Williams later developed a sharp criticism of representative democracy and electoral politics, arguing for the more radical demands of a system of direct rather than representative democracy.
>
> (O'Connor, 1989: 106)

This is the textual tradition in TV studies; a passionate dislike for post-political fun. Here's Williams himself, from a column written in 1969:

> There have been things so bad recently, yet so characteristic, that the struggle over whether to mention them is acute. But what sort of life can we be living if we are prepared to sit down and watch a quiz show between 'the William Rushton trio' and 'the team of the Rt. Hon. Quintin Hogg MP'?
>
> (Williams, 'Watching from elsewhere', in O'Connor, 1989: 67)

What sort of life can we be living? The one where television, like *Picture Post*, suburbia and the Labour Party, was taking the path of social democracy, rather than radical restructuring and resistance. Williams's passionate dislike of its results – having fun in an early version of *Have I Got News for You?* – has its roots in the period before television was around, and interestingly enough it is the passionate dislike that has survived into the textual tradition in TV studies, not the fun.

Interestingly, it is this vision of Left-pessimism that Stuart Hall himself chose to broadcast to a larger audience in the 1970s, as part of the BBC radio series *The Long March of Everyman*. In both the series (preserved in the BBC Sound Archives as T35085) and the book of the series (Barker, 1975), Hall had the honour of making the last contribution, which he called 'Between two worlds'. He introduced voices and ideas from the 1950s and early 1960s, and he too opened his account with a long extract from Phil Cohen's article in *WPCS 2*; he went on to sample teddy boys and telly boys, politicians and protesters, never-had-it-so-good premiers and angry-young-man playwrights, rockers and racists. Hall's conclusion: 'Change, certainly. But a "social revolution"? I doubt it. We need another term for a period of massive social upheaval which, nevertheless, leaves so much exactly where it was: which preserves even as it surpasses' (Hall, 1975: 294).

Hall's analysis of the contradictory developments – where surfaces change rapidly but structures don't – included this reflection on the role of television:

> The real spread of BBC television happened only in the early years of the fifties. Commercial television opened in 1955. This development fed the confusion [about affluence] in two ways. First, by monopolizing the channels of public discussion and debate in the society, television also centralized the power to make its images of social life stick. It communicated, at rapid speed, highly selective, if not distorted, images of one community or section of the society to another. It also helped to form an overall image of where the *whole* society was headed. Secondly, it gave an almost tangible visibility to the quite limited rise in consumption and in spending money. It signified the world in terms of the 'goodies' produced in the new consumer industries and seeking markets among the working class. It created the *spectacular* world of commodities. Advertising, and the spurious social images to which it was tied, represented only one way in which television helped to obliterate the deep sources of change in a veritable cornucopia of goods.
>
> (Hall, 1975: 281–2)

A not entirely charitable reading of this analysis would point out that Hall seemed to be blaming television for its own reputation – something quite out of its control – in his comments about it 'monopolizing the channels of public discussion and debate'. But Hall himself was less than generous about television's cheerfulness: there had been a rise in consumption and spending-power, but television making a spectacle of it merely serves commercial interests seeking new markets. Hall didn't concede that the people watching television might have enjoyed their 'limited' improvements, including television, nor that the significance of the new medium for its viewers went beyond straightforward false consciousness – television 'obliterated' structural change in a 'cornucopia of goods'. He concluded that the extent to which television's 'imagery of consumption entered the lives of ordinary men and women . . . seems, in retrospect, to have been wildly exaggerated':

> The 'telly', like the piano before it, moved into the corner, and was at least partly absorbed by the whole densely textured and structured life around it: it made a difference – but it did not suddenly dismantle the culture of working class people, rooted as it was and remained in the persistent structures of the English class system.
>
> (Hall, 1975: 282)

For Hall, then, television was not to be feared (as it had been in the anxieties expressed by Phil Cohen), but it was also a failure precisely because it didn't effect changes in the 'persistent structures' of class. Although Hall recognized television's great abilities in what I've identified as *cross-demographic communication* ('it communicated . . . images of one community . . . to another'), he was not inclined to read this positively, because the images were 'spurious' and 'spectacular', they spread 'confusion', were 'centralized', and 'selective, if not distorted'. In short, television didn't make enough of the right sort of difference, because it didn't teach the kind of oppositional or resistive class consciousness that Hall's materialist analysis of culture wanted 'ordinary men and women' to keep at the forefront of their minds rather than in the corners of their rooms.

ENOUGH!

I want to close this line of argument by pointing to the damage done, not by television, but by the 'textual tradition' of denunciation it has suffered (as have other popular media, everyday practices, democracy, suburbs and the like). I've argued all along that since this rhetoric predates television it is not strictly about television, and since it seems to be held equally by critics of the Right and the Left it is not strictly about politics either. It is more like the home-talk of the knowledge class; the class which wants to take power over information media and cultural technologies like television, not only by running the business on behalf of the shareholders and stakeholders, but by regulating it, and controlling the literacies and discourses by means of which it is understood culturally. The 'default setting' of this knowledge-class chit-chat about television is as pernicious as it is hypocritical. In a wonderful chapter – ominously entitled 'Acacia Avenue Syndrome' – the television critic Chris Dunkley points out why this is so dangerous:

> As we approach the critical question – what should our attitude be towards television tomorrow? – there is one more major problem to be faced: although in terms of numbers television is the most popular mass medium the world has ever seen, in Britain it appears to have virtually no friends, or none with much influence. Politicians, press, lawyers, police, academics, clergy, the solid centre of the middle-class intelligentsia, all seem more or less inimical to television. There are those who actually work in the industry of course, but even some of them take a remarkably supercilious attitude towards the business.
>
> (Dunkley, 1985: 119)

Dunkley quotes, among others, the teacher who thinks reading the *Beano* would benefit her 10-year-old students more than watching David Attenborough's *Life on Earth* series on the grounds that 'anything's better than bloody television', but he makes an important general point:

Worst of all for the future of the medium is the antagonism not of any particular professional group but of a seemingly large proportion of that band of people known as 'opinion formers': authors, journalists, critics, designers, playwrights, publishers, theatre and cinema producers, and so on. It is depressing to find that the very people who should be leading the way in bringing discrimination to the use of this new mass medium are still dismissing it lock, stock, and barrel.

(Dunkley, 1985: 125–6)

Later on he makes clear why this 'deeply dispiriting array of virulent reactionism, folk mythology and Luddism' should persist. It is, though he doesn't put it this way, a knowledge-class conspiracy against the audience – a conspiracy by 'opinion leaders' against the led:

As viewers what we should be demanding is that we keep the best of what we have got and add as many as possible of the advantages offered by the new technologies: greater choice, more specialization, an increasing shift of power from the broadcasters to the audience, greater convenience in timing and format. . . . We must stand our ground, refuse to be browbeaten or blackmailed, and remind them that the BBC regarded ITV then [in 1954, when ITV was about to begin] as the bubonic plague, yet today they see ITV as brothers in arms, so admirable that they are quite willing to go into business with them.

(Dunkley, 1985: 145–6)

It is quite rare to hear a reasoned argument in favour of popular audience choice, against the interests of broadcasting and critical cartels alike, from a respected television critic. (Dunkley was 'Fleet Street's first mass media correspondent and also television critic' while working for The Times from 1968, before becoming television critic of the Financial Times from 1973.) But as Dunkley suggests, new digital, satellite, cable and multimedia technologies are forcing change, and it is the control of these changes that is sought by the knowledge class (or loss of it feared, more accurately). In this context, the 'textual tradition in TV studies' turns out to be part of the conspiracy; training audiences to discount their own encounters with television, and to speak about it as if they are cultural or social critics still locked into the fears and passions of the 1930s. Certainly much of what we currently 'know' about television's textuality has been taught not by television itself, but by opinions that predate it; perhaps by now, when the 'new mass medium' is sixty years old, the time is ripe for 'the textual tradition' to look to its own past, rather than trying to govern television's future, and everybody else's with it. Meanwhile, the textuality of television remains what it always was, American and proud of it, while the residents of the real East End, where *Housing Problems* was filmed, are re-immortalized in the gritty authenticity of their own TV soap opera, the BBC's acclaimed *EastEnders*. But despite more than sixty years of semiotic and socio-logical investment, they still live in Tower Hamlets – according to official statistics, the poorest borough in England.

10

SCHOOLS OF THOUGHT
Desire and fear; discourse and politics

As my history teacher Mr Bunstein says,
'It's not what you know that makes you smart, it's knowing what you don't know.'
(Clarissa Darling, played by Melissa Joan Hart, 1998: 4)

In this chapter I bring the question of television as transmodern teaching forward in time from the period of its first invention and impact (roughly the 1930s to 1950s) to the period of the 1960s and 1970s, when TV studies began to take recognizable form. My argument is that the form taken by TV studies was by no means determined by developments 'inside' the textual system and social institutions of television as such; it was determined more specifically by critical currents and traditions of the time.

Trying to isolate the most significant of these currents and traditions, it seems possible to observe the operation of two different pairs of 'schools of thought' in relation to TV studies. They are:

1 **'Desire'** and **'fear'** schools of thought
2 **'Discursive'** and **'political'** schools of thought

They were both significant in that they attracted adherents to internally contrasting positions which have remained in fruitful (sometimes hostile) dialogue with each other ever since; but they are unlike each other in that the 'desire' and 'fear' schools of thought represent *currents* in critical and analytical thinking based on a general stance towards modern social life, whereas 'discursive' and 'political' schools of thought represent different analytical *traditions*. Desire for and fear of the consequences of modernization are often mixed together in critical visions of the present and possible future, and this mixture of hope and anxiety is not strictly rational; 'desire' and 'fear' are not theoretical or disciplinary components of knowledge, though they may – and I argue below that they demonstrably do – inform and align what knowledge is looked for, and what it is taken to import. On the other hand, the 'discursive' and 'political' schools of thought are more like differing disciplinary 'takes' on the same object of study, analyzing it (in this case television) using traditions of thought which don't quite share the same questions, vocabulary, corpus of work, theoretical assumptions, methods or expectations.

But taken together, I suggest, the 'desire' and 'fear' schools of thought on the one hand, and the 'discursive' and 'political' schools of thought on the other, explain how TV studies took the shape that it has done in the period of its first enunciation. In this context I would point to the possibility that there may be a historical correlation between the 'desire' and 'fear' schools of thought and the conditions of post-war (post-1945) western development, especially in the USA; i.e. that the current of 'fear' corresponded to the possible outcomes of the cold war, while the current of 'desire' corresponded to the very long period of American economic prosperity and steadily increasing living standards, within which television played its much commented-upon part. Critics active in the generation following the Second World War simply couldn't escape the contradictory realities of unprecedented danger twinned with unprecedented comfort; 'fear' and 'desire' were currents in the climate of the times, and can clearly be observed working their way through otherwise dispassionate and apparently cerebral studies of television.

Meanwhile, the study of television began in a piecemeal way within the disciplinary confines of a number of traditional academic subject areas, for instance in departments of sociology, psychology, history, anthropology, literature, linguistics, politics, government, economics and even in some technological and scientific departments interested in the physical aspects of communication. But the first major public impact of academic studies of television came from mass communications – 'mass-comm' – an American amalgam of socio-psychological and political-economy approaches to the modern media. In the US academic context, 'mass-comm' is distinguished from 'speech-comm' (based on studies of personal interaction, rhetoric and public speaking, language and persuasion). 'Mass-comm' is, however, in my view at least, not the foundation of TV studies, since it is not specifically interested in television, and indeed for many years had very little to say about television programming, preoccupied as it was with questions about the scientificity of its own methods, and the governability and management of vast ('mass'), unknowable populations.

I suggest that it was not from the socio-psychological traditions of 'mass-comm' that TV studies arose, nor from television's own real home in the USA, but from the European (specifically British) context of 'discursive' and 'political' schools of thought which were interested, often in close but not always cordial dialogue with each other, in what television might amount to if it was approached as a general object of study. If television was a distinct textual system, a 'medium' in its own right, and not just a distribution network or a mere instance of larger forces such as 'mass communication' or 'modernity' or 'capitalism', then it would need to be thought about in its own terms. That thinking began away from the US centre of both television culture itself and of the then predominant location for studies of media. It began to take recognizable form *as* TV studies in Britain in the 1960s and 1970s.

This chapter traces the bringing together of desire, fear, discourse and politics in the formation of TV studies, and tries to show that the fundamental issue bringing these currents and traditions together was the question of television as a teacher.

SOMETHING TO TALK ABOUT – DESIRE AND FEAR

What were the uses of television for those present as it became established as a major cultural form? The uses of TV varied according to the user; for instance, it was used:

1   as an investment by shareholders in TV companies;
2   as an object of policy-making and regulation by government departments;
3   as a career and creative outlet by practitioners;
4   as a source of stories by entertainment media such as the daily and weekly press;
5   as part of their information and entertainment repertoire by viewers;
6   as an object of study in TV studies.

However, it is part of the argument of this book that television has achieved its public profile in spite rather than because of the actual use made directly of it by those immediately involved in its production, regulation and viewing. I've already argued that television's reputation – its cultural 'image' – was established very early on, even before it was invented, by discourses that were about something other than television itself. They were interested in questions of cultural decline, commercial exploitation, political danger and social reform. Such issues were fundamental to a society whose democratic institutions were dependent upon the 'will of the people', but in what was called a 'mass society', 'the people' were unknowable; no one was sure who they were, what they wanted, or what they would do or could be made to do. Government by the governed was organized through representative (rather than direct or primitive) democracy, but no one was sure who most truly 'represented' the people. In a century all too familiar with totalitarian politics, total war and crises of legitimacy in regimes ancient and modern, it seemed that modern, industrial, urban, mass society had succeeded in producing an unknowable population served by a representative apparatus of only (at best) contingent legitimacy. At this point, the point of fascism, Hiroshima, Stalin and the post-war boom, along comes television. What is it for? Is it a populist political party? A commercially exploitative cultural monopoly? Does it represent the will of the people? Who controls it? On behalf of whom? Questions of its 'use' by its own makers and viewers seem to pale alongside such grand problems; it becomes 'useful' semiotically in public conversations about something else.

Look at any book on TV studies, or almost any; only very rarely will it contain chapters on 'how to use' television. How to buy and manage shares in TV companies; how to become a TV regulator; how to run a TV station. There are of course plenty of texts on the physical act of recording and editing live image and sound, but technical-creative skill by itself never guarantees anyone access to airtime. There are few chapters on how TV is used by *other* media; by, say, the entertainment editors of tabloid papers, or the TV critics of posh weeklies. And despite the widespread recognition of and concern about media literacy among the billions of people who form the worldwide TV audience, there are no books, as far as I know, on *how to watch TV.* Dorling Kindersley is silent on the subject.

I am arguing, in short, that TV studies has not always been as interested in *television* as you might think. It has been interested in the history of ideas, in general questions about the social production and reproduction of meaning, and in political questions about whose interests are being served by public institutions and culturally pervasive semiosis. And as I have suggested in previous chapters, these questions come not from television itself but were already a running conversation in intellectual, academic and governmental traditions before television came along.

So forgive me, I am not going to expand on television's uses to shareholders, TV executives, producers or even viewers, directly. During the period of the 1960s and 1970s, when writing that is now recognizable as TV studies was first being published, it was television's 'use' as a teacher that preoccupied critics, specifically a teacher of those vast, unknowable, simultaneously desirable and threatening 'masses', rather than its everyday uses by interested parties. Naturally there were differing schools of thought on whether television was a good or bad teacher. A critical community of writers, thinkers and commentators, who were successors to a very long debate (lasting decades if not centuries) about the prospects for successful *cross-demographic communication between unknowable strangers*, discussed whether television, as the latest technology for cross-demographic communication, was good at this job, or whether it was *too* good. Critics and researchers from different disciplinary backgrounds asked how, on present trends, the relationship between TV and its audiences would turn out. They disagreed on whether its social influence was *communicational, behavioural, cultural* or *political.* These were the opening questions of TV studies, and that remains the major 'use' of television in intellectual culture: it sustains the debates of differing schools of thought.

It would be easy to dismiss different academic 'schools of thought' as irrelevant to the main business of making and watching television, but the record shows that television bears the mark of its reputation all the way through from the legislative and industrial set-up in which it operates, through to the details of semiotic presentation on screen, and of course to the framework of understanding and expectation within which it is viewed. And despite the fact that academics, intellectuals and critics are not always held in very high regard, they have nevertheless exerted a disproportionate influence on television by defining and patrolling the limits within which it can operate. Schools of thought, in fact, 'create' television for their societies as an object of the imagination – sometimes, perhaps too often, a somewhat fearful imagination – and the real thing has to limp along in the shadow of this phantasm. In short television is the child of the intellectual climate of its times.

However, times change. During the period of television's ascendancy in the 1950s, the formal study of television in the USA was established as part of 'mass communication' studies; a social-science approach to contemporary mass media that was preoccupied with the issues of the 1930s and 1940s – questions of 'mass society' as outlined above. The predominant discipline was psychology, which was less interested in television as a cultural and historical phenomenon than in its own methodological and disciplinary scientificity; it was interested not in television but in finding scientific ways to describe observable behaviour in individuals, and in finding ways of doing replicable scientific experiments using 'subjects' from rats to students. Using such an approach, researchers in US schools of communication forayed forth, seeking to observe, describe and quantify what 'uses and gratifications' television had for its audiences. They were trained to see audiences as individuals and 'uses' in functional terms – that is, television's 'use' for maintaining (or eroding) individual 'gratifications' in mass society. The most influential studies were those by authors such as George Gerbner, Elihu Katz, Charles Osgood, Percy Tannenbaum, Denis McQuail, Jay Blumler, Hilda Himmelweit (and their many collaborators, students and followers on both sides of the Atlantic), for whom television was not understood as a distinct medium in its own right but merely part of a larger object of study, 'mass communication.'

For these investigators and the 'mass-comm' tradition they represent, television was not cultural but behavioural, not textual but socio-psychological, not historical but functional. 'Uses' of television were understood in straightforward sociological and psychological terms. Questions included how viewers used news to maintain surveillance on their society; how they used drama to satisfy psychological needs; how they used television-watching as escape or diversion; how they used comedy to maintain personal equilibrium. As far as I know, 'viewers' were always understood in the mass – researchers tended to visit places like Normal, Illinois, rather than the White House or Harvard or the Pentagon, to determine how TV was used. In other words, those viewers who were regarded as powerful or as immune, from politicians to schoolteachers, were rarely if ever surveyed, sampled or subjected to experiments as members of 'the' audience. Reading this early American research on television, there is little sense that television (unlike film) was an enjoyable medium to watch (for the researchers, especially), nor that the 'mass' audience's motivations for watching it might be positive, nor that its social, psychological or political impact was anything other than pathological.

The 'mass-comm' tradition I've outlined here certainly continued, and has of course proven very influential in its own right, but it was not within this tradition that thinking about television in *general* began to emerge. So, ironically, it was not in the USA, coping with the twin realities of the cold war (fear) and a boom economy (desire), that TV studies began to take shape in its own right.

131

One neglected reason for the disproportionate attention given to television's effect on *other* people, and the disproportionate credence given to fearful theories emanating from 'schools of thought' rather than from the actual process of cross-demographic communication itself, lies in the social distance between the parties for whom TV is useful. They are not only personally strangers to each other, but they tend to occupy positions in society, and do jobs, that are literally unimaginable to others in the system. The 'ordinary viewer', especially when television first became an important cultural force, had (and perhaps in many cases still has) little access to the 'culture' of the TV producer, regulator, shareholder or commentator. Such figures belong to the depersonalized category of 'They', as in − 'They shouldn't be allowed to get away with it!', 'They say it rots your brain', 'They always look after themselves.' In a situation of social distance, personal strangeness and impersonality, the parts of the system are so separate that the connections are filled by each party *fantasizing* an identity, purpose and usage for the others. Just as viewers are obliged to 'know' only in their imaginations what the uses of TV may be for a shareholder, regulator, producer or critic, since they are never going to run into one at the supermarket, so for these other parties the viewer is an unknown quantity, fleshed out by some rather vivid imagining, much of it in the convincing but often misleading guise of market surveys and academic studies.

It is here, in a context where each TV user only knows the other textually, or in fantasy, or by reputation, that the possibility arises for public discourses about television to assume disproportionate importance. They fill in the social space between the parties to the communication with a set of assumptions and expectations. What are the uses of television? It gives 'society' a way of talking to itself, about itself, in conditions where cross-demographic communications are mutually untranslatable, and inter-societal knowledge is hearsay. Meanwhile, television was coming of age in a society that did not know if it was the luckiest one ever, because of its economic supremacy and standard of living, or the unluckiest, because of the ever-present threat of literal annihilation by 'MAD' cold-war politics (MAD = mutually assured destruction, the so-called balance of terror between NATO and Soviet nuclear deterrents). Clearly, in such a society, discourses of fear on the one hand and desire on the other, of 'mutually assured' prosperity or death between people for whom 'mutuality' was more directly experienced on screen and page than by personal contact, are going to be unusually significant, and unusually applicable to television. It is my own view, then, that the two important 'schools of thought' in relation to the question of television's efficacy in the matter of cross-demographic communication between strangers are not organized around evidence, but around the stance or perspective of the observer.

Between the '*desire*' and '*fear* ' schools of thought, it is noteworthy that the most familiar to the public is the 'fear' school. This includes all those from behavioural psychologists to moral entrepreneurs ('clean-up-TV' campaigners) who believe that television affects its audiences for the worse. They generate the rhetoric of sex, violence and bad language that has heckled television since it started. It also includes the paranoid radicals who believe television semiosis is a conspiracy by the so-called 'military-industrial complex' (the term is President Dwight Eisenhower's) to produce docile consumers. And the fear school also includes those who believe TV is part of a general cultural decline, frequently evidenced by the very prosperity that television itself both promotes and exemplifies ('our materialistic society' seen as a pathology).

On the desire side, where I would place my own work in TV studies, are those who see television as having democratic potential, increasing the intensity of information and experience available to more people and to an extent never before seen. The 'desire' school of thought might also include people who like television and want to study it or work in it; and those for whom television represents hope for a cause or a constituency. It has to be admitted that in the sphere of scholarly and formal intellectual publishing, the 'desire' school is much thinner on the ground than the 'fear' school, and it attracts unusually vehement denunciation by critics from Camp Fear (see the large body of writing around the work of John Fiske).

The earliest major figure to theorize television in general from the 'desire' point of view was Marshall McLuhan. A Canadian working in the US, McLuhan was trained (at Oxford and elsewhere) as a Shakespearian scholar, interested in questions of literary history, the history of ideas, and in the impact of technologies of communication upon whole societies. McLuhan used a 'mosaic' rather than a 'linear' or rationalist form of logic, and was not in the least interested in behaviourist, sociological or psychologistic explanations of the 'uses' of television. He was interested in a much broader, anthropological perspective on human activity, and was better-versed in aesthetic, textual, cultural, dramatic and mythic debates about human sense-making than he was in 'mass-comm' techniques of population-observation. He saw television as an epoch-making development in human history, comparable with, but antithetical to, the invention of printing in the European Renaissance. McLuhan achieved what can only be described as popular stardom in the 1960s and 1970s, trading his original position as a provincial professor for a period of fame and public recognition-value that was itself so remarkable that it could become a topical joke in a popular movie (where he played 'himself' in a Woody Allen film). He was constantly on television talking about television, he released records featuring his cryptic one-line philosophizing, and was of course a best-selling author, especially of the popularizing versions of his work (i.e. *The Mechanical Bride* and *Understanding Media* more than *The Gutenberg Galaxy*). McLuhan was and has remained a controversial, intriguing and much criticized figure. (See Tom Wolfe 'What if he is right?', 1968: 107–33; and Hans Magnus Enzensberger 'Constituents of a theory of the media' in 1970: Chapter 2, especially pp. 42–4.) It is now thought that his intellectual forebears, especially the Canadian scholar Harold Innes (*The Bias of Communication*), may have left a more considerable scholarly legacy than he did. Nevertheless Herbert Marshall McLuhan pointed to an entirely new way of thinking about television and he made 'television' itself into an object of public debate, putting on the agenda questions about its historical, social, technological and mental impact that had not been widely aired before. He *liked* television; liked being on it, thinking about it and he liked the idea that it might reconfigure human relations along lines that were more 'mutual' and 'oral' than those established by literacy in the dominant print-media of modernity. He was the first to think that the prospects for cross-demographic communication among strangers were enhanced rather than damaged by television.

It ought to be noted, perhaps, that a 'disciplinary' distinction exists between the legacy of the 'desire' and 'fear' schools of thought respectively – a distinction between literary and social-science faculties in universities. The work of Marshall McLuhan was certainly influential in discussions of literary history. This is how I first encountered it – as a grad-student puzzling about the place of popular drama in the English Renaissance, recommended to me by my then-supervisor, the Shakespearian scholar and polemicist Terence Hawkes, who also wrote innovatively about TV (see Hawkes, 1973). It was McLuhan's cultural-historical book *The Gutenberg Galaxy* (1962), rather than his better-known writings on contemporary media (McLuhan, 1964), that provoked most thought.

But it was another literary figure with a great sense of history who became perhaps the most influential, certainly the best, of the early European theorists of television – Umberto Eco. Like McLuhan, Eco was intrigued by the relations between contemporary culture and the cultures of the past, especially that of the European Middle Ages. His later work in the book *Travels in Hyperreality* (1987) contains some of the best analysis there is of what I've called 'transmodernity' and he calls the 'new medievalism'. But his earliest work on television (in English, at least), an article called 'Towards a semiotic enquiry into the television message' (1972), was not an attempt to medievalize television but to analyze its semiotic components. Eco was no naïve celebrant at the altar of the new; he understood the politcs of culture and the ideological problems of 'mass' communication. But his solution was to change the literacy of the audience, not the content of the message. He took television to be a communicative opportunity for liberatory as well as for more reactionary politics. His attitude to television was intrigued, if not welcoming; and he used his literary training, both as an analyst and as a writer, to communicate with wider publics. He wrote regular columns in the Italian press, where he was (and remains) a major public intellectual, while simultaneously subjecting the new medium to rigorous analysis in his academic work (see Eco, 1981), and talking to industry-leaders in consultancy and 'policy' work (Eco, 1979). Eco's journalism, theorizing and public profile make him a model of the 'desire' school of thought, not because he was a proponent of the new medium, but because he set about working with what it offered, and trying to understand that.

Among the earliest noteworthy American scholars to take television seriously as a medium without pathologizing it was Horace Newcomb (1974), himself trained in literary traditions. Newcomb has gone on to make a significant contribution to the establishment of television studies in the North American context through his collection *Television: The Critical View*, which has gone through multiple editions, and more recently a project of heroic proportions that could not have been produced by the 'fear' school of thought – the three-volume, 2,000-page *Encyclopedia of Television* (Newcomb, 1997). And, if I may, I'll add here that another work to gain influence on both sides of the Atlantic as an early attempt to study television from a tolerant perspective was *Reading Television* (Fiske and Hartley, 1978), also written by authors with literary rather than social-science training, and leading to our first invitation to speak in America – through the good offices of Horace Newcomb. In such ways did the 'desire' school of thought inveigle its way into parts of the American academy which were until that time bastions of social-science, 'mass-comm', pathologized media and 'fear'.

The desire and fear schools of thought contrast with each other thus:

DESIRE	:	FEAR
ECONOMIC PROSPERITY	:	COLD-WAR ANXIETY
MARSHALL McLUHAN	:	SOCIAL PSYCHOLOGY
LITERARY TRAINING	:	SOCIAL-SCIENCE TRAINING
JOHN FISKE	:	GEORGE GERBNER
TV STUDIES	:	'MASS-COMM'

It is as well to end this section with the observation that these distinctions don't so much mean opposition as *dialogue* – intense semiotic traffic between 'untranslatable' textual systems, and some writers, like Umberto Eco, deftly incorporate the concerns of both sides in their own work. Indeed, the dialogue has been such that they've come together perhaps more than either side would have expected in the 1970s and 1980s. For instance, one of the differences that has always held the 'desire' side apart from the 'fear' side is a presumption of relative activity and passivity among the audience. The social-science approach needs a passive audience, precisely because it is looking for influences *on*, power *over* and manipulation *of* that audience: the thing has to sit still (on the couch) while all this ownership, control, commercialization, consumerism (and so on) is done *to* it. Conversely, the literary-derived approach needs an active audience, since it sees television as communication, and communication as a two-way, interactive practice of meaning-exchange: you *can't* watch television passively at the semiotic level.

But now it transpires that the champion of the active audience, John Fiske (see Fiske, 1987: 62–83), who attracted quite intemperate criticism for his notion of a 'readers' liberation front' (i.e. that participation in media sense-making, even via commercial TV, could be resistive of dominant ideologies precisely because reading is active), has been joined by the champion of the social-science, 'what-media-control-is-doing-to-the-world' school, George Gerbner. In a recent article, Gerbner reports the establishment not of a 'readers' liberation front' but of the 'Viewer's Declaration of Independence', as part of a citizen-activist response to the 'cultural environment' (Gerbner, 1998: 144–5 – you can contact the 'Cultural Environment Movement' on e-mail CEM@libertynet.org). Full circle.

'DISCURSIVE' AND 'POLITICAL' SCHOOLS OF THOUGHT

Given the dominance of the 'fear' school of thought, there is a large archive of writing about the so-called negative effects or influence of television. But since, as I've suggested, such writing is largely a continuation of the questions of the 1930s and 1940s into later periods, I will not survey it in detail. Instead I want to isolate a later question, one that arose in the decades after television became established, i.e. during the 1960s and 1970s, and which holds within it equal potential for the 'desire' and 'fear' schools of thought. This is the issue of teaching – of television's 'use' as a transmodern teacher.

In Britain, a tradition of writing emerged around the issue of television-as-teacher which was to prove decisive in shaping TV studies. It began as a convergence between two schools of thought that were rather different from the 'desire' and 'fear' schools, in debates organized around the question of television's actual (fear) and potential (desire) uses as a teacher of large populations. The two can be identified as **'discursive'** and **'political'** schools of thought respectively.

The 'discursive' school of thought arose from literary studies, the 'political' school from the New Left. Both were ascendant in the early 1960s. Raymond Williams was there at the time. This is his configuration of the situation:

> A current of opinion, and the necessary work to support it, has been decisively introduced into social argument. The great merit of earlier work in this field, of the phase associated with 'Scrutiny', was its remarkable and still growing influence in education: critical work, on the content of popular culture, has now a long and still exciting history in many of our schools. The mark of the second phase, which is normally associated with the 'New Left', has been an extension to the problem of institutions: both their immediate amendment and reform, and the discovery of newly possible institutions for a democratic culture.
>
> (Williams, 1968: 10)

Williams here distinguishes between *discursive* work in formal education, associated with F.R. and Q.D. Leavis's journal *Scrutiny*, and dedicated to 'critical work on the content of popular culture', and *political* work in the New Left, dedicated to institutional reform, renewal and perhaps even revolution. Williams, with one foot in each camp as a literary theorist and critic who was also prominent in the New Left, knew only too well that these two schools of thought, concerned respectively with discursive content and institutional politics of popular culture, did not always see eye to eye:

> There are still many tensions between the two phases: the arguments about a minority culture and a democratic culture often and necessarily divide them. But also, in actual work, there is important common ground, and their combined influence has had an evident public effect.
>
> (Williams, 1968: 10)

The discursive, Leavisite, critical school of thought was identified with 'minority culture' while the political, New Left, institutional school of thought was identified with 'democratic culture'.

DISCURSIVE : POLITICAL
LEAVISITE : NEW LEFT
CRITICAL ANALYSIS : INSTITUTIONAL ANALYSIS
MINORITY CULTURE : DEMOCRATIC CULTURE
SCRUTINY : *NEW LEFT REVIEW*

The 'important common ground' between these otherwise opposing (or at best alternative) projects, was, though Williams doesn't put it this way, their shared suspicion of *popular culture*.

Indeed, it is from within popular culture that Williams discerns his enemies. Having arrived at an intellectual and analytical project based on the 'evident public effect' of the discursive + political approach, the next stage he describes is not further theoretical or analytical advance but defence against reactionary attacks. He says that a 'genuine and powerful counter-attack was mounted and developed' (1968: 11). The counter-attack came from three directions:

1   'fashionable culture' [knowledge-class opponents];
2   from the 'absorption, containment and apparent neutralization of the offending ideas' by 'existing institutions and practices' [owners and controllers]; and
3   'a direct and open attack, from the existing interests', namely 'newspapers themselves involved in commercial television'. (see Williams, 1968: 11)

For Williams, 'democratic' meant anti-capitalist, which is why 'democracy' in the form of a Labour government such as Harold Wilson's (1964–70) was a defeat. The two schools of thought (discursive and political), with their twin concern for content and institutions, and their desire for 'minority' and 'democratic' utopias respectively, working in schools (*Scrutiny*) and in debate inside the 'intelligentsia' or 'knowledge class' (NLR), could only experience dialogue with popular culture as *counter-attack*; scorn by the 'fashionable', neutralization by unnamed 'existing practices', and open attack by the 'existing interests' in the highly suspicious form of those who own or control commercial television. No mention of the audience (discursive) nor the public (political) in all this; the battle was about conflicts within the 'knowledge class'.

The formula was set: discursive + political + counter-attack = TV studies. In other words, from the start, television studies took as its object not *television* but *intervention* into the discursive and political conditions of the time. The idea was not to understand but to undermine television; to train citizens to resist commercial and state ideologies which, it was believed, were what television taught best. Even when, late in the 1970s, the most Marxist and adversarially politicized decade in recent cultural studies, by which time the foremost writers had forgotten the Leavisite origins of the discursive component of TV studies and even Raymond Williams had come out as a Marxist (see Williams, 1977), even then, the legacy of *Scrutiny* was found to be inescapable. Here's an editorial from the influential journal *Screen Education*, presumably by its then editor, James Donald:

> *Scrutiny* must appear a strange model for *Screen Education*, given the explicitly anti-Leavisite impetus of much film and television teaching. The point of comparison is to stress that it is possible to make an effective intervention into education through critical *journalism*. It was through its 'militant, committed, interventionist cultural practice' [Mulhern, 1979], that *Scrutiny* was able to shape the practices of several generations of English teachers (and to win a remarkable degree of hegemony among other sectors of the British intelligentsia). Similarly, it is by putting into circulation theorisations (of the objects of study, of the education system, of pedagogy) which challenge the dominant régime of truth within educational institutions that *Screen Education* can most effectively contribute to bringing about changes in teachers' practices. Critical journalism, then, is a precondition of critical teaching.
>
> (*Screen Education*, 1979: 1–2)

Here then is the reinvention of the discursive + political + counter-attack = TV studies formula in a new guise. The terms have become inflected with Gramscian and Foucauldian accents (hegemony, regime of truth) and, while the language is both more political and more theorized than Williams's on the same theme from the previous decade, the ambition is both much more modest and much more radical.

It is more modest because 'politics' has been reduced to 'teacher-training'. The 'counter-attack' mentioned by Williams must be presumed to have been successful, since the passage above takes for granted that teachers' practices need to be changed, and that there is such a thing as a 'dominant' regime of truth. So now the struggle is not to educate the citizen directly, or to intervene in public debate directly through journals such as NLR, but (militantly, politically) to *intervene* in formal education itself, and thereby to educate teachers, who in turn, presumably, go on to educate citizens. But the struggle is still imagined as taking place wholly within the 'knowledge class'. The chosen weapon, *journalism*, is understood not as reporting for the general public but as academic writing in a journal; it is understood as *Screen Education*. 'Interventions' in this form are strictly pedagogic: the idea is to train a Coleridgeian 'clerisy' of schoolteachers whose duty it will be to tramp the land in search of congregations, in classrooms rather than among social classes, before whom the word of *screen education* may be preached.

The ambition is more radical than Williams because the object is 'to challenge the dominant regime of truth'. This textual radicalism, pulling the rug from under the very notion of truth itself in the name of a goal specified only as 'change' and 'challenge' (not indicating where the change is supposed to end socially or institutionally) points the way to the 'next stage' of *Screen Education*'s development. The journal seeks to move from 'a theoretical concern' with the object of study (cinema, broadcasting, media), towards *activism*: 'an active engagement with the political arguments around the practices, discourses and institutions of cultural production' (1979: 3).

La lutte continue (the struggle continues), it seems, as Parisian walls had proclaimed in 1968, but as in 1968 so in 1979; this theoretical turn away from the training of critical literacy among the population towards *proposed* but unspecified activism inside the institutions of cultural production coincided with an *actual* lurch of mainstream politics to the Right. In Paris the 'événements' of May 1968 were followed by a surprise electoral victory by the rightist Charles de Gaulle; in Britain this issue of *Screen Education*, dated summer 1979, was published at exactly the moment that Margaret Thatcher won her first general election (May 1979). 'Interventionist' activism in the name of radical challenges to the dominant regime of truth became, in practice, defensive critique for its own sake.

Meanwhile, the theme of democracy-as-defeat seemed more than ever justified to those who looked on, powerless and askance, at the triumphalist populism of the Right. An alliance of PR and advertising gurus with Right-wing think-tanks emboldened Mrs Thatcher to appeal directly to the electorate, over the heads of party and parliamentary apparatuses, using television to 'teach' the population her particular regime of truth, which even had a name. It was called 'TINA': There Is No Alternative. And indeed, *Screen Education* was no alternative. Cultural critics and 'activists' had already withdrawn from mainstream politics to the politics of pedagogy, to leftist theoreticism and to utopian or revolutionary political rhetorics that were not even supposed to prove a match for Thatcherism, since they were directed not to the middle ground of ordinary life but to the creation of intellectual cadres and political movements *outside* the mainstream; inside the 'knowledge class'. *Screen Education*'s screen education, then, was intended for critics, not for audiences.

A major 'use' of television has been its use by contending schools of thought to fight out their own differences, and then to 'use' television institutions and discourses to promote (teach) one or other of various forms of cultural citizenship, whether understood as 'minority' culture, 'democratic' culture or commercial culture.

11

PEOPLE WHO KNEAD PEOPLE

Permanent education and
the amelioration of manners

*Spend a week regularly watching television
. . . and you almost feel the cakes of custom being cracked open.*
(Richard Hoggart, 1960: 42)

An early example of a teacherly vision of television as a teacher of cultural citizenship is an article by Richard Hoggart, published in the journal *Encounter* in 1960, called 'The uses of television'. Hoggart was clear about the educational 'use' of television:

> Think of one season's features . . . going into thousands upon thousands of homes, getting behind thousands of lace curtains and potted bulbs, past ranks of chintz settees and modernistic climbing plants. Who . . . can estimate the liberating, the kneading effect of this detailed and intelligent presentation of the day-to-day texture of other people's lives, assumptions, hopes?
>
> (1960: 38)

On the basis of this unique ability to invade its *viewers'* privacy, he concludes that 'television may well be a most important *primary* educator'. Not only can television 'knead' people's interest in *other* people, it can, says Hoggart, inspire a love of knowing on a grand scale: 'The advantage of television is that it can, instantaneously and sharply, offer huge numbers of people a sense of the excitement and variety and possible depths of knowledge' (1960: 39). 'Its limitation,' he adds, careful to remain balanced, 'is that it is a creature of daily or weekly fresh starts.'

Hoggart sees television teaching as a 'kneading effect'. Kneading, perhaps like television, is literally a process of hard, repetitive manipulation. Here's the breadmaking expert Elizabeth David on how it should be done. After being left to rise for an hour or two, the dough 'will look puffy and spongy', she advises (making it sound uncannily similar to the couch potato who's been sitting quietly in the warm, watching television for hours, gradually increasing in size and gas content). Then:

Break [the dough] down by giving it a good punch with your fist. Then gather it up and slap it down hard in the bowl several times. Sprinkle it with flour and knead it by pushing it out and then folding it over on itself in a roughly three-cornered fashion; then repeat the process two or three times. The punching down and kneading, or knocking back as it is also called, redistributes the gas bubbles produced by the yeast, so that it will renew its work and form new air balloons.

(David, 1977: 258)

Well, you can see why this is a lovely metaphor for teaching the public via television. To knead, according to the OED, is 'to mix and work up into a homogeneous plastic mass, by successively drawing out, folding over, and pressing or squeezing together'; figuratively, it is 'to blend, incorporate, weld together, or reduce to a common mass, as if by kneading. To manipulate, shape, form, as by kneading' (OED).

According to the OED, kneading applies not only to breadmaking, but also to the action of the potter on clay, to the kneading of people's bodies in massage, and to the kneading action of cats' paws as they make themselves comfortable (this feline kneading is said to be what kittens do to stimulate mother's milk – otherwise known as 'pap'). It seems, then, that being 'reduced to a common mass' by 'manipulation' can be a pleasurable/nurturing (cat), healthy/sensuous (massage), and creative/productive (potter) experience for the recipient, despite the temptingly pejorative connotations of some of the terms if you apply them to TV audiences. But in Hoggart's hands it's an entirely positive image; he's watched a lot of kneading, at his grandmother's kitchen table, and likes the idea of people's consciousness being drawn out, folded over, squeezed, and occasionally even slapped down hard. Even if TV audiences' brains hurt because they're looking at lives unlike their own, thinking about issues otherwise avoided, or beginning to glimpse, through news and drama, horizons previously unimagined, Hoggart believes the effect on the audience is desirable – it will cause them to *rise*.

As a television teaching method, kneading is not a passive metaphor for either party involved; it's not of the 'sitting with Nellie' school of education. For the televisor (broadcaster), kneading is a vigorous and rewarding activity, and as anyone who's done it knows, an enjoyable and therapeutic one too. For the audience, being kneaded is a more internal and molecular experience, but the 'dough' is still very much alive; the more it allows itself to be knocked into a cocked hat by the kneading process, the more 'air balloons' of inspiration it forms. Hoggart does not imagine the audience individually as a 'puffy and spongy' airhead, but collectively as a living dough to be 'broken down' and worked on as part of a process known in breadmaking, and in life too, as 'proving'. Television 'proves' popular consciousness by aerating it and allowing the mixture of 'detailed and intelligent presentation', and 'the texture of other people's lives, assumptions, hopes' to ferment in the warmth of the suburban kneading-trough until 'general education' has occurred. Here's Hoggart on how it is done:

141

In some respects *Dixon of Dock Green* [a classic police series – in Britain its current successor would be *The Bill*; in the USA perhaps *NYPD Blue*] is probably a more powerful factor in general education than a whole range of evening institute classes in non-vocational subjects. . . . Each instalment is really a dramatised secular parable played by characters who are almost alive. And all the time, consciously or unconsciously, it is trying to ameliorate manners. . . . No doubt the effect of such half-art is slow, but it may eventually (in combination with the other forces of which it is both a part and a reflection) be considerable.

(1960: 42–3)

Hoggart sees television trying to 'ameliorate manners' as one of its major uses; it is here, he suggests, that TV already is a teacher:

I have already suggested that television can be an important primary educator. In a much wider sense it will be an important general educator, an educator in manners, a way of transmitting . . . attitudes and assumptions different from those many of its audience have previously held. In any society a medium so intimate and pervasive will do this; it is bound constantly to be putting before people other ways of shaking hands, of sitting down, of wearing clothes, of reacting to strangers, of eating, of carrying on conversations; it is bound constantly to be setting in motion numerous slight but widespread reactions.

(1960: 41)

'NICELY WEATHERED BY SINLESS WINDS'

However, for Hoggart, who hasn't got time in 1960 to wait for forty years to see how those 'slight but widespread' reactions turn out, television should not only prove *useful* in this longue-durée, anthropological, breadmaking sense; but more immediately it can also be *put to use*. He wanted its users – both producers and audiences – to work to television's own strengths, to make it do imaginatively what it can do generically:

Some people are thinking about the more tractable educational possibilities of television; few have thought much about its imaginative possibilities. . . . Whatever the developments in the imaginative use of television, its basic work must always be direct and discursive. It must try, clearly, helpfully, and demotically, to speak to and for the variety and the strengths of its society.

(1960: 40)

Television as teacher is best when it recognizes the quality of its audience and provides them with the means to meet and learn from each other:

> If we believe that 'ability' is . . . widespread and complex, . . . if we believe that many . . . people . . . can think responsibly and feel deeply, then we have to try . . . to create more areas for demotic meeting.
>
> (1960: 41)

Although he wasn't particularly well-disposed towards commercial television in 1960, Hoggart was nevertheless aware that one reason for ITV's success was 'their sense of this need'. Used as a 'demotic meeting place' for the 'amelioration of manners' by the 'kneading effect', television could add to the repertoire of sources for *continuing education* by groups who were then, and still are, underserved by formal education:

> [Despite their decline,] local, face-to-face . . . communities, whether of a neighbourhood or a workbench, will still be important educators: talk at work or round the lamp-post or at the edge of the dance-hall or in a coffee-bar, and the acceptance of the habits of these groups, will all have their persistent educative effect. And teen-agers in particular pay comparatively little attention to television. But for most of us the box in the corner will have a relatively more important place as a moderator of manners.
>
> (1960: 41)

Aware as he is of the educationally leavening potential of television, Hoggart is keen to have its ingredients pure. He sees contemporary popular media as guides to choice, or guides to the attitudes that inform choices, in conditions of increasing social affluence, mobility and openness. So it's not a matter of manners only; it's also a matter of consumption, and here, for him, lies a problem. The people who were exploiting the educational potential of television most deliberately, for Hoggart, were not formal educationalists at all, but advertisers. So the 'moderation of manners' was being done in the service of cocoa powder:

> In the present situation the single most powerful attempt to alter attitudes – to educate manners – in Britain is being made through the advertisements on ITV. . . . It is a bright world and a congenitally innocent world, a world prior to the knowledge of good and evil, in which all the young girls have that wonderful Jamesian exclamation mark between their eyebrows (see the Mirandas of the cocoa-commercials) and even the middle-aged fathers look no more than nicely weathered by sinless winds. . . . It is . . . important to realise the essential childishness, inadequacy, euphoria of this world; and so to question the quality of the life which is being promoted.
>
> (1960: 43–4)

Improvements to the quality of life, encouraging the imaginative meeting of the variety and the strength of society, were being pursued most vigorously, and the population kneaded most effectively, by those who would educate them not out of, but into 'childishness'.

THE EFFECT OF THE AUDIENCE ON TELEVISION

This childishness, for Hoggart (and this is where I part company from his position), is not a positive condition to which his notions of 'primary education' and 'general education' properly apply, not child-likeness, but a negative condition produced by having to address an unknowable population. Whereas 'commercials . . . are forms of bastard art, based largely on emotional appeals often irrelevant to the rational case for using their products'(1960: 43), says Hoggart, a '"pure artist" . . . is not aware of a vast, unknown, unassessed, varying audience which has to be *won*' (1960: 44). So Hoggart's language changes – from 'kneading' to 'winning', from knowing to feeling, from educating to appealing, from 'speaking clearly, helpfully and demotically', to a world of 'childishness, inadequacy and euphoria'. It is pretty obvious that he was making the standard distinction between 'public service' and 'commercial' television, a distinction that lasts to this day, and with the evaluative implications of which (i.e. 'public service = hooray!; commercial = boo!') I for one do not agree. But it is important to realize that Hoggart is doing something else within this rather conventionally pejorative account of commercials and commercial TV. He is showing that television does have a teaching function, which he places at an almost anthropological level, and that the most 'advanced' exploitation of this function was to be found in commercials.

Hoggart was worried about something that most of television's critics have failed to think about; not the effect of television on the audience, but *the effect of the audience on television*: 'one of the strongest limitations on the mass media – simply because they are mass media – is their pressing awareness of a huge audience' (1960: 44). This insight is of general importance to television studies, where it has almost been forgotten; it is counter-intuitive, but nevertheless in line with my argument in this book, that television as an institution and a textual system can best be explained by coming to an understanding of the discursive and institutional effects of a fear of, or anxiety about, the audience among those who made, regulated and criticized the new medium.

Hoggart himself was interested in pursuing the effect of the audience on television semiosis. He believed that the unknowability and size of the audience restricted the imaginative licence of the TV artist.

A 'pure artist' . . . is not aware of a vast, unknown, unassessed, varying audience which has to be *won*. This situation is not wholly discreditable, but at the best it is extremely inhibiting. How will a

Figure 11.1 'Blond or Brunette!' Ad for General Electric TV, USA 1951
Source: *Saturday Evening Post*, 24 March 1951

miner in South Wales or a woman on a North Yorkshire farmhouse or
a solicitor in London take this? Will some be dangerously shocked?
Dare I assume this? How far will most people go along with me if I
risk this?

(1960: 44)

Figure 11.2 Dressing up and celebrating TV, Germany, 1950s
Source: Postcard from the Deutsches Historisches Museum, Berlin

For Hoggart the discipline of having to 'win' (seduce?) something that is vast and unknowable has had three related effects on television 'art':

1 it reduces the ability of television to take imaginative risks: 'it can rarely be, in a sustained way, radical or searching' (1960: 44);

2 it promotes a spurious 'objectivity': 'Part of the trouble here is, once again, that the audience is undifferentiated . . . so mass communications tend to seek an "objectivity" which can be pretty well statistically demonstrated, and, if necessary, defended' (1960: 39);

3 it is done most successfully by those who *want* 'mass audiences, mass audiences of masses', namely advertisers and hence commercial television.

146

Figure 11.3 A family night with Rowntree's Fruit Gums (but what are they watching?)
Source: Woman, 31 March 1956; courtesy of Nestlé UK

Figure 11.4 Television celebrates its 21st birthday: Jimmy Edwards entertaining the Picnic Girls
Source: *Illustrated*, 31 August 1957

Figure 11.5 The TV audience becomes a pastiche of its former self: 'Soap Crazy'

The effect of the audience upon television, according to Hoggart, is to make it bland. The 'interests of the advertisers' mean that commercial television makes a different kind of bread:

> They want to push [this society] towards a generalised form of life which looks much like the life we have known and for the rest looks nicely acceptable – but whose texture is as like that of a good life as processed bread is like home-baked bread.
>
> (1960: 45)

More kneading is needed, evidently. Hoggart sees television as a 'general educator' of the people, but is not happy about the 'education' of television by its audience; not happy with rule or government by the audience, or by the conception, fear or desire of it by television-makers. It tends to produce the very kind of bread most demanded by *children*. The effect of the audience on television is *paedocratic*, and like the good grown-up he is, Hoggart resists this form of government. He ends his meditation upon the 'uses of television' with a vision of a society subjected to the 'processing of attitudes' by broadcasters:

> It is a processing which tries to produce what I have called a cultural classlessness. . . . Such a society would not be ostensibly hostile to 'culture'. It would make culture a commodity. . . . But the disconcerting force and personal humility of genuine imaginative or intellectual

activity would have been lost as surely as both the crust and the taste have been lost in that processed bread.

(1960: 45)

PERMANENT EDUCATION

It is significant that Richard Hoggart's gentle breadmaking metaphors (associating television's outcomes with warmth and time, nurturing and kneading) have been forgotten in more recent cultural and television studies. The 'tradition' most widely remembered is the theoretically more militant and radical but politically more modest tradition of *Screen Education*. Like *Scrutiny* before it, this and other journals of the 1970s and 1980s assisted in the training of those who went on to write the TV studies textbooks (including me). The study of television, from discursive and political points of view, grew into television studies. Meanwhile, direct address to the population at large, the audience, was progressively abandoned. My own version of 'intervention', which I called 'intervention analysis', was an attempt to bring television studies back into contact with those who would form television audiences, but still via educational strategies; I saw my own version of TV studies as being 'dedicated to making the existing practices of reading and understanding television better informed, less unselfconscious and more systematic. . . . It develops readings which are intended to intervene in the way people might want to watch television. Its perspective is that of the audience' (Hartley, 1992a: 6). In fact, my version of 'intervention analysis', published in this form in 1992, is no more than a return to what Hoggart was proposing in 1960 and what Williams, in his own way, was also arguing in 1968. But while Hoggart was exclusively concerned with the direct relationship between television and its audiences (desire), and the teaching function contained in that relationship, Williams introduced the virus of pessimistic adversarialism (fear). He recognized that television was a teacher, but he opposed what it was teaching, in whose interests, for what purposes, by what means, root and branch. He wanted to supplant this kind of teaching with one of his own, which he called 'permanent education':

[The idea of 'permanent education,' which is now so important in French cultural thought] . . . seems to me to repeat, in a new and important idiom, the concepts of learning and of popular democratic culture which underlie the present book. What it valuably stresses is the educational force . . . of our whole social and cultural experience. It is therefore concerned, not only with continuing education, of a formal or informal kind, but with what the whole environment, its institutions and relationships, actively and profoundly teaches. To consider the problems of families, or of town planning, is then an educational enterprise, for these, also, are where teaching occurs. And then the field of this book, of the cultural communications which, under an

150

old shadow, are still called mass communications, can be integrated, as I had always intended, with a whole social policy. For who can doubt, looking at television or newspapers, or reading the women's magazines, that here, centrally, is *teaching*, and teaching financed and distributed in a much larger way than is formal education?

(Williams, 1968: 14)

So, for Williams, 'permanent education' is a reality; but it is currently being pursued most actively and successfully by television, the press and magazines, understood as the enemy:

> The choice then is clear. The need for permanent education, in our kind of changing society, will be met in one way or another. It is now on the whole being met . . . by an integration of this teaching with the priorities and interests of a capitalist society. . . . a capitalist society . . . which necessarily retains as its central principle . . . the idea of a few governing, communicating with and teaching the many. I have been deeply impressed, looking again at this material, by the extent to which it is itself integrated. Organized economically, in its largest part, around advertising, it is increasingly organized culturally around the values and habits of that version of human personality, human need and human capacity. This strong and integrated world is capable, I believe, in the coming decades, of adapting to its own purposes both politics and education.
>
> (Williams 1968: 14–15)

Williams observes with alarm the integration of government, education and media; viewing it as an *invasion* of media and education by political forces to which he is opposed. He is therefore not minded to see such integration positively, and rather than asking how it might be done well, or how well it is doing, from the perspective of the audience, he seeks to set up something completely different, and educate the population with that:

> Against this kind of permanent education, already well organized and visibly extending its methods and its range, an integrated alternative is now profoundly necessary. I have seen something of the plans, in many countries, for a permanent education of a democratic and popular kind: programmes for family care, for the improvement and extension of schools, universities and further education, for the public safeguarding of natural beauty, for the planning of towns and cities around the needs of leisure and learning, for the recovery of control and meaning in work. It is in the spirit of this kind of programme that I discuss communications, the field in which one or other version of a permanent education will be decisive.
>
> (Williams 1968: 15–16)

I have no wish to engage in posthumous point-scoring with Raymond Williams, but I do think his pessimism was misplaced. He locates his desirable 'plans' *outside* of the postmodern agora of the integrated relationship between government, education and media; in fact he removes them to a popular-democratic utopia called 'many countries' (but not this one). But looking back from the late 1990s to the late 1960s, it is at least arguable that many of these plans, for social welfare, education, the environment, leisure and work, have been achieved, or at least realistically fought for, and are still very much alive as desirable plans among large and demanding populations *within* the 'version of a permanent education' that he hates most. He doesn't trust the established interests of commercial and governmental power to 'educate' the citizen via television, but instead fears that these interests will use television to 'educate' the citizen into permanent subjection to advertising. Therefore, it follows, he places too little trust either in television itself as a medium or in the popular audience itself. This pessimism of the intellect, which sees television from the point of view of the intelligentsia, whether discursive or political, but not from the point of view of the audience, leads Williams to betray the very purposes he seeks to represent. He turns attention away from the *audiences* and *readerships* of 'permanent education' to the *interests* and *institutions* which are taken to control it.

I don't think TV studies has ever quite recovered from this move. Rather than thinking through the implications of how to address an 'unknowable' audience, this tradition in cultural and television studies has more or less forgotten that the audience is taking a permanent 'teach yourself' course in life (but see Brooker, 1998), using resources to hand, such as commercial television, and has instead retreated either to top–down schemes to 'school' the population in alternative truths deemed important by the teachers, or else into instrumental 'audience research' which gets to know the popular audience less to discover how it is teaching itself than to measure how successfully some *interest* or *institution* has been pushing it around.

The model of permanent education that I prefer is supplied by Umberto Eco: 'If you want to use television for teaching somebody something, you have first to teach somebody how to use television' (Eco, 1979: 15). Accepting that television does teach, Eco wants 'education' to start from there:

> I think that the first duty of a teacher is, if not to say, 'Don't trust me', at least to say, 'Only trust me within reason'. I think in fact that this attitude is one that every reasonable person takes when watching television. . . . Television is the school book of modern adults, as much as it is the only authoritative school book for our children. Education, real education, doesn't mean teaching young people to trust school. On the contrary, it consists of training young people to criticise school books and *write their own school books*. It was like that at the time of Socrates, and I don't see any reason for giving up this attitude.
>
> (Eco, 1979: 16, 22)

It is this emphasis on young people, and on the possibility and desirability of empowering them to 'write' their own education rather than receiving it passively from either school or television, that I want to take through into the next chapter. If there is such a thing as a permanent education in the discursive and political components of cultural citizenship, then it is organized around the figure of 'young people', specifically, most recently, the teenage girl. It seems to me that the teenage girl is the figure in popular semiosis that stands most perfectly in the place of, and as the figure for, the popular audience itself. How does she teach herself; teach 'us'? It is towards this figure that the remaining chapters of the book will wend.

12

DEMOCRATAINMENT
Television and cultural citizenship

My whole trick is to keep the tune well out in front. If I play Tchaikovsky I play his melodies and skip his spiritual struggles. Naturally I condense. I have to know just how many notes my audience will stand for. If there's time left over I fill in with a lot of runs up and down the keyboard.

(Liberace, quoted from *Jazz Monthly*,
in Hall and Whannel, 1964: 70)

LOVE, NOT QUITE REQUITED

In previous chapters I have traced the development of the discourses and concerns of TV studies over the period between the 1930s to 1950s when television itself was first established, and in the period of the 1960s and 1970s when TV studies were first established. In these final chapters I wish to bring the narrative more up to date. What is the use of television at the turn of the millennial century, when it is a well-established medium? With the development of new communications technologies and semiotic systems, from non-broadcast television by video, cable, satellite and digital systems, to the newer virtual and interactive computer- and telecommunications-based technologies, it seems that interest in television as such has declined, at least among marketeers and policy-pundits, whose attention seems entirely fixed on newness. But television in its 'classic' broadcast form is still culturally, if not technologically, pre-eminent. Once the promoters of newness have passed on to new excitements, television is still there – just as its own predecessors, cinema, the press and books are thriving despite television's own much-feared expansion. Among audiences, publics and consumers in all known countries, it is television programming and television culture, not new technology as such, that attract attention. So much of the rhetoric of promotion for new technologies has to do with business expansion, national self-aggrandisement and individual emancipation that their 'functions' for the communities who eventually take them up is forgotten. A question for television as a cultural and historical fact of the last half century, then: what was that all about?

In this context, the argument of this chapter is quite simple. Television is used, both in its original 'mass' broadcast form, and now in its emergent subscriber-choice forms, to teach two new forms of citizenship, which I am calling

154

'**cultural**' and '**do-it-yourself**' or **DIY citizenship** respectively. I've argued that as a 'transmodern' medium television shares many of its teaching characteristics with pre-modern 'media', especially the European medieval church, and it takes its own cultural place in the 'institutional' setting of talk and the family, which I would designate as essentially pre-modern in its everyday conduct; more anthropological than industrial certainly. In such a setting, during the second half of the twentieth century, television has reached and sustained a position as the foremost medium for cross-demographic communication. Meanwhile, a largely successful campaign has been mounted by government regulators and professional broadcasters alike to stop it becoming directly political in this usage. So its impact for its unprecedentedly large but politically unfocused audiences has been cultural and personal rather than political in the formal sense. However, I argue that exactly these cultural and personal usages have themselves contributed to new forms of citizenship, thereby becoming political in unexpected ways.

If television is a transmodern teacher, the question of what it teaches has eventually to be addressed. But this is not just a matter of describing the content of its 'lessons'. Certainly it teaches general knowledge and facts about the world, and about the day to day conduct of public and private affairs. As Richard Hoggart suggested in 1960 it also teaches 'the amelioration of manners' (meaning the manners of the age rather than table manners); teaching different segments of the population how others look, live, speak, behave, relate, dispute, dance, sing, vote, decide, tolerate, complain; television is a major source of 'people-watching' for comparison and possible emulation. And no doubt television teaches various ethical, ideological and moral precepts, prejudices and perspectives too. But if the television medium as a whole – as a cultural-historical phenomenon – can be characterized as a teacher, then it ought to be possible to identify a similarly general addressee to whom its teaching is directed.

What 'addressee' does the teaching discourse of television call into being? Traditional schooling calls into being the student addressee; one who is self-motivated by a perceived lack of some knowledge or skill to subject themselves to the regime of schooling, including its forms of collective organization and discipline, teaching practices, subject-taxonomies, assessment methods, certification and cultural expectations. By contrast, the 'addressee' of advertising is the consumer; one who is chatted up by the advertising text, which performs all manner of flirty, attention-attracting tricks in the full knowledge that the 'addressee' of advertising has made no prior commitment, expressed no lack and is not self-motivated to see things the same way as this or any advertisement, but who may be entertained, intrigued or informed by what is shown and said, sufficiently to maintain awareness of, interest in and sympathy for a particular brand or product, based on the addressee's 'literacy' in the ways and wiles of advertising, itself built up over a long period, and requiring some degree of mutual trust between advertising and its addressee in order for the system to work at all. Whether the elaborate display of commercial courtship sparks a response powerful enough in the consumer-addressee to result in a consummation (a purchase

. . . ; a marriage . . .) is by no means a foregone conclusion, as both parties perfectly well know.

These two extremes of 'addressee' – one purposeful, institutional and regimented, the other based on the rhetoric of declarations of (unrequited) love – show that the 'addressee' of television in general, the audience, may vary, since television addresses its viewers in a variety of ways, ranging from the 'love-object' of advertising to an addressee-position much closer to that of the traditional student in certain types of 'public service' factual and educational programming, for instance. But television in general is neither potential lover nor formal schoolteacher (nor is it, as some critics have long feared, a scandalous mixture of these) – the addressee of television teaching is neither student nor consumer, but the audience.

Having called this entertainment-seeking, voluntary (uncommitted, fickle) addressee into being, television 'teaches' it, first of all, to continue to watch television, for example by providing narrative and dramatic genres that promote reconsumption (serials, series, news, weather, sport), and by using semiotic devices at every level from dialogue to plot, characterization to casting, language to location, that might help to carry viewers through, continuing from the heyday of the nineteenth-century novel the famous Wilkie Collins school of good tale-telling – 'make 'em laugh, make 'em cry, make 'em wait'. The 'literacy' of the television viewer in watching television is the first priority of television teaching. Such literacy may be understood as very basic, but it may also become quite sophisticated, especially over a lifetime of viewing, or where individuals become fans for particular shows, stars or series, and it has the unplanned outcome of promoting relations *among* television audiences, not just between the addresser and addressee. Indeed, investigations into fan cultures have been at pains to point out how active, astute and 'literate' such viewers are, frequently knowing more about a given television show or genre than the best-funded academic or commercial researcher, and investing considerable resources – both of self and money – into conducting a relationship with the show, other fans and the outside world based on their television-literacy. They attend conferences, produce and consume fanzines and websites, buy the clothes, collect the gadgets, live the life (see Jenkins, 1992; Tulloch and Jenkins, 1995; Miller, 1997).

Of course not everyone who watches television goes to such lengths about every or any show, but it is impossible to watch television in a settled context (i.e. in a given country) for long without beginning to participate in an intersubjective conversation with all the anonymous others of that context about the fashions and celebrities of the season, the politics and insider gossip of the production process, the ups and downs of the ratings, the joys and horrors of the great shows and the not-so-great, and the vast, rolling, cumulative oral 'archive' of common knowledge that is both mined and made by television. So 'how to watch television' is a lesson in cultural (intersubjective) as well as media literacy from the start – from the first lessons in repetition (*Tellytubbies*), in generic recognition and media-allusiveness (*Sesame Street*), to full-scale self-reflexive homilies in the micro-politics of everyday life in TV-Land (*The Simpsons*). Television promotes reconsumption of its own forms by teaching lessons in cultural literacy, and within this context it promotes among its 'subjects' – the audience – both 'identity' (sameness with others in TV-Land) and 'choice' (difference within an intersubjective field). It is my contention that what arises from long-tutoring in this non-purposeful cultural-personal semiosis is a new episode in the historical development of modern citizenship (but see also Ellis, 1982; Ang, 1996; and Hartley, 1987 for a previous debate about the implications of seeing the television viewer as what Ellis called the 'normal citizen').

CITIZENS OF MEDIA

Does television teach citizenship? How does it? How should it? Once again, the issue is not television itself (as a social institution or on-screen discourse), but the relations among the populations it serves: how these populations can be known, reached, taught; turned into citizens. In previous work I have suggested that citizenship is profoundly *mediated* in the modern/postmodern period – we are all 'citizens of media' (Hartley, 1996: Chapter 3) in the sense that participation in public decision-making is primarily conducted through media (and that this has been true since at least the French Revolution). Traditional political theory sees citizenship as something prior to, separate from and if anything damaged by media relations. But in the modern/postmodern period, citizenship needs to be seen in historical rather than categorical terms; it is an evolving and cumulative concept adapting to changes in western development. As new philosophical, political and industrial conditions became established through the period of the eighteenth to the twentieth centuries, so new rights and claims came to be associated with citizenship. And because development for different social groups was uneven, so citizenship rights varied for different populations; rights tended to be claimed first by urban adult white men who might at first have enjoyed citizenship rights unheard of (if not undreamed of) by colonized and 'ethnic' populations, women, children or people of various 'minorities' from gypsies/ Romanies to gays and lesbians. Nevertheless, the promulgation of rights, free-doms and responsibilities associated with citizenship among one group set up an inevitable standard or yardstick for others, promoting a logic of equivalence by which those whose rights were denied or unrecognized might move forward in their own particular struggles (see Enzensberger, 1970; Laclau and Mouffe, 1985; Hartley, 1996). Hence, at any one time, there may be different forms of citizen-ship in existence even within the same population. It may need to be stressed here that this 'historical model' of developing citizenship recognizes that there is continuing struggle both to attain and to maintain existing levels of citizenship – this is not a 'treacle-flow' view of history (a slow tide, inevitably rolling forward, outward), but a history of uneven development; one step forward, but sometimes two steps back or, for some, no step at all.

Television has an important bearing on this historically complex and 'mottled' situation, because it is no respecter of differences among its audiences; it *gathers populations* which may otherwise display few connections among themselves and positions them as its audience 'indifferently', according to all viewers the same 'rights' and promoting among them a sense of common identity *as* television audiences. At one and the same time, then, people can experience political differences based on territory, ethnicity, law and heritage between one another, but also, simultaneously and conversely, they can enjoy undifferentiated 'identity' with others based on television audiencehood. While television promotes loyalty among its audiences, and tries to 'subject' each and every viewer to its 'regime of viewing', it does not (on pain of regulatory intervention by the 'secular branch' of government) interfere with people's existing political rights and citizenship. Much of the anxiety about television's social impact rests on the riskiness of this situation – television is seen by some viewers and many governments as a usurper of their own rights and privileges, but at the same time television enjoys unparalleled success in turning actual populations into its 'subjects'.

It seems to me that what has in fact been occurring over the fifty-odd years that television has become established as the world's number-one entertainment resource and leisure-time pursuit is that a new form of citizenship has overlain the older, existing forms. In the long-term perspective of history, this new form of citizenship may be seen not as a competitor with traditional 'political' forms, but a successor, covering and further embedding previous forms certainly, but cumulatively, not supplanting them. However, as it has evolved and spread, observers have frequently taken fright at the apparent *removal* of hard-won civic rights and their *replacement* with 'media citizenship'. My own view is that citizens of media remain citizens of modernity, and the rights struggled for since the Enlightenment are not threatened but further extended in the so-called 'post-modern' environments of media, virtuality and semiotic self-determination.

What's new is that with television, the potential community of 'media citizens' has now run to several billions of people around the world. Populations have been gathered, and cross-demographic communication established with them, beyond the reach of secular states and nations – the television audience has truly become the 'laity' of a new supernational community, exceeding the scope but not the ambition of the medieval Catholic church, overlaying traditional citizen-ship with something new. Television corporations are the new ecclesiastical bureaucracies, vying with mere governments for the hearts and souls of the laity, ostensibly tending to non-secular needs but actually in constant dialogue with the political and territorial powers, negotiating precisely the extent (possible or permissible) to which each can authentically claim to be speaking and acting on behalf of most people, both in terms of absolute numbers and in terms of their most vital interests, opinions, will or needs. Since it is the case that public participation in terrestrial politics is predominantly conducted through the media (although the traditional apparatus of political parties, local activism and asso-ciative democracy still continue inside the envelope of the mediasphere), and since in addition 'media' now means television before other forms such as newspapers, it follows that television has become implicated in civic issues in new and complicated ways.

Looking at the rest of the world through television, it is inevitable that differences can be both celebrated and erased, recognized and removed, insisted upon and ignored. So there's a curious 'toggle' switching between television as a teacher of 'identity' among its audiences, and as a teacher of 'difference' among the same population. It seems to me that this 'toggle' switch is itself historical – it was set to 'identity' first, promoting what I've called 'cultural citizenship' and identity politics (during the era of 'golden-age' broadcast television), and to 'difference' more recently, promoting 'DIY' citizenship and semiotic self-determination. It follows from what I've argued above that both types of citizenship may be found in social circulation simultaneously; some groups may have moved beyond 'cultural citizenship' and identity politics to 'DIY citizenship' and semiotic self-determination, while others are still struggling for identity and see newer developments as irrelevant or dangerous. For instance, some sections of the women's movement and feminist theory, and some thinking within the politics of sexual orientation in the gay and lesbian movements and queer theory, have moved beyond 'identity politics', while many ethnic groups, including first peoples, are still struggling for their identity and for the rights of 'cultural citizenship' to be recognized. Television has, it seems to me, moved historically in a similar way, from the promotion among its audiences of an 'addressee position' based on common identity and 'cultural citizenship' during its first half-century, to a more recent acceptance of difference in its audiences, promoting 'DIY citizenship'.

Various semiotic developments can be explained by this schema. For instance, in the area of factual television and actuality reporting, I would argue that a definite move can be observed during the television era from news or journalism as a discourse of power to news or journalism as a discourse of identity. Concomitantly, the 'object' of news was once the decision-maker, now it is the celebrity. News was once about security (i.e. national security – defence and war, policing and civil order) and was based on conflict. Now it is about personal comportment and is based on confession.

In drama and other TV genres such as chat shows (both celebrity-guest and audience-talk shows), as well as in advertisements, television has grown in importance as a promoter of difference understood as 'neighbourliness'. Even when the audience is treated to the pathological side of neighbourly conduct – not least in the rivetting new genre of 'neighbours from hell' documentaries – the overall perspective is to posit a level of civility, tolerance and acceptance of difference that is being breached in whatever spectacular way in any one show. Hospital dramas tend to pivot around neighbourliness; the hospital standing for the local community, and the doctor/nurse/patient/administrator relationships standing for neighbourly ones. Just as people tend to choose both sexual partners and enemies from neighbours (not from near family or far strangers in both cases), so hospital dramas find sexual and other tensions inside the virtual community of the fictional hospital. They share the unspoken presumption of neighbourliness with recent genres like the 'world's most gruesome police-chase videos' and 'world's funniest home-video clips'. What's regarded as dramatic, uncivil or funny in each genre is directly related to the audience's sense of virtual community, since dramatic conflict/romance, moralistic discourses about get-away cars or amusing ruptures to family and bodily equilibrium can only work for the audience on a prior presumption of neighbourliness and civility in personal, social and domestic comportment. This is cultural citizenship on show.

Meanwhile, the cumulative growth of a new form of citizenship raises socio-political as well as semiotic questions. If there are citizens, then traditional citizenship theory will be looking for some kind of formal, contractual or legislative relationship with a state – citizens of media are presumably 'subject' to some institution which is doubtless seeking to lead them, to take power in their name, to mobilize them in one cause or another. 'Someone' is usually taken to be the much-maligned media corporation: the 'mogul' or 'baron' – in the present era often personified by Rupert Murdoch – whose 'power' is deemed to derive from their subjection of populations to their political and cultural agenda, rather than from their economic or corporate dominance as such.

Rupert Murdoch's career has indeed spanned the change from cultural to DIY citizenship: News International, his corporate vehicle, has shifted progressively from print (originally the Adelaide *News*), to broadcast-network television (Fox), then to non-broadcast television (Sky, Star) without abandoning the earlier forms (he retains newspaper titles in several continents, although he has closed the *News*). Meanwhile his own citizenship moved from 'identity' (he's a native of Australia) to 'DIY' (he took US citizenship to comply with federal ownership regulations). However, despite the alarming extent to which this individual is demonized and held to be personally responsible for the lives and politics of whole populations, I don't think it is Rupert Murdoch who explains the phenomena of 'cultural' and 'DIY' citizenship, or the 'use' of television as a transmodern teacher, that I've been trying to explain, but precisely the reverse. It is television's propensity to establish new versions of community that explains Rupert Murdoch. He has simply ridden the regulatory wave as governments and media organizations have coped with the democratization of media semiosis. In short, my model of citizenship is more interested in the process of citizenship formation among the populations that might be collectivized as citizens of whatever community, than in the formal relationship between any one citizen and any one 'state' or power. In this I am following the tradition of thinking about cultural citizenship that is derived from cultural criticism – the Arnoldian, Leavisite tradition which was developed by Hoggart and Williams – rather than social and political theories of citizenship, which focus on the civic rights and obligations that take legislative form. In my schema, Rupert Murdoch and all the other moguls, barons and 'kings of the world' who from time to time proclaim themselves sovereign *over* the people are certainly important figures in the landscape, but they're all temporary usurpers: more important is the truly sovereign community in whose name they operate – the populations among whom relationships, decisions and ideas are negotiated and arbitrated. Hence cultural citizenship is better seen as a historical activity among audiences, not as a conspiracy by corporate raiders. It is in process of formation – being made to mean something – long before it can be institutionalized and legislated. In my view 'cultural citizenship' is at a late stage of rights-formation, moving into formal legislative existence in a number of contexts, while DIY citizenship is much more recent, fleeting and of uncertain outcome. But it can be seen as 'citizenship' nonetheless, because semiotic self-determination is 'claimed' as a 'right' and 'taught' as a mode of civility or neighbourliness by those within its purview. It is – or could be – the citizenship of the future; decentralized, post-adversarial, international, based on self-determination not state coercion right down to the details of identity and selfhood. Its model is the 'remote control' exercized by television audiences, and its manifestations include fan cultures, youth cultures, taste constituencies, consumer-sovereignty movements and those privatizations of previously 'public' cultures that succeed in democratization without politicization: extending to everyone membership of the republic of letters that was once reserved for literate/clerical elites.

The progressive fragmentation of sources of television, as the medium very slowly evolves from broadcast to non-broadcast (cable and satellite) forms, and from free-to-air to subscriber services, and from one-way transmission to various types of interactivity (ranging from the phone-in to full computer compatibility), and from broadcasting seen as 'national culture' to television as part of consumer choice, means that technologies of communication are evolving from what may be recognized as a *national semiosis* model in the period of broadcast network television, to a *semiotic self-determination* model in the post-identity era of DIY citizenship.

No wonder critics are concerned. But as always, advertisers are quick to see the positive aspect of such developments. There are many advertising campaigns, for international brand names in particular, that promote DIY citizenship in a field of 'identity-within-difference'; recognizing 'cultural citizenship' and identity, but playing with it. One such is on air as I write; a British television commercial (TVC) for Coca-Cola. It features an Aboriginal boy from what looks like the central desert of Australia, who is found at the beginning of the ad within his 'identity' group, painted up in traditional patterns and dancing traditional movements alluding to a corroborree. As the TVC progresses, refreshing water/Coke begins to abound, having the effect of transporting the boy directly from pre-modernity to 'DIY citizenship': the white paint is washed off the tribal bodies, the boy's own body gets a red T-shirt, emu-steps turn to breakdancing and clap-sticks turn to a bottle of Coke. The TVC alludes, consciously or otherwise, to the South African film *The Gods Must Be Crazy* (Jamie Uys, 1984), but it is also clearly promoting a worldwide citizenship of people of colour as the Aboriginal boy breaks into the urban rhythms of African America, while suggesting to the predominantly Anglo-Celtic but also multicultural British audience that their semiotic self-determination allows them access to and pleasure in these other identities, and indeed promotes respect and fellow-feeling for the co-consumers of Planet Coke. In this the advertisement is by no means alone. McDonalds TVCs in Australia play with the very same ideas, including the use of Aboriginal characters as part of their world community of Citizens of the Golden Arches. Benetton has for over a decade been promoting its United Colors; and internationally branded goods from IBM ('solutions for a small planet') to Microsoft ('where do you want to go today?'), from cars to beer, vie with each other to promote – to *teach* – cultural identity and semiotic difference all at once. As I write, Benetton is running an advertising campaign celebrating the fiftieth anniversary of the Universal Declaration of Human Rights. The print media advertisement features some of O. Toscani's familiar 'united colors' multicultural portraits, surrounding an excerpt from the Declaration: 'ALL HUMAN BEINGS ARE BORN FREE AND EQUAL IN DIGNITY AND RIGHTS (art. 1)' (*Vogue* (UK), April 1998: 68–9). It is in the spaces created by commercial culture, sponsors of highly capitalized innovation in the mediasphere, i.e. in upscale advertising, that the connections between culture, difference, identity and human rights are being visualized and made both appealing and accessible in the era of semiotic self-determination and DIY citizenship. The idea that a company specializing in the sale of franchises for clothes shops may also be a radical, avant-garde producer of cutting-edge ideas about citizenship and social relations in an international media economy still jars with many commentators; but it is at least arguable that the 'message' of the United Nations is getting across at least as effectively via Benetton as it is via formal schooling. Popular commercial media are certainly not *outside* the process of citizen-formation. They may even be making a good job of teaching its latest potentialities, to a public that can participate in the communicational exchange of ideas about selfhood and citizenship, rights and differences, without any requirement to buy a sweater (much less a franchise for a Benetton shop). Advertising on television and elsewhere is now a fully emancipated component of the general mediasphere, a bastion of what I will call, in deference to other recent Government-Education-Media hybrids like 'infotainment' and 'edutainment,' **democratainment.**

FROM CIVIL, POLITICAL AND SOCIAL TO CULTURAL CITIZENSHIP

What forms of citizenship do these new forms (cultural and DIY) overlay? In a classic account, T.H. Marshall (1992, first published 1950: 8, 10) argued that the history of citizenship in modernity comprises three evolving components, each one building on rather than supplanting the one before. These are:

1 **civil citizenship** – Enlightenment rationality leading to individual rights

and the 'bourgeois freedoms' (freedom of accumulation, contract, labour and exchange: see Macpherson, 1973);

2   **political citizenship** – the ascendancy of 'representative' (as opposed to direct) democracy and government by consent expressed in the vote;

3   **social citizenship** – welfare and education understood as rights.

Marshall's plan is explained by John Chesterman and Brian Galligan's helpful summary in their book on indigenous citizenship:

> According to Marshall's influential account, which has shaped modern thinking on citizenship, there are three main components of citizenship, or three kinds of human rights, which have developed cumulatively during the last three centuries: the civil element, which developed largely in the eighteenth century, consisted of the rights necessary for individual freedom, such as the right to freedom of speech and the right to own property; the political element, which largely arose during the nineteenth century, entailed the right to take part in political processes, most importantly as a voter; and the social element, which has received its greatest definition during the twentieth century, was the third and least easily defined category, to which Marshall most closely connected the educational system and social services. This social element covered a range of rights, from one's right to a modicum of economic security to the 'right to share to the full in the social heritage and to live the life of a civilised human being according to the standards prevailing in the society'.
>
> (Chesterman and Galligan, 1997: 5)

Chesterman and Galligan, tracing the history of Aboriginal citizenship in Australia, are at pains to point out that indigenous people throughout the modern period have been 'specifically excluded from certain rights in all three of Marshall's categories'. So while it is clear that a cumulative progression from civil to political to social rights of citizenship can indeed be seen to underlie the history of industrializing western commercial democracies since the Enlightenment, it was by no means a universal history, even for the inhabitants of the countries involved. A similar caveat would have to be made for women, non-heterosexual identities, various ethnic groups and colonized peoples, and children; their 'progress' is not necessarily in convoy with that of the white adult European male who is the 'universal' subject of civic discourse since the American, French, Industrial and Russian Revolutions. However, it is among the disenfranchised or unenfranchised so-called 'minorities', such as indigenous people, that a fourth type of citizenship has clearly and now irrevocably arisen:

4   **cultural citizenship**, or identity, as in 'identity politics'.

Chesterman and Galligan concede that 'new understandings of citizenship' have been informed by, for instance, the recognition of Aboriginal rights, and that 'these less formal social and cultural aspects of citizenship and community structures, practices and values are crucially important' (Chesterman and Galligan, 1997: 5), although in their own study they leave the articulation of 'cultural aspects of citizenship' to the experts, who in this case are Aboriginal people themselves:

> There have been two great themes to our struggle: citizenship rights, the right to be treated the same as other Australians, to receive the same benefits, to be provided with the same level of services; and indigenous rights, the collective rights that are owed to us as distinct peoples and as the original occupiers of this land. *Lois O'Donoghue, chairperson of the Aboriginal and Torres Strait Islander Commission, 1996.*
>
> (Quoted in Chesterman and Galligan, 1997: 193)

Lois O'Donoghue's distinction between 'citizenship rights' and 'indigenous rights' points to something more than the particular circumstances of indigenous people in Australia. It is a version of a much more general tendency which has gathered pace globally since Marshall's tripartite model of citizenship was used to describe mid-century Europe, namely a tendency towards the articulation of cultural citizenship and identity rights as a separate category from social, political or civil citizenship. 'Indigenous citizenship' stands therefore for a fourth type of 'cultural' or 'identity' citizenship more generally; 'collective rights that are owed' to any group as 'distinct peoples', be they ethnically/territorially organized as with Aboriginal people, or 'virtual' communities, as with women, children/youth or even 'mass' media audiences. David Trigger says that this kind of ('indigenous') 'cultural citizenship . . . would imply that real moral weight should be accorded to world views and practices that are at times inconsistent with predominant sentiments' (Trigger, 1998: 164).

'Mass' media audiences have been the focus of public and cultural policy since there were masses to mediate. They were for decades regarded as relatively undifferentiated, unknowable, by turns desirable (redeemable) and threatening (revolutionary). The technologies of communication characteristic of the twentieth century have been designed to reach them and regulate them, influence them and stop them being influenced. Oddly enough, these great unknowable masses that have stalked the pages of social and media theory, government legislation and cultural criticism since the nineteenth century have themselves been the locus of the development of the form of citizenship based not on sameness (undifferentiated mass), but on difference. The so-called 'masses' – the citizen-consumer audiences of 'mass society' – are historically the site whence the fourth type of citizenship has arisen, taking *difference* to the point where it can be claimed, and increasingly recognized, as a human right.

I am arguing, indeed, that a theoretically influential and historically significant 'model' of modern humanity – the model of unknowable and undifferentiated sameness among the industrialized, urban, popular classes – has completely collapsed in the very place where it was most expected and most feared; the 'mass' audience. Television is far and away the most 'mass' of the mass media, its audiences are still (despite computer-based and non-broadcast new technologies) the biggest collective communities our species has yet called into being, and it is still the site where advertisers and politicians most *desire* what social scientists most *fear*: an undifferentiated viewer (buy ours!; vote for us! . . . will they buy that?; vote for them?). But it is here, in the cultural sphere of privatized, individuated, mediated consumption, where audiences gather to partake of *mass* entertainment, that the form of citizenship that most *denies* massness has pitched its tent most securely.

13

INFLUX OF THE FEARED

Democratization, schooling, cultural studies

Shortsighted and contemptuous dismissals of commercial culture often fail to appreciate the seminal importance of the constant articulations or linkages at play in the relation between representational practices and social locations, dynamics and relationships.

(Herman Gray, 1995: 5–6)

Fear of populations in modernity is always the same – it's a kind of latter-day Canute syndrome, where those who believe themselves to be sovereign over a given territory fear their own failure to turn incoming tides. It is a fear of influx, fear of being altered or submerged by dissolved boundaries between 'we' and 'they' identities. An example will serve, I hope, for other versions of the same. The fear of indigenous populations by colonizing settlers is the same fear as that expressed about 'popular' classes in established but industrializing and democratizing societies. The fear of being swamped by influx is thus so strong that it can be turned into its own opposite – fear of influx by the *indigenous*. The policy that arises from such fears can be illustrated (because of their clarity) through the words of A.O. Neville, writing in the first half of the twentieth century, during the very period when, in western countries generally, civil and political citizenship (voting) was being actively extended into 'social' citizenship (welfare). Neville asked a rhetorical question about this very process:

> The different States are creating institutions for the welfare of the native race, and, as a result of this policy, the native population is increasing. What is to be the limit? Are we going to have a population of 1,000,000 blacks in the Commonwealth, or are we going to merge them into our white community and eventually forget that there ever were any aborigines in Australia?
>
> (Quoted in Chesterton and Galligan, 1997: 150–1)

As Commissioner for Native Affairs for his state (Western Australia), and therefore as the government official responsible for 'protecting' Aboriginal people, it fell to Neville to put his theory of assimilation into practice, by means whose brutality has been chronicled elsewhere (e.g. Haebich, 1988), but which bore a remarkable similarity to the measures taken in the previous century to govern another kind of indigene, this time the London poor; measures simultaneously to *correct and protect* them, that is to control their threat and ameliorate their conditions, by forcible removal to orphanages, manual work, adoption by white/middle-class families, education into Christianity, backed up by criminalization, coercion and street-clearance. Neville published a book in which he proudly displayed photographs showing how Aboriginality could be bred out in three generations – he called it 'biological absorption' (Neville, 1944; see also Leslie, 1993: Chapter 3). A 'white' Australia was to be protected not by exterminating its original inhabitants (a popular policy up to that time at least), but by turning threatening others into white Australians and thereby obliterating them.

Now we recognize this as genocide, when applied to ethnic/territorial populations such as indigenous people, though not to the urban poor, who are still more subject to assimilationist than to liberationist rhetorics. However, the same mechanisms were first developed not for other races but for the masses – this policy reached the outback of Western Australia via the tenements of Glasgow and London. Indigenous Australians were to be treated as if they were the urban British poor (see Sidney Godolphin Osborne, 1853; Henry Mayhew, 1968).

The populations most feared by those who feared influxes changed according to the 'progress' from the modernizing energies of imperial colonization in the nineteenth century to its latter-day 'postmodern' successors. First it was the metropolitan urban poor and conquered races and nations; then it was 'virtual' demographic groups based on gender (feminism and the women's movement), ethnicity (the civil rights movement), sexual orientation (the gay and lesbian movement), age (youth culture) and lifestyle (from hippy subcultures to the environmental movement). What links such disparate groups is not only the attempts by 'educators' to colonize and assimilate them, but also the basis of their organized response in each case. Sooner or later each demographic group that has been subjected to the 'fear of the influx' has turned into what it was feared to be – an *identity*, separate, distinct and often binarily opposed to that of the favoured 'we' community, and equally often justified by reference to unarguable essences such as biological determination, ancestry (blood) or genetic predetermination. 'Identity politics' is the politics of the internally colonized demographics of modernity.

Identity politics became 'popular' – widespread, widely understood and widely adhered to – during the period of most intense territorial *decolonization*. The struggle for national freedom among the imperial 'possessions' gathered pace after the Second World War. India and Pakistan achieved independence in 1947; Harold Macmillan heralded the 'winds of change' in sub-Saharan Africa in 1959; the last significant British colony, Hong Kong, was handed back to China in 1997. This half-century is exactly the period of television's global ascendancy – indeed, one of the facts of life it has had to contend with is the colonialist legacy to which the television industry is itself an inheritor, certainly in its patterns of ownership, international exchange and Anglo-American textual forms. But identity politics is itself a 'decolonizing' discourse; the insistence on

Figure 13.1 'Dear Sîan'
Source: *Girl Talk*, 47, 11 December 1996. © Girl Talk/BBC Worldwide 1997, used with permission

'identity' by one community results in an opposite (though not always equal) insistence on difference by other groups, who then coalesce into anti-colonial movements in opposition to whatever 'identity' is held to be dominant. In short, post-imperial, decolonizing societies are characterized by internal secessionism,

168

internal colonialism and an increasing fragmentation of populations – and this applies to the former colonizing nations as well as to their colonies. 'Identity politics' is susceptible to the 'fear of the influx' – whether the actual or virtual community experiencing that fear is dominant (Balkanization; racism) or not (first peoples; secessionists). States practising 'unifying' or assimilationist policies aimed at integration of difference frequently succeed only in provoking a response by those feared that takes the form of resistance, aspiring to the *liberation* of the very identity that is feared; 'unity' results in the paradoxical insistence on what it most wants to obliterate.

But meanwhile, throughout the period of national decolonization, television was quietly gathering populations, achieving success most comprehensively among those most feared as masses. Working-class and female audiences, people of colour and ethnic minorities, subcultural and 'oppressed' groups from gays to children, have historically been among the heaviest and most appreciative ('uncritical') audiences for television, while governmental, professional and intellectual classes – the 'knowledge class' – have historically been both low users of television (at least in their own estimation) and suspicious of popular media. Television supplied a form of citizenship that colonized and 'internally

Figure 13.2 'Too much telly sex is making young girls pregnant!'
Source: © *Woman's Own*, 7 July 1997, used with permission

169

EXCLUSIVE: Tough new package will protect children from squalid and seamy programmes

CURB THE DARK AND BRUTAL SIDE OF TV

Diana's parting of the waves

A SWEEPING purge on the dark and brutal side of television will be declared today.

Virginia Bottomley will unveil a package of measures to clean up pre-watershed programmes which feed children a degrading diet of sex, drugs and violence.

EastEnders, The Bill, Brookside and Neighbours have all faced criticism for their treatment of issues such as incest, rape, adultery, prostitution and murder.

The Heritage Secretary has made it her priority to tackle the major concentration on the seedier side of life.

She has emerged with an agreed

By PAUL EASTHAM
Political Correspondent

four-point initiative which they will present jointly with her today.

● TV bosses will tighten their codes of practice in the New Year to curb gratuitous violence.

● More, better and clearer information will be published to warn parents what kind of material programmes will contain.

● Broadcasters will launch a campaign to 'educate' parents on what sort of programmes are banned before the 9pm watershed so they can protect children and complain when it is breached.

● Possibly most controversially, Mrs Bottomley will formally revive

the idea of installing a 'V-chip' in every new television set enabling parents to censor programmes.

She will insist that the EU funds research into the technology, as it already has for wide-screen high-definition broadcasting.

A source close to Mrs Bottomley stressed her determination to make the measures stick. 'Any broadcaster who fails to live up to these promises will be dealt with very firmly,' the source warned.

The breakthrough will be announced this afternoon at the end of a summit with BBC chairman Sir Christopher Bland, the Independent Television Commission, which regulates ITV, Channel 4 and the Sky satellite network,

Turn to Page 2, Col. 1

MASTERY of the zig-zag parting will become a must for hairdressers — thanks to Princess Diana.

Long a trendsetter in matters of coiffure, she has gone, well, short. Her new style, remarkably similar to that worn by Prince Edward's girlfriend, Sophie Rhys-Jones, (inset) relies on a zig-zag parting to give just the right amount of lift.

Diana showed off her new image as she addressed the 30th anniversary convention of the International Federation of Anti-Leprosy Associations in London.

High at the back and softly layered at the front, the cut is also faintly reminiscent of the 'Rachel' cut worn by Friends actress Jennifer Aniston.

— Splitting images: Pages 30 and 31 —

Figure 13.3 'Curb the Dark and Brutal Side of TV'
Source: *Daily Mail*, 10 December 1996 © *The Daily Mail*, 1996, used with permission

colonized' communities did not enjoy in the political and social spheres (even where they did enjoy individual freedoms). Cultural citizenship allowed such communities among the 'masses' both to participate freely as audience along with all the other people in the mediasphere, and to observe an official culture that was not comfortable with their presence.

Figure 13.4 'Man who Died of TV'
Source: *Express on Saturday*, 19 April 1997

Television promoted identity politics by modulating between 'we' and 'they' identities for such groups – addressing them as 'we' in entertainment (citizens of media), and as 'they' in the reporting of formal politics and official discourses. Television did not *represent* all the different demographic groups in a given polity, and has often been criticized for not pursuing a policy of 'proportional representation' of gender, ethnicity, age, body-shape, sexual orientation, class and so on. But it was doing something much more profound than this; it was providing a general sense of intersubjectivity among such groups, and allowing cross-demographic communication despite such differences, and giving those activists who wanted to know evidence of how other identities were forming and faring. Television, the medium that is often seen as most 'mass', least sensitive to 'identity', presided over the era of identity politics; taught *cultural citizenship* equally to those whose identity made them subject to assimilationist and liberationist rhetorics alike.

Television was, in short, the teacher of cultural *neighbourliness*. Just as neighbours may differ markedly even though they live next door, so the mediasphere juxtaposed difference. Just as 'good' neighbours learn to stand back from insisting on their own 'rights' and learn to tolerate the peculiarities of those around them, so television taught that families can get along internally (sitcom) and alongside one another (soap opera). Television avoided political partisanship, tried hard not to insult anyone, chatted up in ads and gameshows people who had no history of public esteem or even self-esteem. It was a truly caring neighbour.

Meanwhile, the people for whom television in its most commercial forms cared most – i.e. the so-called masses – were beginning to find their way into parts of the body politic and folds of the social fabric that had previously been thoroughly disinfected against them. The consequences of nineteenth-century political and twentieth-century social citizenship were being felt. Democratization was reaching into culture, education, lifestyle and intellectual life. Suddenly, the neighbourhood was changing.

CULTURAL CITIZENSHIP – SCHOOLING *VERSUS* TELEVISION

One particular manifestation of the fear of the masses took the form of a cultural and educational rhetoric that resisted or regretted the 'influx' of 'masses' into literate culture and higher education. That fear is historically the very tap-root of cultural studies, despite its leftist, libertarian line. How to cope with mass schooling, mass leisure, mass culture? What to teach the children of the poor? How to cater for a mass influx of working-class and female students into universities? These are the questions of the 1960s and 1970s, and they have never entirely subsided or ebbed. The founders of cultural studies were all in some way concerned with popular education, and all were interested in the question of what and how to teach the popular classes made free, affluent and choosy by civil, political and social citizenship. They all had an interest in how television fitted into this pattern.

The most magisterial of these founders were themselves drawn from the 'influx'; the provincial working class (Hoggart), Welsh border-country (Williams) or colonized populations (Hall). They came into a polity whose public conversations were traditionally about preserving purity and privilege. British popular politics and populist journalism routinely called for the preservation of territorial and racial purity against the threat of influx. This for instance:

> Every country is privately determined not to become the spiritual home of the Great Unwanted. . . . Money we will provide, if need be, but the law of self-preservation demands that the word 'Enter' be removed from the gate.
>
> (Cited in MacShane, 1979: 91)

That was the London *Evening News* of 13 July 1938, referring to Jewish refugees from Nazi Germany. Denis MacShane (who at the time of writing the article in which this is quoted was President of the National Union of Journalists) quotes other headlines of 1938: this from the *Daily Mail*: 'ALIENS POURING INTO BRITAIN'; this from the *Sunday Express*: 'Just now there is a big influx of Jews into Britain. They are over-running the country' (June 1938). Just to show that what he calls 'journalistic hand-me-downs' have a long shelf-life, certainly in the *Mail* and *Express*, MacShane cites a *Daily Express* headline of May 1976: 'ASIAN INFLUX WILL SWAMP US' (MacShane, 1979: 91). Such stories are recognizable as routine, low-grade, 'rivers-of-blood' fear of difference. The same fear, more respectable but the same all the same, prompted calls for the preservation of privilege — that is, scarcity, exclusivity and purity — in education. Here's a routine editorial from the politically liberal *Guardian* newspaper:

> A comprehensive system in higher education . . . seems to mean opening all forms of higher education to all comers, regardless of aptitude or attainment. As such, it must lead either to a tremendous dropout rate . . . or to a disastrous decline in standards.
>
> (*Guardian*, 18 September 1973)

Democratization of higher education cannot be allowed because such an influx would damage either the people allowed in (tremendous dropout rate) or the education (disastrous decline). As a contemporary newspaper put it: 'When everybody is an M.A., nobody is' (quoted from the *Yorkshire Post* in Rubinstein and Stoneman, 1972: 9). As Rubinstein and Stoneman comment: 'This comes close to claiming that knowledge and research, even education itself, are of value only in so far as they control entry to the elite.' The solution desired by those who oppose mass higher education is the same as that proposed by A.O. Neville for Aboriginal people: those who come from poor families and educationally disadvantaged backgrounds can only be allowed into higher education and thence intellectual culture if they *become the same* as those already there. It's an assimilationist policy, recognizing the difference between the influx and the elite only by seeking to erase it.

Until the late 1980s, formal higher education in Britain was based on keeping the 'influx' out by means of competitive entry and examinations, and on training the few successful immigrants from 'under-privileged backgrounds' (like Hoggart, Williams, Hall, and me too, come to that) in the values of formal education. These traditional school values had been spelled out as early as 1916 by the philosopher Bertrand Russell:

> Certain mental habits are commonly instilled by those who are engaged in educating: obedience and discipline, ruthlessness in the struggle for worldly success, contempt towards opposing groups, and an unques-tioning credulity, a passive acceptance of the teacher's wisdom. . . . [A fundamental cause of these evils is] the fact that education is treated as a means of acquiring power over the pupil, not as a means of encoura-ging his own growth.
>
> (Bertrand Russell, *Principles of Social Reconstruction*, 1916, cited in Rubinstein and Stoneman, 1972: 13)

Perhaps things have changed by now, but perhaps they have not changed as much as they should have. (This description of formal pedagogy is very familiar to me, from my own schooling in the 1950s and 1960s, from the educational ideologies of right-wing populist rhetoric of the 1970s and 1980s such as Thatcherism, now adopted by 'New Labour', and from some of the things that come back from my daughters' primary school in the late 1990s.) Be that as it may, in relation to the development of television, of TV studies, and of their respective attitudes to teaching, the point is that since *formal* education was not a very welcoming place for people from ordinary backgrounds, formal educationalists had an uphill task if they hoped to teach ordinary people. They were tainted by formal education itself; coming over not so much as the necessary democratic antidote to 'mass' culture, but more as a partisan power-elite in competition with media for the rights to dictate citizenship formation. Here, of course, they suffered from a double disadvantage: television, especially commercial television, was a form of comprehensive education, it *liked* its masses of ordinary viewers and tried its very best to accommodate 'all comers, regardless of aptitude or attainment'; while formal education tried to take power over them or exclude them. Small wonder that viewers preferred to take their lessons in cultural citizenship from entertain-ment rather than from education.

This is the context for the public writings that launched cultural studies and with it the study of television in Britain. Its founders – Hoggart, Williams, Hall – were simultaneously 'beneficiaries' of formal higher education with its fear of influx and part of the influx feared by educational traditionalists. Informed, tempered and made sympathetic though they may have been by their own origins, all of these figures were also *teachers*, and their intellectual concerns were about how to know the 'masses', and about what the popular classes were learning from the media environment, to what political and cultural effect. Here's Stuart Hall and his colleague Paddy Whannel, introducing their version of

174

cultural studies; an early but neglected book which shows how the later magisterial Hall grew directly out of the seedbed of schooling, nurtured by a
Hoggartian-Leavisite concern for aesthetic politics. The book was called *The Popular Arts*, and this is how Hall and Whannel explain their project:

> The origins of this book can be traced back to the period when we
> were both teaching in secondary modern schools. This is a sobering
> experience for any teacher. . . . During the succeeding years we have
> been lecturing on and arguing about the cinema and the mass media
> with a variety of audiences – film societies, teacher training colleges,
> youth clubs and youth leaders, adult education classes, students in
> further and higher education. The arguments in this book grew directly
> out of that experience.
>
> (Hall and Whannel, 1964: 13)

So, from the beginning, cultural studies was about teaching. Williams and
Hoggart too make frequent reference to the importance of their periods in
both universities and in adult education. The teachers who invented cultural
studies, and with it the formal study of television (in the English language),
were interested in what television taught. Given the weight and prestige of the
social theory that had made up its impersonal mind long since that what 'mass'
media taught was to be regretted and resisted, they were always going to find it
hard to be positive about television as a teacher.

What is the process by which cultural citizenship is formed? The early writers
on what I am identifying as 'cultural citizenship' believed that it comprised the
two components discussed in Chapter 10: *discursive* and *political*. In the discursive
field such writers belong to the Arnoldian (literary critical) tradition, and in the
political field I have in mind reformists from the Fabians (e.g. G.B. Shaw and H.G.
Wells) to the New Left. Theorists of both the discursive and the political aspects of
cultural citizenship believed that it could not be formed unconsciously by a
process of simple maturation within a culture; they saw 'culture' as something
that had to be taught. Looking around the modern landscape, they saw three great
institutions with a stake in such an enterprise: government, education and the
media. They sought to yoke government and education together; to bring about
an alliance whose explicit purpose was to counter the perceived influence of
commercial, industrial, urban life – a context within which the media were
firmly located. The alliance of education (including a vocal and militant intelligentsia, not just those involved in formal education) with government (in the
form of 'public' institutions), in opposition to commercial media, is now so
familiar a part of our cultural and institutional citizenship that we find it hard,
perhaps, to remember that it was an invention, created in the pursuit of governmental control over the formation of cultural citizenship. The emblem of the
success of this policy is the BBC, an agent for educating cultural citizenship so
influential in Britain that its ethos of 'public service broadcasting' has been

imposed by successive governments on its commercial rivals, producing an entire media sector that for several generations was dedicated to teaching cultural citizenship to the entire population, no matter what they were hearing or watching, or on which channel.

Cultural citizenship, then, was taught by television; the only dispute was about whether the teaching was done by public or commercial interests, and whether it was done well or ill.

14

CLUELESS? NOT!

DIY citizenship

Adults need kids, they just don't realize it. . . .
So . . . we are going to create a country in cyberspace, not defined by geography or
race, but by technology and age: Nation.1 — a country populated and run by kids.
(Junior Summit II, MIT: http: //www.jrsummit.net)

Umberto Eco organizes his thoughts on television and teaching around the figure of the audience, his young daughter:

> When my daughter was beginning to watch the world through the window of a television screen . . . I once saw her religiously following a television commercial, which, as far as I remember, was assuming that a certain product was the best in the world, and was able to satisfy all your needs. Educationally alerted, I tried to teach her that television commercials usually lie. She understood that she shouldn't trust television (since for oedipal reasons she was yearning to trust me). Two days later she was watching television news, informing her that it would be imprudent to travel on the northern [Italian] highways because it was snowing (information that met my profound wishes, since I was desperately trying to stay at home that weekend). She glared suspiciously at me, asking why I was trusting television as I had suggested, two days before, that television does not tell the truth. I was obliged to begin a very complicated dissertation in existential logic, pragmatics of natural languages and genre theory in order to convince her that *sometimes* television lies and *sometimes* it tells the truth.
> . . . Only the psychiatrist that my daughter will probably summon on arriving at the age of wisdom will, I suppose, be able to say to what extent my pedagogical intervention has damaged significantly her mind or her Id. But this is another story.

(Eco, 1979: 15)

Characteristically, Eco locates television teaching around the context and discourse through which it is received, rather than assuming that it's merely a matter of one-way influence of child by TV set. He allows the idea of a critical, interrogative and alert audience to emerge out of a conversation with his young daughter; this is no image of an ignorant, passive or child-*ish* consumer, but rather a conceptualization of an audience that knows how to 'use' television for their own purposes, and moreover an audience that can deal appropriately with a 'dissertation in existential logic, pragmatics of natural languages and genre theory' from the Professor of Semiotics at Bologna University without confusion, despite her tender years. And even though Eco has nothing but positive feelings for his audience, and a truly Hoggartian desire to be her teacher 'in the best sense', he wryly concedes that his 'pedagogical intervention' is more likely to do this audience harm in the long run than the television news . . . .

Well, I hope she's forgiven him for introducing her to the vicissitudes of semiosis; meanwhile, this astute young girl can still serve as the model of the television audience. She is the 'D-I-Y' or Do-It-Yourself citizen. In Britain, 'DIY' is familiar as the amateur end of home-improvement − installing the material basis for the ideology of domesticity in the form of particle-board, paint and a patio. I borrow the term to describe the Do-It-Yourself citizen; the practice of putting together an identity from the available choices, patterns and opportunities on offer in the semiosphere and the mediasphere. Whether it's a full 'fitted' identity, expensive, integrated and in a recognizable off-the-shelf style, or an identity more creatively put together from bits and pieces bought, found or purloined separately, is a matter of individual difference. The point is, 'citizenship' is no longer simply a matter of a social contract between state and subject, no longer even a matter of acculturation to the heritage of a given community; DIY citizenship is a choice people can make for themselves. Further, they can change a given identity, or move into or out of a repertoire of identities. And although no one is 'sovereign' in the sense that they can command others, there's an increasing emphasis on *self*-determination as the foundation of citizenship. How do you learn this difficult trick of 'suiting yourself', as it were, while remaining locked in to various actual and virtual, social and semiotic communities? Television audienceship provides the training ground. And the focus for this new direction in self-determined citizenship is that previously unenfranchized, silenced subject, the teenage girl.

DIY CITIZENSHIP

Television teaches cultural citizenship, and this builds on and extends the civic citizenship of the Enlightenment, the political citizenship of the French Revolution and the social citizenship of industrialization into new rights, namely rights of identity. Paradoxically, then, the era of 'mass' communication and 'commodity' culture is the time when *difference* is established as a human right. Here we have a vast and unknowable audience, 'bombarded', as the usual phrase has it, with commercial messages of childlike simplicity, and instead of turning into an undifferentiated mass of infantilized consumers, we find they produce an endless succession of ever more weird and wonderful, actual and virtual cultural identities, each one carefully differentiated from the one next door. While cultural identity has classically been conceived as proceeding from natural or territorial authenticity, being determined in other words by heritage and territorial location, more recent identities arise from the private, domestic world of individual life-style, choice and preference; identity based on sexual orientation and preference, for instance, and subcultural identities based on youth, taste or fanship of various kinds. Now we are moving rapidly past 'identity' politics towards something new; citizenship based not on an authenticist notion of cultural identity, but on a radically decontextualized network of meanings which locate identity in the mediasphere, not the public sphere; we're moving to the fifth form of citizenship:

1 **Civic citizenship**;
2 **Political citizenship**;
3 **Social citizenship**;
4 **Cultural citizenship**;
5 DIY – *'Do-It-Yourself'* – *citizenship*.

The places where you find DIY citizens exercising their semiotic self-determination are on television and among its audience. But the relationships of the mediasphere are not like those of territorial polities. For a start, the intentions of the addresser and the 'use' of semiosis by the addressee are not causally related; as Umberto Eco said a long time ago, all mass communication is 'aberrantly' decoded, not in line with the intentions of the producer. Indeed, this insight has been a constant theme of cultural and television studies:

> We have a situation in some ways more similar to that of television, where the use intended by the provider and the use actually made by the audience of the particular style never wholly coincide, and frequently conflict. This conflict is particularly marked in the field of teenage entertainments, though it is to some extent common to the whole area of mass entertainment in a commercial setting.
>
> (Hall and Whannel, 1964: 269–70)

In this context, television may be used by its audiences in unintended, even aberrant, but profoundly *public* ways. Here's Richard Hoggart again, with some observations discussed previously:

> In any society a medium so intimate and pervasive will do this [be an 'educator in manners']; it is bound constantly to be putting before people other ways of shaking hands, of sitting down, of wearing clothes, of reacting to strangers, of eating, of carrying on conversations; it is bound constantly to be setting in motion numerous slight but widespread reactions. . . . And all the time, consciously or unconsciously, it is trying to ameliorate manners. . . . No doubt the effect of such half-art is slow, but it may eventually (in combination with the

179

other forces of which it is both a part and a reflection) be considerable.

(Hoggart, 1960: 41–3)

I think Hoggart is on to something really important here, although there's no chance at all of being able to 'prove' this particular thesis by other than bread-making methods (waiting for it to rise) – it cannot be 'proven' scientifically (by statistical means). But as Hoggart himself remarked in the same article, the sway held by scientific methods is itself an effect of the need to address vast, undifferentiated audiences: 'It may be, too, that there is a more general tendency among individuals – perhaps more widespread to-day than it used to be – to hold to the semi-scientifically demonstrable in preference to that which is called "mere impressionism" or even "mere interpretation"' (1960: 39–40). It can only ever be an impression gained from watching television over several decades, and an interpretation based on my own desire to 'describe popular culture in different terms, which neither claim to speak on its behalf, nor to reform it, nor to discredit it' (Lucy, 1993: 288–9), and so to find terms that are not 'objective', but nevertheless it is in fact my settled impression that television has been influential in just the way Hoggart describes in the period since he wrote this appraisal more than a generation since.

Its rather simple and therefore frequently overlooked 'power' to bring social, geographical, environmental and demographic variety into the home makes television the greatest 'variety show' in history. Coming out of the 1950s, and, as Hoggart says, in combination with forces of which it is both a part and a reflection, television showed the domestic audience something of 'nature', as it was innocently called in those far-off days of Hans and Lotte Hass, Armand and Michaela Denis, long before Jacques Cousteau. Now we have environmentalism, eco-warriors and the million-member RSPB (Royal Society for the Protection of Birds) – 'nature' with political teeth, backed up by quite unusual public tolerance for activism, by such groups as Greenpeace, 'Swampy' and others, and unprecedented dialogue between governments, corporations and activists in the formulation of public policy, for instance around the fate of the Shell vessel Brent Spar, and roadbuilding policy in the wake of the by-pass era (see McKay, ed., 1998: chapters 4–7). Of course David Attenborough didn't 'cause' all this, but it is my belief that year after year of Anglia's *Survival*, Oxford Scientific Films, the Nature Unit productions of BBC Bristol, not to mention the strange 'nature-logues' imported from all the continents of the earth to the hearths of East Finchley, have done just what Hoggart said they would; they've 'ameliorated our manners', in this case persuading millions of the need to tread more lightly on the natural environment, and to temper production with conservation. Television showed, still shows, without becoming 'political' about it, what is there to conserve. And in a semiotic full circle, staid, conservative characters in soap operas – the tweedy, mature women of Radio 4-land – can be shown both sympathetically and reinvigoratingly as eco-activists, standing firm in green wellies on muddy fields defending trees against developers – semiotically appropriating the political iconography of 1960s and 1970s radicalism in the cause of conservative con-servation. Meanwhile, the wheel turns again, and law-defying Swampy becomes the not-so-secret pin-up of Home Counties ladies, appears as a guest on the comedy TV quiz *Have I Got News For You*, and eventually announces his retirement from eco-activism because his recognition value as a celebrity is now so high he is always the first to be arrested whenever he appears at a protest site.

I believe similar arguments can be made about the visions of cultural identity we've taken from decades of television – women's issues in particular are now literally more visible than they were in the official cultures of the 1950s; television has always been slightly ahead of public acceptance in its 'manners' in this respect. It is not that the representation of women on TV *satisfies* women, much less that what's on TV featuring women's issues 'represents' activist and feminist groups; what I'm suggesting is that TV made visible the 'culture' and condition of women to *others*, including those who didn't want to know, and has made certain kinds of assertion, assumption and abjection simply unspeakable. Television (among other 'mass' media) made women visible, their issues and 'culture' normal; brought them into the everyday conversations of the whole nation-audience-public.

Without wishing to push the point beyond your willingness to consider it, I'd say that television's approach to teaching is to use the scatter-technique of broad-casting (a metaphor derived not from breadmaking but from the causally prior activity of wheat-sowing) to knead 'cultural citizenship' – preparing populations for difference, mobility and change; easing the way for communities based on ethnic and sexual difference to be treated with respect; creating the first levels of demand (i.e. awareness) for travel (outward), migration (inward) and tolerance. A chequered history, all this, of course; but we're not where we were in 1960, and we didn't experience the 'rivers of blood' confidently expected by those for whom the politics of ameliorated manners was too tough to trust.

If he is right, then, Hoggart's point about 'secular parables' (i.e. 'transmodern teaching' in my terminology) working 'consciously or unconsciously' to 'ame-liorate manners' to 'considerable effect' describes the process of 'kneading' out of which has arisen cultural citizenship; social cohesion based not on sameness but on difference, identity not shared with the whole population but nevertheless shown to them; television teaching populations who their 'others' are and how usefully to *de*-politicize that knowledge.

A TRUE PAEDOCRAT

Now is the era of what I call DIY citizenship. In a period of consumer choice, computer-aided interactivity and post-identity politics, semiotic self-determina-tion is emerging as a right, not just a market segment over-populated with early adopters, nerds and geeks, and other denizens of Californicated computer culture. What does semiotic self-determination look like? Let Clarissa explain it all.

Clarissa Explains It All (Nickelodeon/Viacom) – Clarissa Darling is smart, garru-

Figure 14.1 Clarissa Explains It All: Melissa Joan Hart as Clarissa Darling
Source: Courtesy of Tom Hurst/Nickelodeon

lous, talks directly to camera and is at the centre of her show's semiosphere. It's not that this is a unique or especially brilliant show, though Melissa Joan Hart is very good as the feisty teenager; what's unusual about it is the control her character exercises over the space, pace, mood, gags and wisdom of the show. She's unusually young and, of course, she's a she. So *Clarissa Explains It All* is emblematic of feminization and juvenation (Hartley, 1998) and is a teacher. The show teaches family comportment and self-realization through knowing how things work. Clarissa learns in each episode the limits to her control of the situation and finds ways of exercising what control she does have imaginatively and amusingly. For the rest, she can loll on her bed, accommodating to the realities where her control does not extend (to her brother Fergus, for instance).

I watch *Clarissa Explains It All* with my own daughters, and we look, laugh and learn together. I think Clarissa/Melissa is cute; they think she's funny. I think the show teaches self-esteem for girls, the girls think it's cool TV with good characters, dialogue, stories. They like her to talk to us, sharing confidences, dilemmas and quips; I wonder whether this mode of address is a postmodernization of a very much earlier *Clarissa* - the epistolary novel by Samuel Richardson (1747–8) which some count as among the founding texts of the modern novel, of modernity itself in writing. We all like the way her best friend (a boy) always arrives by climbing up a ladder into the ever-open window of her room, and that everyone is nonchalant about this. We all hate her clothes sense. We relish her schemes to best her brother. We learn how to get through a half-hour plot by attending to Clarissa/Melissa's frank, open face, constantly upraised optimistic-encouraging eyebrows, and to the wisecracking quickfire soliloquies she delivers direct to camera. She's a smart teenager teaching by example how to survive family life, which is no easy matter. We're her diary.

Clarissa Explains It All sums up so much of what television does as a transmodern teacher that I take it to be an emblem of the 'uses of television' in which I have most intellectual investment: it really does 'explain it all'. Like so much in popular culture, if you take a single episode or even the whole show by itself without thinking about what it does, where it fits and who it is for, it may seem an unworthy object. It is not serious, deep or 'critical' television, and may present to the new viewer as banal and ordinary, but of course that's the point. It is doubtless not reckoned to be more than a repetition of a familiar genre even to its own creators – it is not formally, aesthetically or ideologically innovative, not narratively adventurous, not avant-garde television at all. It's right there at the centre of cultural 'law formation' (Lotman, 1990); an absolutely rock solid family sitcom.

So *Clarissa Explains It All*'s uniqueness lies within this field of sameness. It is TV that is not trying to play any clever tricks on the viewer – not presenting them with the opportunity to be stretched, tutored, discomfited or embarrassed by its formal apparatus; viewers can trust it and therefore ignore it and, of course, by that very fact, can enjoy the repetition of its familiar semiotic and narrative rhythms in a way that assists with (teaches) the cultural transmission of story-telling structures, narrative and plot sequences and television semiosis. The show quietly teaches its viewers cultural-linguistic form, genre, character and action by being *reliable* in these matters, allowing the viewer to apprehend them while actually attending to the 'surface' structures of plot, scene and dialogue.

Just as researchers in the Netherlands have recently discovered that readers of Asterix comics are in fact better and more accurately informed about actual ancient history than those who learnt it at school, so *Clarissa Explains It All* teaches by entertainment and by drawing viewers to it by its charm and cheer, not by the more militant techniques of formal schooling. And just as some colleges have decided in the light of the Dutch research that if they can't beat popular entertainment they may as well learn from it, and have therefore adopted Asterix comics as course reading for ancient history programmes, so *Clarissa Explains It All* has something to offer beyond its own pleasures, which is why I have appropriated it for the more formal purposes of this book.

Clarissa/Melissa 'Explains It All' by focusing the familiar apparatus of the family sitcom on the figure of the teenage girl. Of course there have been teenage girls in sitcoms before, from two of the three sisters among the *Brady Bunch* and the *Cosby Show*'s cool but dutiful daughters to Julia Sawalha's naff but pivotal Saffy in *Absolutely Fabulous* and Christina Applegate's definitive dumb-but-sexy teenager in *Married . . . With Children*. Indeed, there was a spate of 'Generation X' teenage stars, from Winona Ryder (*Heathers*) on the darker side, to Alicia Silverstone in *Clueless* (also echoing the early-modern novel; this time Jane Austen's *Emma*). *Clarissa Explains It All* is more comparable with (the really excellent) *Press Gang*, a British drama series (as opposed to sitcom) that preceded *Absolutely Fabulous* in the early 1990s, co-starring Julia Sawalha as a student-newspaper editor and made for 'youth TV'. More recently there is *Moesha* (1996–8), a family sitcom with an all-black cast that is also based on the teenage girl of the house, starring the singer Brandy Norwood.

What makes *Clarissa Explains It All* unique, or at least trend-setting, is the *age* of its star, and the fact that she is the undisputed centre of her show, portrayed as a very young teenager, starring in a show that is certainly aimed at pre-teen children as well as adults. So she's an example of *juvenation* in contemporary semiosis, placing the young girl centre-stage of situations and ideas that are by no means 'childish'. She is presented here not as young girls tend to be in news or actuality in both print and electronic media, as attractive victim or unruly body in need of protection or correction, nor as they appear in drama shows made for the protected 'C' (children's) slots of public-service broadcasting, but on the contrary Clarissa appears as a mainstream, fully-formed, 'adult' character, articulate, interesting, full of initiative, clever and congenial.

She's clearly a *citizen*, a 'first citizen' among her probably much younger viewing peers, perhaps, someone to admire, but only for qualities which are understood to belong to the 'polity' she serves, namely children. Here it is worth pausing to remember how badly served children are in formal civics, both in theory, where they are excluded from almost all forms of citizenship, and in practice, where they are ignored or made subject to the will of others. Similarly, in *Moesha* the eponymous character is the centre of the Mitchells, her fictional family, keeping them together for better or worse. However, in addition to being child-led, *Moesha* takes on even more aspects of normally-neglected semiosis – it features an all-black cast, and for this risky innovation was hailed at the time of its premiere as 'a sitcom variation on the verdicts in the O.J. Simpson trial – it's a payback for all those times when talent of color couldn't even get second or third leads on shows already capped by white stars' (Michael McWilliams, *Detroit News*, 23 January 1996). What's more, *Moesha*'s sitcom 'situation' is that the Mitchells are a melded family, and Brandy/Moesha has to get used to a new step-mother in a household where she had been the female head. Luckily Moesha at 15 is older than Clarissa, but the point is the same – *Moesha* and *Clarissa Explains It All* (and their like) teach semiotic citizenship to their child-constituency. They are *paedocratic* shows in the strict sense that they portray a world governed by a child, and they present that world, that government, to young viewers not only for their entertainment but also – I contend – their edification.

Clarissa, Moesha and their semiotic sisters are personifications of the 'unknowable audience'; each is the 'per-sona' of the young girl who, having entered history in the news media as an attractive victim and/or unruly body, begins to speak for herself in the drama-fiction media as the figure of the DIY citizen. She takes what she needs from the identities and differences available in the mediasphere and claims her rights of semiotic self-determination. Unlike the classic bearer of individual rights (civic citizenship), voting rights (political citizenship), educational and welfare-to-work rights (social citizenship) or even identity rights (cultural citizenship – though these are often semiotically represented as feminized), the DIY citizen appears as under-age, female, 'powerless' in traditional terms of territory or force; her 'appeal' to her constituency is just that, her attractiveness as a 'per-sona'. Her value as a teacher – the one who 'Explains It All' – is that her teaching is 'useful' only if wanted by viewers, for whom she is paedocratic democratainment incarnate.

CONCLUSION? NOT!

> I have been an advocate for commerce, because I am a friend to its effects. It is a pacific system, operating to cordialize mankind, by rendering nations, as well as individuals, useful to each other. As to the mere theoretical reformation, I have never preached it up.
> (Thomas Paine, *Rights of Man*, 1792: 188–9)

If television can teach any lessons about the future, as we use it windscreen-wiperistically to peer into the unknown, what might those lessons be? Television's 'classic' phase is broadcasting. This period has by no means come to an end even though broadcasting has already been succeeded by cable, satellite, digital and video-cassette forms of non-broadcast television. But during the fifty to sixty years of broadcasting, television has become an 'old' medium – not supplanted but joined by new technologies – and it has lost some of the attention it attracted during its youthful period. Whether it is growing old gracefully or disgracefully, it is not quite so hemmed in by moral entrepreneurs, regulators, pundits, promoters and techno-prophets as it used to be, largely because these characters have moved on to worry about computers and computer games, the Internet, and the dawn of the age of inter-activity, connectivity, cyber-democracy and the 'ünternet' (all those not www-wired).

Does television have anything to teach this new phase in the expansion of difference, capitalization of language, politics of information? As telephony, television and computers integrate, it seems likely that the 'fear' and 'desire' schools of thought, and the 'discursive' and 'political' schools of thought, will still have plenty to occupy them. The 'fear' and 'desire' schools of thought have

185

turned their attention from 'massness' to 'globalization', either fearing it (loss of identity; invasion of alien content; domination by 'bad' corporations; difficulty of controlling access) or welcoming it (usually for commercial reasons, but also to welcome the chance to extend the 'republic of letters' into cyber-space, and to integrate the species at the level of individual choice if not of government policy). This is certainly a case of 'Play it Again, Sam', as all these issues were thoroughly rehearsed in relation to television.

Similarly, the 'discursive' and 'political' schools of thought have turned from concerns about the content (discursive) and ownership (political) of television to the same concerns in relation to new information media. The moral entrepreneurs have gathered once more around the figure of the innocent child, just as they did when television was young, to worry about 'pornography on the net' or worse still 'paedophile rings' – bad cyber-citizens who lurk in dark websites waiting to pounce on the unsuspecting paedocratized user. Meanwhile, the 'political' school of thought has much to worry about as Microsoft gains ever-further control of the global market, and back-room boffins make progress towards the solution of the problem of financial security online, after which scarcity and thus profit can be introduced more comprehensively into the currently rather libertarian World Wide Web, by charging for access – just the situation that television went through, as it moved from being treated by its users as public utility, to being stratified into free-to-air broadcasting and user-pays narrowcasting.

Beyond these institutional and industrial issues, there are also lessons to be learnt from television's cultural form, and from the relations it has established over decades with its audiences, and they with it. Such issues include a vast increase in visual literacy associated with television – a literacy that the currently rather wordy and stills-based computer-media cannot match. Similarly, television has extended the range of 'common knowledge' by its internal allusiveness as a textual system, and by the success it has achieved in bringing to people's attention things they would not otherwise have chosen to attend to – from the daily news and factual programming to the 'Hoggartian' encouragement of 'virtual' neighbourliness and fellow-feeling by showing other people from their own point of view. The new information technologies are based much more on targetted and ideally individual choice, so one of the things television can teach them is the need for sociality, porousness, what Hoggart calls 'air-holes' (Hoggart, 1998) for ideas to breathe.

Indeed, if there is a 'lesson' to be learnt from television, it is that the commercial, technological and industrial aspects of a new medium are nothing like as important as its cultural and political 'use' for its users. Just as television has had a hard time establishing itself *as* culture and *as* politics, so new modes of communication will meet resistance to their emancipation as independent, autonomous modes of human interaction unbrokered by control agencies, even if this is the very 'culture', the very 'politics' they offer. I have argued that television, presiding over the move from 'mass society' to 'cultural citizenship', and from 'identity politics' to 'DIY citizenship', is the place where people have learnt to 'do it themselves', making centralized, propagandistic, ideological, populist and persuasive modes of communication bend to other, more demotic purposes, allowing individual packaging of identity and the right of what I've called semiotic self-determination to vastly more citizens than have hitherto been able to exercise such choices. The new media technologies make 'DIY citizenship' not only easier because of extended choice (they're like publishing in this; a move non-broadcast television has also made), but also mutual, because of enhanced interactivity and connectivity.

The 'interactive' technology can also be a video (television) camera; and it too can be used to develop semiotic self-determination. Gerry Bloustien, for instance, explores the 'use of the camera by the teenage girls [members of an Aboriginal all-female rock band] as a means to "play with" and "explore" possible identities through particular generic styles and televisual forms': she is interested in analyzing the 'effect of self-recognition and self-creation through the mechanism and the power of the camera lens' (Bloustien, 1998: 129, 116–17). She comments:

> The girls could see the possibilities of alternative gendered identities in their world. Their language was replete with references to images from advertising, film, television, magazines and music videos suggesting the opportunities and possibilities for change, transformation and control.
>
> (Bloustien, 1998: 130)

However, in more cautionary mode, she notes that 'the girls also knew simultaneously that such "freedom" was romantic and fantastic. In spite of the media hype, self-making is hard work. Identity is not like a fashion item that can consciously be put on or off at will' (1998: 130). It might be said that fashion is not so easy either, nor is it voluntary in any individual sense, but what's interesting here is both the desire among the teenage girls to explore identity through televisual codes and technologies and the analyst's desire to have 'media' as hype, romanticism and fantasy. If it is the case that television and popular media proffer dreams of possible identities, and if it is inevitable that such 'freedom' collides with other, 'grown-up' realities, it still ought to be remembered that dreams of freedom have had a historic hand in creating the very 'possibilities for change, transformation and control' desired by the Aboriginal teenage girls – who as a community are among the twentieth century's least 'free' citizens. Their desire for semiotic self-determination based on dreams is nonetheless real for that, and it has long and honourable political credentials too: here, for instance, is the song of a Chartist from the mid-nineteenth century on the same theme:

> A boy I *dreamt* of liberty;
> A youth – I said, but I am free;
> A man – I felt that slavery

Had bound me to her chain.
But yet the *dream*, which, when a boy,
Was wont my musings to employ,
Fast rolling years *shall not* destroy,
With all their grief and pain.

(Cited in Gwyn Alf Williams, 1975: 81)

And so, as Kurt Vonnegut might have said, it goes.

Meanwhile, an activist version of DIY citizenship has emerged in the counter-cultural form of 'DiY Culture', described by George McKay as:

> a youth-centred and -directed cluster of interests and practices around green radicalism, direct action politics, new musical sounds and experiences. . . . DiY Culture is a combination of inspiring action, narcissism, youthful arrogance, principle, ahistoricism, idealism, indulgence, creativity, plagiarism, as well as the rejection and embracing alike of technical innovation.

(McKay, ed., 1998: 2)

Not unlike TV itself, then, 'DiY Culture' is a contradictory, limited but also empowering version of what the 'selves' of do-it-yourself might actually *do* with their citizenship.

What sorts of communities, what kind of neighbourliness, what variety of citizens, might arise from the extension of DIY citizenship? Television has provided some hints. As government, education and media integrate, the cultural forms and political outcomes of media citizenship will continue to proliferate. Feminization, juvenation, population-gathering, cross-demographic communication, transmodern teaching, cultural and DIY citizenship, democratainment – these are some of the legacies that television can bequeath (not that it's near its demise yet) to the next phase of development. It can stimulate the desire for freedom, comfort, politics, culture. That's what it has been 'for'. Those are the 'uses of television'.

15 (POST-SCRIPT)

SUBURBANALITY
(IN CULTURAL STUDIES)

Again, it is difficult — far more difficult than most of us want to recognize — to describe a poor childhood, to avoid dropping into either harshness or sentimentality.

(Richard Hoggart, 1970: 170)

ON SEA

In 1956, aged 34, Richard Hamilton popularized British Pop Art with a poster for an exhibition called *This is Tomorrow*, by the Independent Group at the Institute for Contemporary Art in London. Appropriately, this is not only art, it is also an ad; and it is not a painting, it is a collage. It is called *Just What Is It That Makes Today's Homes So Different, So Appealing?*

In 1956, aged 7 or 8, two years after my father died, I was wondering much the same thing.

I lived over the top of a Catholic church, which was itself located in a large, nineteenth-century house in the seaside resort of Westgate-on-Sea in south-east England. I thought it was beautiful, this bulbous house (long since demolished to make room for link-housing) with floral patterns etched into its stucco walls. It had lots of gables with lots of different slate roofs, the slates laid in patterns of blue and green. It had a short drive, at the gate of which was a lodge in the same style, in which lived the parish priest, Father Dunstan, a Benedictine from St Augustine's Abbey in distant Ramsgate.

Ramsgate Abbey suited the Benedictines to their hearts, being built of black flint. It was Victorian-medieval, large, dark, authoritarian and rich, built during 1845–50 by Augustus Pugin, who is buried in a splendid, isolated, glowering side-chapel, and who also co-designed the Houses of Parliament (1840–70). Its exotic black bulk squatted on the chalk cliff-top of a respectable little English seaside resort, right next to one of the town's best-known tourist attractions, the Model Village. But the main attraction for me was all inside that low anonymous doorway; a most un-English glimpse of ancient rites and fabulous Roman ecclesiastical wealth, of costume, incense, ritual, song, terror, guilt, glory and eternity, all in Latin. The Benedictines like to lay such things on with a trowel, especially when the Abbot processes in state for Pontifical High Mass.

The house where we lived was in the English William Morris rustic style, and

189

had presumably once been a Residence for a Gentleman or better, for it was imposing, and called Westgate House, suggesting the town was named after it, rather than vice versa. It was of an age that made it a relic of the Victorian fashion for sea air; opulence in illness, tubercular grandeur, empire and enervation, with rich, tiny, English detail, medieval in conception but concrete in execution, perfection of drawing with resplendence of colour, as John Ruskin says (Ruskin, 1907: 1), dedicated to the eternity of art and certainty of death. Soon after I was born, it seems, my family moved from London to Westgate-on-Sea for my father's health, although he continued to commute by train to London (72 miles each way) to work as a clerk in the civil service. It didn't do much for him; we'd hardly settled in before he dropped dead on the stairs; in the middle of a parental row, goes our family mythology. After that, for mysterious, adult reasons, we couldn't stay in our terraced house called Summerdene, and we moved into a flat over the church. He was not a Catholic.

Westgate-on-Sea is just down the road from a town called Birchington-on-Sea, famed for its bracing sea air, packed full of consumptives, where the Pre-Raphaelites had gathered, and where both Dante Gabriel Rossetti and Christina Rossetti are buried; that is, where English opulence and death are coterminous, or at least siblings. Margate, on the other side of Westgate, had, besides my father's grave, its curative Royal Sea Bathing Hospital, on the beach, opposite Dreamland pleasure park. Westgate, while I was there, claimed its share of the health trade too; it boasted more bath-chairs than motor cars. Next door to Westgate House was a convent called Les Oiseaux, which, like the Abbey in Ramsgate, was a colony of French Benedictines (not the more usual Irish missionaries to Protestant England); our continental catholicism felt closer to Cluny than Canterbury. My sisters were sent to school at Les Oiseaux; I was sent to school at St Augustine's Abbey Day School.

AT HOME

In the midst of all this, it's no wonder that I'm familiar with opulence in poverty, the hovel in the mansion, and with the ambiguity of death – death in a health town, death in religious rituals of eternity, death in art, death in youth. And so I'm familiar with ludicrousness, the drollery of tragedy, the not-quiteness of subjectivity. In fact, it is *Just This That Makes Today's Homes So Different, So Appealing.*

Ludicrously, in a kind of performance – or at least a rehearsal – of these dances with death, I used to have little fits (opulently called 'petit mal' by those who wanted to honour them, otherwise dismissed as fainting), and I mostly had them when I knocked my funny bone or my knee, droll jerkings which merely frightened the onlookers while I had blissful, golden, Klimtian dreams. In 1956 I went to school on a steam train from Westgate station, through Margate, Broadstairs, Dumpton Park (a greyhound racing track) to the Abbey at Ramsgate. I returned the same way. Up the drive past the lodge, I piddled into a puddle, exulting in my puerile parabola, without noticing until too late that Fr Dunstan was looking, aghast and threatening, out of the window. Is pissing at the priesthood a mortal or merely a venial sin? Never mind, run for it; up the drive past the circular flower bed, which my mother weeded, and on which grew irises which Fr Dunstan painted (and Van Gogh had lived in Ramsgate too, alleges a blue plaque in Spencer Square). Here I fell, had a fit.

And so into the house. I went in the big front door and up a big, wide, staircase that turned around the part of the house that had been converted into a church, and on the first floor there were three doors. The first one, on the left, was sealed shut, as it gave on to thin air, where a floor had been removed over the altar area of the church below. The second door, also on the left, gave on to a gallery looking down into the church; this was used by worshippers, including us (worship required for my sisters, though not for me, wearing a hat). The third door was on the right, and it gave on to three flats. First was old, kind Mrs Moore (who cooked potato chips on her stove, and gave me – or was it my sister? – a treasured sandalwood box, which I still have). Then through a door beyond her rooms were the family whose eldest son had died as a baby, but before you got there, there were some steep stairs, running counter to Mrs M's hall, up to the attic area, and that's were we lived.

Our flat was called The Eyrie, St Peter's Church, Westgate House, Canterbury Road, Westgate-on-Sea, Kent, and so on up to The Universe. The name Eyrie referred not only to its height and inaccessibility, but also to a brass door-knocker in the shape of a spread-eagle that was a prized signifier of 'our place' long before we had a front door to place it on. The flat had no ceilings, no electricity. It had very large, gurgly water tanks, built to serve the whole house, and it had big beams traversing the middle of the main rooms, sticking up about a foot, presumably holding the rest of the building rigid, but just the right height to crack even habituated shins on a regular basis. Our mother's bedroom was up still more stairs, to what must once have been either an observatory or a smoking room; a single square room atop the whole pile of the house, with its own pyramidal slate roof. I'm not sure about our rooms (there were three children); I remember only those tanks, and a little dais or stage by the window, and a lack of plaster but not of laths on the walls. Cooking was done on a primus and on an oil heater called an Aladdin, upon which a kettle always simmered.

Improvements were made while we lived there, a peculiar little Catholic-charity family, which happened to include my mother's live-in lover (who was not Catholic and not a man) and, for a while, a kitten called Marmalade, who escaped into the church and sat under the altar-boys' seats during mass. We eventually got our own front door, at the top of the steep stairs, and proudly fixed the eagle. We had partitions put up between the tanks and our beds, between the two girls and me. A painted garden trellis went up over the beam that divided the kitchen from the sitting room; we children took our meals at the table on the kitchen side; the grown-ups on little individual nest-tables in the two armchairs in the sitting area. Cross-trellis communication was not encouraged.

The proud shiny brass eagle did not repel boarders; we had an egg-stain as a semi-permanent fixture on the kitchen wall after another lesbian couple came round for a row with our lesbian couple. Other alien innovations included getting inexplicable presents like a hard-leather cigarette case inscribed with the words 'Smoke Like Helen B. Merry', and a pen with a woman on it whose dress drained off when you up-ended it. Mother's lover wore trousers with turn-ups, had a name that sounded like a man's, had been an NCO in the army, came from Broadstairs and sustained some running jokes with me, like being able to click her nose and make her false tooth come out, and teasing me with scissor-hands if anything poked through the customary gap in my pyjamas. She smoked Kensitas (like hell, but not all that merrily).

ON TV

We had light from gas in the wall; also from paraffin lamps which were portable, hot, dangerous and seriously attractive with their glass flues of heavenly length and their magical incandescent mantles. But then a real improvement came: the introduction of an electric cable, swung up from the nether regions of the house and into the flat by a kindly bus driver. He was there because his bus had knocked me down while I was hurrying home from a corner shop with a bag of sugar. Terrified of getting into trouble, apparently, I had scarpered at top speed after feeling the bus hit me, falling under it, having my shoe and sock blown off somehow and slithering out from the side, between the front and back wheels, neither set of which ran me over (this seemed to diminish its status as a pratable accident). I was caught, hospitalized, released, taken home, then visited by this kindly bus driver. Later, electric light appeared.

Later still, swung through that cable, came the power that lit another light in our Eyrie: television. Mind you, I wasn't at home when it arrived, having been sent to an orphanage in Wolverhampton (250 miles away) in the meantime, along with my sisters, returning to the church on holidays (as if from a boarding school of the posher English sort, or so it was, I think, supposed to seem). On one such return, as a surprise, there was the television. It was in the room with the egg, on the sitting side of the trellis, the room where I'd been caught calling one of my sisters 'sloppychops' (which sounded much more heinous to me than to anyone else), the room where I'd inhaled a spoonful of stolen cocoa powder with near-fatal consequences, where I'd knocked my knee on the sideboard door with predictable consequences. Here then; home and television.

IN QUOTATION

One of the mysteries of capitalism and pop art alike is the simultaneous presence of individuality (uniqueness) and interchangeability (sameness). It is the essence of what has come to be known as Fordism. My car (a Chevrolet, actually, not a Ford) is uniquely, individually mine (it's a '68 pillarless Impala), yet every part in it is interchangeable for another identical part (which is why it's still on the road thirty years later). Every capitalist commodity has, like Salvador Dali and Elvis Presley, a dead twin, an identical other that does but does not exist. So it is with pop art. Richard Hamilton's Pop Art collage *Just What Is It That Makes Today's Homes So Different, So Appealing?* is unique and therefore valuable, but all of it, and all of its parts, are interchangeable (by definition, since it's a collage), including a Ford logo stuck on a lampshade slap bang in the middle of the picture. And the skill required to exchange parts is that of the mechanic, not the artist (painter) or engineer, so Hamilton's collage has been quoted and plundered and remade, as it should be:

> I quote [Dick Hebdige] here not just because he is an 'authentic' spokesman for the popular arts, not just because like Lichtenstein, Barker, Bailey, Warhol, he refuses to comply with the perennial art or music critic's request to talk 'in depth', to explicate, to 'get to the heart of the matter'. I quote him because if pop art teaches us nothing else, it teaches us the art of facetious quotation, of quotation out of context. After all, pop art was initially provocative precisely because it quoted 'matter out of place'.
>
> (Hebdige, 1988: 136)

(The name in square brackets should be James Brown: I have taken liberties with Hebdige by making his quotation about quotation refer to himself; which in this instance he isn't doing. That comes later (p. 154).)

The Hamilton collage is quoted, for instance, by Dick Hebdige, in his book *Hiding in the Light* (Hebdige, 1988: 131). But the reproduction is not direct; it's a 'quote within a quote', showing the collage as used on the cover of an Open University textbook for their Popular Culture course.

Or Hamilton is recollaged, each item artfully replaced by a new generation's rereading, in a process that is itself neatly ironized by Tom Lubbock in a witty critique of Pop Art – done as Pop Art – which appeared in The Sunday Review section of the *Independent on Sunday* newspaper. The *Independent* was itself co-sponsor, with the phone company Mercury, of the Pop Art Show at the Royal Academy in London in 1991, and Lubbock's illustration accompanies one of the many reviews of that event. It is called *just what is it that makes yesterday's pop art so familiar, so appealing?* And the answer is also an alphabet:

anonymity
brand names
cartoons
design

Figure 15.1 *Just What Is It That Makes Today's Homes So Different, So Appealing?* Richard Hamilton, 1956
Source: Courtesy Alan Cristea Gallery and DACS

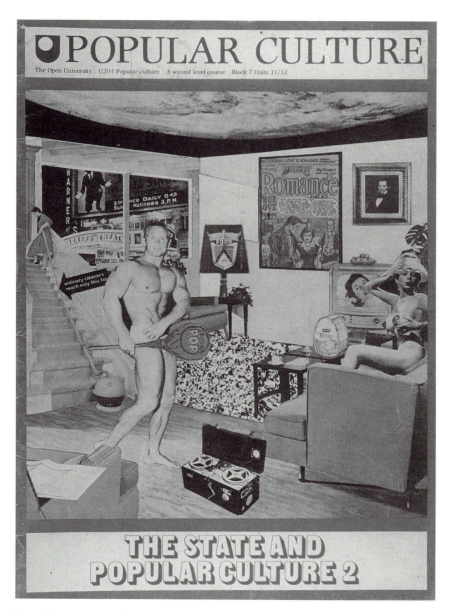

Figure 15.2 A quote within a quote: Hamilton in Hebdige in Hartley. Collaging popular culture, the state and university study, 1981
Source: Courtesy of the Open University and DACS

expressive brushstrokes
furniture
groceries
household appliances
icons
just what is it that makes yesterday's pop art so familiar, so appealing?
knowingness
lips
muscles (this one illustrated by a detail of the Hamilton)
numbers
old masters
pin-ups
questions
repetition
stars
& strips (comic)
typography
USA
violence
WHAAM!
XYZ (on an artwork)

(*Independent on Sunday*, 1 September 1991: 8–9)

Figure 15.3 just what is it that makes yesterday's pop art so familiar, so appealing?
Source: First published in *Independent on Sunday*, 1 October 1991. With permission of Tom Lubbock ©
Tom Lubbock.

The theme of unique reproducibility as icon is the sales gimmick of the first issue of *The Modern Review* (first series), a publishing venture launched in London by Julie Burchill under the slogan 'all academics are wankers' in 1991, and sporting on its cover a complete recollage of *Just What Is It That Makes Today's Homes So Different, So Appealing?* (*Modern Review*, 1.1, Autumn 1991: 1). It was edited by Toby Young, but it was Burchill who was chosen to infuriate the potential readership into fascination with an appearance on BBC Radio 4's *Start the Week* show. The artist who recollaged Hamilton is not credited, but it was Anthony Costin.

Hamilton transforms the traditional nude into a straightforward, Charles Atlas-type body-building guy and a complicated, maybe-girlie, body-baring woman, wearing something metallic on her nipples and something like a lampshade on her head, he standing, she sofa'd. In the *Modern Review* the suburban Adam and Eve become Schwarzenegger and Madonna. Of course there's a television in the Hamilton, but it has disappeared completely in the post-*Modern* version, to be replaced by the opened top of a laptop, almost elbowed aside by Madonna's lingerie and designer ice-cream. Hamilton's *Young Romance* comic-as-art (hung on the wall, that is) becomes a poster for *The Modern Review* itself (though the items mentioned are not quite as published in the magazine). Art or ad, self-reflexivity or self-regard, *Modern Review* or postmodern preview, critique or consumption, it doesn't matter, it's all interchangeable, just as so-called 'non-genuine' parts will fit a Ford even if Ford doesn't make them. It's what Hebdige calls the 'simultaneous articulation of the fact of *accessibility* and *reproducibility* (a million streamlined Chevrolets, a million streamlined radios)' (Hebdige, 1988: 72).

That's what modern art and modern cultural critique rely on and too often simultaneously despise. As Anthony Hanania argues in his review of the Pop Art Show in the same issue of the *Modern Review*, the 'moribund irony' of the pop artist was not interested in pop culture itself, but in High Culture. He writes:

> While trading off the iconic power of pop, Pop Art never *connected* with [it] on any level; it saved itself for High Art alone, rather like a prostitute who reserves her kisses for her beloved boyfriend. The artists themselves – colder, older, balder men, educated beyond all instinct and honesty . . . – were simply not Pop people; they could not comprehend that innocence could co-exist with a flip, hip sensibility, as it did in pop music. They couldn't understand that being dumb or being cynical are not the only choices.

Hanania exempts Hamilton himself from this critique, however, allowing him benefit of fanship: 'It is this strange and sleazy Martian sexiness of America which is celebrated in Hamilton's *Just What Is It* . . . .' ('The Parasites of Pop', *Modern Review*, 1.1, Autumn 1991: 23–4).

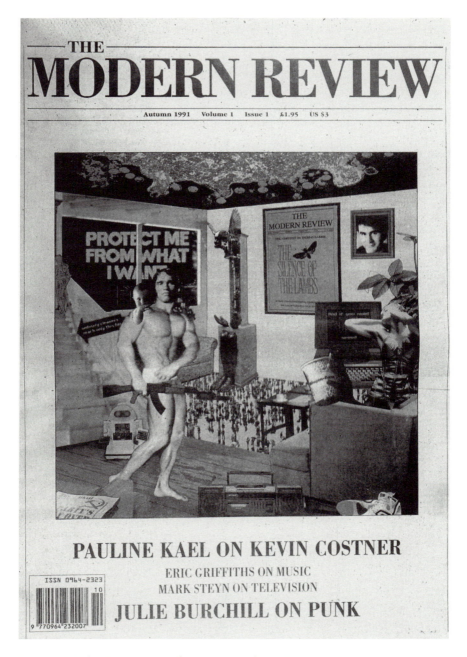

Figure 15.4 Modern Review inaugural cover art, Anthony Costin 1991
Source: The Modern Review, 1:1, Autumn 1991. Courtesy of Anthony Costin

SAME DIFFERENCE

But the question remains: *Just What Is It That Makes Today's Homes So Different, So Appealing?* The question remains, that is, for pop artists and their critical metafriends, for it is in these circles — art, criticism, modernism, postmodernism and the academy — that the question of the *Appeal* of the home is posed. Mostly, the answer given is this: The trouble with *Today's Homes*, the very thing that makes them *So Different, So Appealing*, is that they're interchangeable, individuated but indistinguishable, and they traverse the earth in an ecocidal sprawl, and the people who live in them suffer from a condition that can be summed up in one word, albeit a composite word of my own manufacture — *suburbanality*.

'Suburbanality' is of my manufacture, but only possible, like any manufacturing, thanks to some bought-in components. Dick Hebdige identifies where the parts come from: 'to find artful fragments from leading Left Bank theorists like . . . Meaghan Morris . . . is only to be expected' (Hebdige, 1988: 160–1). The components come from Morris's machine tool for critical engineering, itself made by H. Lefebvre & M. de Certeau Bros, Left Bank, Paris, France. With such machinery Morris is able to cut a precision swathe through 'Banality in cultural studies' (Morris, 1990), throwing up lots of swarf, which she called John Fiske, along the way. In fact, in that article, Morris perfected the art of swarf-throwing. After that, 'suburbanality' was easy.

And this is where I came in, for the peculiar household arrangements of my preliteracy were decidedly not those of Hamilton's *Today's Home*, even though he liked the ordinary; seeing consumer goods as sexy and everyday attitudes as 'epic' (Hebdige, 1988: 132). For my attenuated family, suburbanality was not a pretext for ironic homage, but a condition of stability, visibility and competence to which we *aspired*. Not for me at least the contempt of the artist, despair of the critic. In 1956 we were already living in an ambiguous virtual reality of postmodern not-quiteness (which we called 'being poor'), in which nothing was certain; not our faith, our sexuality, our housing, our history, our next season. Actually one thing was certain; we were 'matter out of place' (trying to forget that this is a well-known gloss of 'dirt'), interchangeable with others by mere deixis (we were the 'There' in their 'There But for the Grace of God Go I'), but uniquely we were our own peculiar selves too. In short, our uniqueness was experienced as tragedy, others' sameness as happiness; we were living clichéd quotations, since Tolstoy had sorted all this out eighty years earlier in *Anna Karenina*'s first sentence, which can be glossed (misquoted) as: 'Happy is the family that has no history (but there's no novel in it either).' With a home and family like ours, I couldn't look at contemporary popular culture with lofty metropolitan disdain or artful critical contempt. With my history, suburbanality is not to be sneezed at; not envied or scorned, not over- or under-valued, but not to be taken lightly either.

THE YOUNG ONES

Enter television: Is it a symptom of suburbanity, of banality, the suburbanality of the creme soap and the shower-caddy and the Italian tiles and the massage shower-head and the en-suite bathroom and the whole house itself, in the midst of which the postmodern nude stands, not naked but wet and soapily semioti-cized, amid the products and actions and hygiene and housing which surround the TV set which advertises them? Is it hell! Television doesn't belong to the world of the interchangeable individual, the mythical suburban family, the semio-con-sumer whose image it endlessly euphoricizes, any more than it belongs to the world of the disparaging cultural critic, the pop artist, the canny Left Bank Intellectual, the Biff-cartoon intelligentsia. In *Hiding in the Light* Hebdige devotes a chapter to Biff cartoons, in which the simulacrum of the Intellectual is sus-pected to be a mixture of Roland Barthes (sign) and James Brown (soul), as misquoted on a Harrods advertisement (sell). 'Nonetheless', it turns out in the end to be Dick Hebdige; he's the po-mo lecturer lampooned in a Biff cartoon that he then ('nonetheless') subjects to a postmodern analysis (Hebdige, 1988: 147–54). Too canny by half for TV.

No: television belongs much more than is admitted in its official histories (where too much is decided by supposed height of brow) to the ambiguous not-quiteness of people like me. It is made by, and it makes, oddities. It uses up people who cannot be certain of their origin, class, faith, sexuality, family, housing, history. It revels in us.

I went to an orphanage (though not quite an orphan), which was run like a public school in the tradition of Lindsay Anderson's film *If* (though it wasn't a public school). For what is this school renowned? The Royal Wolverhampton Orphanage Asylum, the 'Ofny', home (though it wasn't a home) for peculiar pupils and crazed staff, does have some claims to fame, namely its 'Old Royals'. For such are its survivors called, unless they're women, like my sisters, who're 'Old Rowans', which is etymological (but not ideological) nuts. Here are three Old Royals:

1   **Gilbert Harding**, the irascible, ubiquitous radio and TV star of the 1950s, more famous in his day than any of the names you've read so far, known as 'Britain's rudest man' and 'TV's top personality'. These lines are on the blurb of his autobiography (Harding, 1953). He tells of his time at the Royal Wolverhampton School in detail, though not of his gayness; the illegal 'love that dared not speak its name' at that time. He does tell of his first encounter with the attraction of catholicism; this took the form of seeing a dead but authoritative man (the Ofny's late headmaster) dressed in catholic clerical costume for his laying out. Harding empathized with a man who wanted to profess in eternity what had been impossible for him to admit in life (if he was to keep his job). The attractions of men in strange dress, death, authority, and the peculiarities of English catholicism can

perhaps still be sampled; you might try looking at an odd but all too plausible thriller by 'Robert Player' (pseudonym of architect-historian Robert Furneaux Jordan) called *Let's Talk of Graves, of Worms, and Epitaphs* – where an Anglican country vicar can murder his wife and still become pope (Player, 1977). Harding had been a pupil at the Ofny from 1916 to 1925, while I was there from 1957 to 1962, so we were hardly contemporaries, but he did live long enough to visit the school for a Speech Day during my time; I remember him as authoritative, strange, attractive, and when he died soon after I felt personally touched, though at the time I knew nothing of his 'not-quiteness', his gay, Catholic, 'rude-boy' Englishness.

2   **Alan Sinfield** was Head Boy of the Ofny during my time, and I became his fag for a short while, cleaning his shoes in exchange for vicarious prestige and real kindness (a quiet, educative warning to put polish on the shoes but not the laces). Now Sinfield is a well-known scholar and gay activist, a Shakespearian who reads the Bard against the grain, anti-canonically. Sinfield writes: 'Once the canon has become established (in the full range of that word) it seems "natural" – so much so that the reader perhaps doubts my seriousness' (Sinfield, 1983: 1–2). Another career not-quiteist.

3   And then; an almost invisible figure, ghost-faced in the school photograph like his own dead twin, but unmistakeable – **Eric Idle**. He was my con-temporary, but I don't think we ever spoke, given his exalted status (his 5th or 6th form to my 2nd, I think). He was one of the older boys who impressed not by prefecture and authority but by larrikinism, along with De Marco whom I admired, and Dennis, on whom my sister had a distant crush. He probably never knew this, given the rigid segregation of the sexes. The Ofny's two 'Sides' were separate girls' and boys' schools at the opposite extremities of the same long building, divided by a tower and taboo in the middle. Contact was almost exclusively visual, at the joint Sunday chapel, although intelligence could be gleaned from siblings at weekly 'soeur's meetings' (I know: I was that sibling).

My favourite Eric Idle is the one who emerges from the suburban fridge in the Python film *The Meaning of Life*, glittering pinkly like a gameshow Klimtian dream. He takes Mrs Suburbanal on a walk through The Universe, concluding with the hope that there's intelligent life somewhere up there in the billions of galaxies, because there's bugger-all down here. He has caught my mood exactly, and I know just where he caught it.

Television; made for suburbanality, but made by misfit not-quites like Idle and Harding and interpreted by the likes of Sinfield and me. Notice this, and then you begin to realize that the characters entertaining the suburbanal millions *on* the little screen are as weird as the people *behind* the screen; right through TV history from Lucille Ball (see Mellencamp, 1992: 322–33) to Stephen Fry (and any number of buggered-up boarding-school-misfits in British comedy). Why, then, is it a commonplace, taken-for-granted truth

Figure 15.5 'The Ofny', 1960: Idle top; Hartley, bottom
Source: Royal Wolverhampton 'Orphanage Asylum', 1960

that those in front of the screen – the audience – are an interchangeable, undifferentiated mass, suburban, banal, beneath comment but not contempt? It may well be that they – you too – are all as weird and not-quite as the weirdos they and you are watching.

That, in the end, is *Just What Makes Today's Homes So Different, So Appealing*; their occupants' interchangeability not with each other but with those on whom their weekly gaze falls in a not-quite unrequited crush. Potentially, we're all Gilbert Hardings, 'laying the foundations of unorthodoxy from the start' (Harding, 1953: 25).

Compared with the artful dodges of critical-pop-art irony this insight may not be much to write home about. But never mind the insight; look at the *home*.

APPENDIX 1
Glossary of concepts and neologisms

'Newspeak' is the modern version of the English tongue ordained by the Party. It has given to the world such remarkable words as doublethink, thoughtcrime, plusgood, and sexcrime ('love' in to-day's English).

(George Orwell, *Nineteen Eighty-Four*, inside-cover blurb)

TV studies is a new subject and it needs new concepts, new specialist terms – a new jargon – to describe the new landscape of the mediasphere. One of the pleasures of writing about it is that you get to name things you find. It's not as exact a science as the naming of fossils, flora or fauna, because there's no obligation on anyone else to follow your nomenclature. But it can't be avoided. I'm probably one of the worst offenders in the coinage of neologisms. So here's a glossary to explain some terms I've used in this or other books that may not be familiar or not used in ways currently recognized by the OED, but which have a bearing on the study of television.

One of the reasons for my profligate neologizing is that television is a familiar socio-semiotic experience for everyone; like breathing it's easy to do, but like breathing the mechanics of what is actually going on are not necessarily made visible via the usual resources of ordinary language. It has therefore always seemed useful to me to try to think about television in new ways, using concepts not commonly applied to it, precisely because it is so obvious. Now this habit can seem like unnecessary obfuscation, or a perverse delight in making difficulties, and perhaps it is, but the idea is to elaborate a 'specialist language' of terms, metaphors, concepts and notions by means of which television can be 'triangulated' against three reference points:

1   the viewer's experience, which is both individual and social, using personal and 'common' resources (ordinary language, common knowledge, common sense);
2   television itself, in any of its textual, industrial-institutional and historical forms;
3   the formal apparatus of TV studies, including the inherited store of philosophical, theoretical and conceptual tools for thinking, analyzing and criticizing, as well as newly-minted notions – such as some of the terms below – which serve to show that the analytical process is as creative as any other,

204

and that the object of study may require new ways of thinking, to say new things in new ways.

However, bearing in mind that theory and analysis is also a 'lingua franca', it is important not to use specially coined words as if they're common currency – these days a concept is not necessarily self-explanatory, but needs to be understood as authored. Just as you can't say 'public sphere' without invoking Habermas, or 'governmentality' without Foucault, or 'semiosphere' without Lotman, so I can't claim that even useful terms like 'paedocracy', 'juvenation' or 'mediasphere' (never mind wilder coinages like 'blivit', 'frocks pop' and 'windscreenwiperism') have achieved that impersonal status where they may be used freely as descriptive concepts. As yet, they're language, not learning, thinking aloud and making mistakes in public, not achieved knowledge. They make progress by taking an existing idea or term and changing or twisting it (most of the terms originate from other authors), and putting it to new uses; it's the 'advancement of knowledge' at the margins, moving forward floe-ly, as it were, amoeba-style. When a word does capture a thought or clarify an observation, however, that's not 'doublethink', it's 'doubleplusgood'. But in deference to anyone who finds such stuff trying, here's the explanation (if not the apology) they may feel they are owed.

Some of the terms haven't cropped up in this book, although they're all part of the 'semiosphere' within which the present text was generated; to help the interested reader track them down I've indicated in brackets where each term is deployed more fully, except in a few cases where a term is in general use.

ACCESSING

Television 'accesses' voices and viewpoints from the general public. 'Accessed' voices can be distinguished from 'institutional' voices (i.e. from professional broadcasters) but are always narratively subordinate to them. (*Understanding News*; *Tele-ology*; *Key Concepts* with O'Sullivan *et al.*)

AGORA / AGORAPHILIA

The 'agora' was a place of public meeting in classical Greek city-states comparable with the Forum in Rome. It allowed citizens to assemble in sight of one another for democratic will-formation, judicial decision-making and dramatic edification, as well as for commercial exchange. It is therefore the archetype of the 'public sphere', and can now be found only on television. 'Agoraphilia' is the opposite of 'agoraphobia' – it is the love of public space. It describes the condition of those who like public life. (*The Politics of Pictures*)

ANAMNESIA

Not to be confused with 'amnesia', the rhetorical practice of forgetting, anamnesia is the rhetorical practice of reminder, 'bringing to mind'. It is what television does well; advertising especially so. (*Reading Television*; *Tele-ology*)

AUDIENCE, AS GOD

Studies of audiences often credit them with supernatural characteristics; they are unknowable but all-powerful. They have to be propitiated. This is the purpose of academic audience ethnographies and commercial ratings agencies alike. (*The Politics of Pictures*)

BINARISM

The practice of rendering the world as a two-term universe, ranging from male: female and land:sea to high-culture:popular culture and art:commerce. The world isn't like this, but a great deal of thinking about and on television is. (*Key Concepts*; *Tele-ology*; *The Politics of Pictures*; *Understanding News*)

BLIVIT

A term from Kurt Vonnegut, denoting an incommensurable mixture of genres, styles and forms. Television is 'blivitous' because it mixes fact, fiction, faking and forecasting, and it is not always clear where one forms ends and another begins. Vonnegut himself characterizes it as 'two pounds of shit in a one-pound bag'. Blivitous media such as television produce excess meaningfulness in the connections between incommensurate textual forms (fact v. fiction) – it is impossible to watch TV and completely separate rational discourse like news from emotional or persuasive discourses like chat shows and advertising; over decades each form begins to partake of attributes of other, neighbouring types not only in the activity of watching but in production practices and textuality too. (*Tele-ology*)

CITIZENS OF MEDIA

An attempt to connect political participation with media-readership, rather than seeing the media as opposed to the public sphere or a contamination of politics. Audiences are understood as 'citizens of media' in the sense that it is through the symbolic, virtualized and mediated context of watching television, listening to radio and reading print media that publics participate in the democratic process on a day to day basis. It may be right to go so far as to argue that citizenship, traditionally understood, is impossible without media. (*Popular Reality*; *Uses of Television*)

COMFORT / FREEDOM

The twin energies of modernity. Modernity is not only the pursuit of (political) freedom, but also the pursuit of (material) comfort. Thus, it is as much commercial as it is democratic. (*Popular Reality*)

CONTINUITY

The television that isn't there; even though it occupies many hours of screen-time and a significant proportion of what broadcasters transmit. It's made of station IDs, announcements, promos and trailers, time-checks, news-bumpers, advertisements and special items like the close-down sequence or national anthem, where played. (*Tele-ology*)

CORDIALIZATION

A term I borrowed from Thomas Paine (1792); he uses it in *Rights of Man* to describe the cumulative *political* effect of *commercial* dialogue or traffic between nations: for Paine, commerce was preferable to war, and cordialization was the purpose of international politics. That he saw no difficulty about the 'commercialization' of international relations perhaps explains his neglect as a political philosopher by the adversarialist Left in the twentieth century, but that he was right seems clear. There has been an upswing in cordialized politics since the end of the cold war, and the concept applies convincingly to the general international situation of television traffic and audience-education. (*Popular Reality*; *Uses of Television*)

CROSS-DEMOGRAPHIC COMMUNICATION

'Mass' media messages that are designed to communicate across boundaries of class, age-group, gender, ethnicity, region, nation or even language-group. Hollywood cinema, broadcast television and either mass-circulation ('tabloid') newspapers or global-circulation magazines (e.g. *Elle*) come into this category. Cross-demographic communication is a preferred term for what we used to call 'ideology', 'populism' – it describes what 'mass' media do without pre-judging it as an exercise of power, persuasion or manipulation. (*Uses of Television*)

CULTURAL CITIZENSHIP

A term from the literary tradition, referring to participation in the cultural life of a nation, adapted to describe a new phase in formal citizenship understood as mutual rights and obligations between an individual and a community, although without being confined to a nation or state. Cultural citizenship overlays earlier forms (civic or individual rights; political rights or popular sovereignty; and social, welfare-work-education rights) with rights to *identity* understood as membership of an actual or virtual community based not on nation but on, for example, ethnicity, gender, sexual orientation, region, age, etc. (*Uses of Television*)

CULTURAL STUDIES

Originally the study of relations of inequality in class societies within the general areas of sense-making and everyday life; the application of theories of power to conditions of ordinariness. Latterly it has evolved somewhat beyond its adversarialist beginnings, returning to a more 'Hoggartian' project that addresses the democratization of meaning without necessary recourse to notions of power and struggle. It may be characterized now as an anthropology of the everyday, a semiotic history of ordinariness.

CULTURE / POLITICS / ECONOMY

The three spheres of analysis in Marxist and post-Marxist social theory. Marxism predicted that social change would arise from the structure of economic relations and from historical activities in the economic sphere, and tried to base a 'politics of the factory gate' on this assumption – the trades union movement and workerism in particular. When it was discovered that economic activism did not produce social change, and that the political sphere was relatively autonomous from the economic sphere, attention moved to a two-pronged political movement, seeking change through representative politics (party, parliament) as well as through the labour movement. When it was discovered that politico-economic activism did not produce social change and that the cultural sphere was relatively autonomous, attention moved to culture, especially through the work of the Italian Marxist theorist Antonio Gramsci, in an effort first to explain why working-class people think, act and vote against what have been identified as their class interests, and then to produce a 'counter-hegemonic consciousness' that will reinvigorate the politico-economic struggle. This explains why Marxist theorists took such an intense interest in television. It was understood equally as the (cultural) means whereby populations were persuaded to live in structures of domination, and also as a potential source of counter-hegemonic consciousness.

DEFERENTIAL / MOTIVATED CAMERA

Two ways to shoot an actuality sequence. Either the camera can follow a subject — a talking head especially — with micro-shifts of focus and framing, giving the subject priority over the semiosis (deferential camera), or it can choose what to put in the frame at any one time, and by a combination of zooms, pans and tilts take control over the representation of a place, person or event (motivated camera). The ideological significance of this distinction is when it is employed in a single news story; a politician might be given 'deferential' camerawork while protesters might be treated to 'motivated' camerawork. Viewers may see this as stability and calm contrasted with incoherence and disorder. (*Tele-ology*)

DEMOCRATAINMENT

The means by which popular participation in public issues is conducted in the mediasphere. (*Uses of Television*)

DEMOCRATIC EQUIVALENCE

A term from Ernesto Laclau and Chantal Mouffe that describes the 'logic' whereby groups or subjects may claim democratic rights on the basis of equivalence with others who already hold them. In western modernity, the original 'subject' of democracy was the Parisian, adult, male, non-aristocratic citizen. The logic of democratic equivalence was used to demand extension of citizenship rights to groups at first excluded from popular sovereignty — women, non-metropolitan and colonized people to begin with, but over the years the demand has extended to 'virtual' communities based on, for instance, sexual identity, age, body-size or taste constituencies, and eventually to animals, whose 'rights' are modelled on democratic equivalence with universal human rights. The logic of democratic equivalence is important in TV studies because it is through cross-demographic communication — largely via television — that the logic extends. (*Popular Reality*)

DESIRE V. FEAR (SCHOOLS OF THOUGHT)

Two schools of thought about 'popular' and 'mass' society and communication. The 'fear' school of thought sees 'massness' as a threat to existing civilization, governement, taste (etc.,); the 'desire' school of thought sees 'the popular' as an opportunity for democratization and cultural, political and economic extension. Both schools of thought are meditations on the 'founding' problem of modernity, which is that an unknowable and vast population is nevertheless sovereign. (*Uses of Television*)

DIRT, POWER OF

The propensity of television, like other blivitous semiotic systems, to produce more meaningfulness than can be policed by the producer/textual apparatus. 'Dirt' in anthropological terms is the ambiguous terrain between two opposing elements in a system, where overlap creates the possibility that something may be understood as 'both/and' or 'neither/nor' at the same time. Television is structurally 'dirty' in this way. (*Tele-ology*)

DISCURSIVE AND POLITICAL (SCHOOLS OF THOUGHT)

Two intellectual traditions contributing to the contemporary study of television. The 'discursive' school of thought derives from literary and cultural analysis, and is concerned with the 'content' and meaning of media. Traditionally such analysis concerned itself with notions of quality and was a minoritarian pursuit; but it has contributed a strand of non-judgemental textual analysis to TV studies. The 'political' school of thought derives from Fabian and New Left political theory, and is concerned with the institutional organization of television as a politico-economic social force. Traditionally such analysis is focused on strategies for democratization of media in terms of both ownership of the airwaves and access to them; it has (paradoxically) tended to encourage critical (adversarial) analysis and hence a minoritarian stance comparable with that of the discursive school. The two schools of thought were first integrated (into 'cultural studies') by Raymond Williams and Richard Hoggart. (*Uses of Television*)

DIY (DO-IT-YOURSELF) CITIZENSHIP

Semiotic self-determination based on mobility and choice in identity. 'Nations' based on 'virtual communities': e.g. 'Nation.1', an online country inhabited entirely by children; fanship groups from Trekkers to music-based subcultures; feminist communities sustained through communication-networks in various media from print (journals) to dance. 'DIY citizenship' is a concept intended to emphasize the decentralized, deregulated 'suburbanization' of community, and the paradoxical tendency towards *difference* (based on voluntary as well as inherited or regulated identification) rather than sameness in an era of '*mass*' media. (*Uses of Television*)

DRAMA / DIDACTICS / DEMOCRACY –
MEDIA / EDUCATION / GOVERNMENT

The 'three Ds' of drama (performance), didactics (pedagogy) and democracy (participation) were integrated in classical (Greek/Roman) political organization, where citizens gathered in sight of one another for plays, persuasion and politics – each understood as a facet of the others. In modern public spheres, these functions were dis-integrated, each forming the basis for three very large but formally separate social institutions – government (democracy), education (didactics), and media (drama) (see also G-E-M). In what is often described as postmodernity, it is possible to see these three great social institutions of government, education and media converging, with the 'three Ds' most prominently re-integrated in media such as television. (*The Politics of Pictures*)

EUPHORICIZATION

The presentation of popular participation in social, family and public life as if through the optimistic perspective of characters in advertisements. The euphor-icization of democracy is inevitable in countries where political participation, like media audience- and readership, is strictly voluntary. Audiences who have made no prior commitment to participation in democratic will-formation and political/ judicial decision-making have to be won over to the cause of public participation, and commercial(ized) media who wish to hold their audiences while fulfilling their public role have to appeal to audiences as citizens, at the same time as they are informing and educating them in a particular cause. The techniques of publicity are essential for the maintenance of the public. (*Tele-ology*)

EXCESS

All semiosis produces more meaningfulness than is required for the simple transfer of messages, information or instructions. Semiotic excess is a structural condition of television, resulting in a difference between the meanings for a given text as understood by different viewers, or by viewers compared with producers, and so on. Since all 'messages' have an excess of meaning, all understanding ('decoding') is aberrant (this idea originally came from Umberto Eco) – all interpretation is 'wrong' in the sense that alternatives are always both possible and warranted by textual features. (*Tele-ology*)

EX-NOMINATION

That which is so obvious it need not be named (nominated). This is a feature of ideological discourses, first suggested by Roland Barthes, where for instance in the designation of gender or ethnicity in news stories it may be seen as right or even natural to 'nominate' someone's gender if they're a woman, or ethnicity if they are people of colour, while white men are not designated as such. The effect of ex-nomination is to naturalize ex-nominated characteristics, and conversely to attribute the actions or newsworthiness of people whose characteristics are nominated to the nominated feature, not to the person. (*Tele-ology*; *Key Concepts*)

EYEWITNESS IDEOLOGY

The 'dominant ideology' of western journalism, news and current affairs; the preference for 'being there' in the reporting of events. This is a version of nineteenth-century scientific ideologies of positivism and empiricism. It is useful when combined with investigative scepticism and research (i.e. when done 'scientifically'), but less convincing when done merely 'semiotically' (e.g. by flying a celebrity presenter to a trouble-spot so they can do a scripted piece to camera, or even by using backgrounds and voiceover presentations that suggest 'being there' when in fact all that is being conveyed is television's love of liveness). (*The Politics of Pictures*)

FICTIONALIZATION OF DEMOCRACY

Because modern societies are so large, people don't know each other – their co-presence within the process of choice and decision-making is literally a matter of 'representation'. Democratic participation is mediated, and citizens are citizens of media, so 'democracy' itself is textualized, and inevitably takes on features of textual/semiotic 'representation' along with direct/political representation. In this context, democracy is 'fictionalized' to the extent that it obeys textual imperatives. (*The Politics of Pictures*)

FLOE

Not Raymond Williams's concept of 'flow' but a concept to describe knowledge in TV studies. Instead of seeing knowledge as a continuous field of causally connected information, knowledge of such a complex object of study is better understood as discontinuous blocks, like floes of ice in an Arctic or Antarctic sea, which meet and part, combine and split, and may have little to do with each other even when stuck together. Travelling through such a domain of knowledge is hard work for the investigator and liable to the kind of upsets routinely experienced by polar explorers (blindness, falling down holes, disorientation). (*Tele-ology*)

FORENSIC ANALYSIS

'Forensic' means 'of the Forum'. It refers to the process of argumentation adopted in classical Rome to arrive at judicial truth, by means of adversarial argument.

Such argumentation is now wholly identified with the establishment and import of evidence in courts of law, hence the contemporary idea of 'forensic science'. Combining the notion of argumentation in search of the truth with the idea of investigating truth by the minute examination of evidence offers an appropriate 'method' for TV studies. The 'scene of the crime' is the TV text; forensic examination of this is conducted 'scientifically' by semiotic methods, and this evidence is then available for argumentation, including adversarial argument, in search of the truth about textual meaning and communicative relationships. (*The Politics of Pictures*)

FRIDGE, THE

An icon and enabler of the ideology of domesticity; it precedes, accompanies and allows the adoption of television in the home as a mass but private medium. What makes it an interesting 'concept' is that the domestic refridgerator is just as important to twentieth-century cultural change and development as is television, but it has never attracted the public discourses, either of condemnation or celebration, that have circulated around television from the outset. The fridge is therefore an interesting 'control' or 'placebo' to help determine the epidemiology of television's negative 'effects'. (*Uses of Television*)

FROCKS POP

The representation of popular reality via the bodies and actions of attractive female presenters and performers. It is a punning corruption of 'vox pop' or *vox populi* – 'voice of the people' – the broadcasters' term for interviews with ordinary people. (*Popular Reality*)

FROTTAGE

In lexicons of sexual behaviour, frottage refers to sexual arousal from rubbing against the clothed body of another person. It can also refer to the taking of impressions by rubbing, for instance the craft of brass-rubbing. Combining these meanings, 'frottage' in TV studies refers to the pleasure viewers gain from contact with others via television – taking impressions of and pleasure in human contact via television, and thereby sustaining membership of the given 'we' community. (*Tele-ology*)

G-E-M

G = Government; E = Education; M = Media. These three great social institutions of modernity, bureaucratized, specialized and functionally separated as they have been for 'mass' societies, are converging and integrating in 'postmodern' conditions. Each corresponds functionally to the activities carried out as one integrated practice in the classical agora or Forum: combining decision-making (government) with oratory (education) and drama (media) in the conduct of public affairs. In contemporary media, drama is once again being used to educate the public and to assist the process of democratic will-formation (whether that drama takes fictional or factual generic form); and meanwhile, the formal institutions of both government and education are integrating with media and with each other to reach and teach, regulate and mobilize a public that now takes the form of audiences and consumers. (*Uses of Television*)

GLANCE / GAZE

Cinema theory makes much of the notion of the 'gaze'. TV studies requires more attention to the 'glance', because the mode of looking at television is more varied, less intense and more 'anthropological' – the 'glance' being a human technique of the first importance for assessing the status and intentions of other people; you can 'tell at a glance' by people's dress, posture, movements and so on who they are and what they may be doing or meaning (Sahlins, 1976). Television relies very heavily on the practical reasoning associated with 'people-watching', which is itself based on the glance. (*The Politics of Pictures*)

HELIOGRAPHY

Writing with light. The dominant metaphor for journalism – it enlightens, by bringing to light, very often by means of sources of light (the Sun) or techniques for maximizing light (the Mirror). The notion of journalism as enlightenment ties it in with 'heliological' traditions of western philosophy as analyzed by Jacques Derrida. (*The Politics of Pictures*)

INTERNAL COLONIZATION / VIRTUAL COLONIZATION

Internal colonization is a term coined by Michael Hechter (1975) to describe the relations between the British state and stateless countries within Britain such as Wales and Scotland – these are Britain's 'internal colonies'. In the era of media citizenship and identity politics the term can be extended to other 'colonized groups', most obviously indigenous peoples, but extending to 'virtual' communities within a given country who enjoy no distinct representational or representative rights, but whose advocates insist on separate identity and community. Such groups have included proletariats, women, gays and lesbians, youth, and various ethnic or national minorities. The politics of 'internal/virtual colonization' are that rhetorics and policies of assimilation and integration invariably produce their own opposite among the communities so colonized, resulting in political struggle for 'national' liberation and independence on behalf of a given group. Separatism has extended from the Scots to feminism, from the Welsh to the workers, in certain political creeds and ideologies, and is an inherent tendency in identity politics. The pressure of such movements towards separate identity and self-development on the modernist concept of national sovereignty has yet to be worked through, but it is clear that nations founded on territory, ethnic unity and popular sovereignty that is 'indifferent' to difference at the very least coexist with shadow states existing in people's hopes and through transnational communication networks such as television, feminism, etc. (*Popular Reality*; *Uses of Television*)

INTERVENTION ANALYSIS

TV studies has become established not only as an academic subject but also as a 'site of struggle'; there are contending views of society, politics and preferable futures. Knowledge, even academic knowledge, is not neutral in such struggles. Intervention analysis describes work done in research and publication that is self-reflexive about its political affiliations, and seeks to analyze a given situation in order to change it, not just to understand it. (*Tele-ology*)

JUVENATION

The 'younging' of culture. Juvenation refers not only to the representation of, address to and stories about young people, but to a wider process whereby other cultural domains and even politics are also 'juvenated' – represented via youthfulness. Juvenation attracts contradictory journalistic and dramatic coverage, corresponding to the tensions between truth-seeking and communication in media: to attract readers and audiences, texts are juvenated by showing young people as attractive and often eroticized; to fulfil their truth-seeking mandate the same media emphasize stories in which the sexualization of youthful attractiveness is pathologized and condemned. Meanwhile, juvenation does not mean that young people have much say in the uses to which their images and stories are put – they are an 'internal colony' of semiosis. (Hartley, 1998)

KISS

A semiotic device used in visual media to represent relations between textmakers and their audiences; between opposing or distinct social categories. (*Popular Reality*)

KNOWLEDGE CLASS

Traditional class theory in the modernist Marxist tradition posits the division of social relations into opposing classes organized around the mode of production: 'capital' and 'labour' being the fundamental classes for industrial societies, while 'landlords' (aristocrats) and 'peasants' can form mutually antagonistic classes in agrarian and feudal societies. However, certain groups, intellectuals and white collar workers in particular, have never fitted these categories very well. During the twentieth century, increasing social power was exercised around control of information, knowledge, symbol and communication, rather than through control of land or industrial production. Such production cannot be achieved without the active and creative input of professionals who 'make' knowledge, information, communication and social semiosis, but these are rarely the same people as the capitalists who own the means of knowledge production. A 'class' has arisen of those who produce knowledge (broadly defined), who are neither 'owner' nor 'worker' in traditional terms, who have great collective social sway but little individual power, who are not internally organized into class-conscious parties or movements, but who nevertheless represent the most advanced and cutting-edge aspect of socio-commercial development outside the finance industry. The knowledge class, from media professionals to intellectuals, computer software firms to government scientists, educators to archivists, journalists to activists, are the de facto controllers of popular media, which they use to disseminate their faction's truths to audiences in whose name they speak and whose power they represent. (*Popular Reality*; *Uses of Television*)

LAW-FORMATION / ANOMALIES-ACCIDENTS

Two contrasting modes of narration in the semiosphere; the terms are taken from Yuri Lotman (1990). Narratives of law-formation are conservative (small 'c'), myth-making stories at the very centre of a 'we' society's sense of itself; while narratives about anomalies and accidents tend to refer to the margins and boundaries of the semiotic universe, where 'they' communities (both human and supernatural) might be expected to present threats and promises. Television as a medium features both of these narrative types, with law-formation at its most intensive in fictional genres like soap opera, sitcoms and drama series, while news and current affairs specialize in narratives of accident and anomaly. However, because of television's 'blivitousness', news is sometimes active in law-formation and drama in narrating anomaly; this leakage and dialogue is especially interesting to the analyst because here can be traced the shifts in meaning and changes over time needed to understand culture. (*Popular Reality*)

LOOKING – HISTORY / ANTHROPOLOGY / TECHNOLOGY / MODES OF

Looking is not just a natural facility but also a cultural one – how 'we' see depends not only on what's there, and on the physics of optical perception, but also on who 'we' are. Hence looking is a province of social and historical inquiry, and it is found in institutional forms as well as in people's inherited faculties. The history of looking was founded in cultural studies by John Berger in his book *Ways of Seeing* (1972); the anthropology of looking in contemporary societies has been hinted at by Marshall Sahlins (1976) in his structural analysis of western clothing systems (the meaning of apparel must be apprehended 'at a glance'). The institutionalization of looking has been studied most intensively in terms of various technological inventions, from the printed book, via photography, cinema and television to the computer screen – the first influential theorist of the technology of social looking was Marshall McLuhan (1962, 1964). In this context, television can be understood as a technology of looking, promoting specific and historically unique ways of seeing among its users on both sides of the screen, and it may therefore be taken as evidence for both a history and an anthropology of looking – this is what TV studies as a collective discourse is slowly elaborating. (*The Politics of Pictures, Popular Reality*)

MARGINALITY

In textual systems like journalism and television, indeed throughout the semiosphere, it is at the margins of established domains that new meanings, practices and dialogues are most intensively initiated. Margins may be undervalued or overvalued by any given 'we' community (or in its media), but it is precisely this attribution of special or ambiguous status to them that makes them semiotically 'excessive' – productive of more meaningfulness than their position as margins appears to warrant. (*Tele-ology*)

MEDIASPHERE / PUBLIC SPHERE / SEMIOSPHERE (RUSSIAN DOLL)

The 'mediasphere' is the whole universe of media, both factual and fictional, in all forms (print, electronic, screen), all genres (news, drama), all taste hierarchies (from art to entertainment) in all languages in all countries. It therefore completely encloses and contains as a differentiated part of itself the (Habermasian) public sphere (or the many public spheres), and it is itself contained by the much larger semiosphere (Lotman, 1990) which is the whole universe of sense-making by whatever means, including speech. It would be a matter of debate as to whether elaborated textual systems like literature belong to the mediasphere or the semiosphere, and whether it is fruitful to take a whole-earth view of the mediasphere or to posit separate mediaspheres for different nations, speech communities or international culture-cousins, but it is clear that television is a crucial site of the mediasphere and a crucial mediator between general cultural sense-making systems (the semiosphere) and specialist components of social sense-making like the public sphere. Hence the public sphere can be rethought not as a category binarily contrasted with its implied opposite, the private sphere, but as a 'Russian doll' enclosed within a larger mediasphere, itself enclosed within the semiosphere. And within 'the' public sphere, there may equally be found, Russian-doll style, further counter-cultural, oppositional or minoritarian public spheres. For instance, an indigenous public sphere, a feminist public sphere, even a music sphere. (*Popular Reality*)

MULTI-CONSCIOUSNESS

The 'mindedness' of readerships, audiences, viewers and listeners – the ability to attend to more than one level of meaning, genre of discourse, pattern of narrative unfolding, and/or ideological register at once. The term originated with the literary historian S.L. Bethell in the 1940s to describe how popular audiences of the Elizabethan and Jacobean theatre would need to have attended to Shakespeare. It is a useful term to remind critics that people don't need to be scholars or courtiers to 'get' complex drama, even by the great Bard himself, who was a commercial entrepreneur supplying a capitalized commodity to an unknown audience for profit – just like commercial television. (*Reading Television; Tele-ology*)

PAEDOCRACY

Government by children. Television's address to its viewers historically, i.e. in the era of broadcast network commercial TV, has been paedocratic, since childlike attributes are positive and can be assumed to be shared by viewers with few other attributes in common. Paedocracy – government *by* children – is not the same as childishness (it doesn't have to be understood pejoratively), it is not 'dumbing down'. Nor is it the same as pedagogy, which is not government by but (attempted) teacherly control of children. Indeed, paedocracy, taken seriously by both addresser-organizations and by literate addressee-audiences, and understood to allow for both children and television to be *liked*, can be entirely positive as a 'regime of viewing'. However, a paedocratic mode of address has to be chosen from possible alternatives – citizenship of a paedocracy is different from that of traditionally imagined adult-franchise polities. See also JUVENATION. (*Tele-ology; The Politics of Pictures*)

PAINISM / LANGTONISM V HALLISM / ERICSONISM

Painism = Secular, democratic, cordializing political theory on the model of Tom Paine in his books *Common Sense, Rights of Man* and *The Age of Reason*. Langtonism = Intersubjectivity of populations that recognizes and respects ethnic and gender identity, but conducts cultural politics on the basis of what might be termed fellow-feeling across demographic difference, on the model of indigenous intellectual and activist Marcia Langton in her monograph *Well I Heard it on the Radio and I Saw it on the Television*. Hallism = The theory that media are best explained as agents of ideological management of a crisis in hegemony in class-divided and capitalist societies, on the model of the work of Stuart Hall and his collaborators in *Policing the Crisis* (1978). Ericsonism = the analysis of media as functional components of a knowledge society, working to assist in control functions in administration and to provide surveillance over both governmental and social apparatuses, on the model of Richard Ericson and his collaborators' books *Visualizing Deviance* (1987), *Negotiating Control* (1989) and *Representing Order* (1991). In general terms, Painism and Langtonism represent a cordializing, population-gathering approach to political and cultural affairs, while both Hallism and Ericsonism represent an adversarial or managerial approach. (*Popular Reality*)

PERVASION

The condition of television. Often described in negative, pathological terms, for instance as invasive not pervasive, or as 'bombardment' of self and society by semiosis, or as mere industrial distribution not creative production, television's pervasiveness in personal and social life has had a bad press in critical intellectual traditions. But pervasion can be understood as democratization not populism, as anthropological not pathological. (*The Politics of Pictures*)

PHOTOPOETRY

Literally *creation* (from the Greek 'poesis') with *light* ('photo'); hence, photopoetry is making or creating with light. It is what cinema and television do. The word may be useful to remind those who think of popular TV as trash that it inherits a long tradition of creativity going back to Aristotelian aesthetics; and equally it may be useful to remind those who think poetry is hopelessly compromised as an elitist form in contemporary society that the stuff is interwoven into the ordinary now just as it ever was in traditional oral societies. Television is a secularized, pervasive 'poetics' of the ordinary. (*Tele-ology*)

POLITICS OF PICTURES

Politics conducted in and via visual, representational, semiotic, media contexts; see also MEDIASPHERE. (*The Politics of Pictures*)

POPULATION-GATHERING

A concept designed to capture television and other popular media's propensity to address vast cross-demographic audiences, without using pejorative terms inherited from critiques of populism, imperialism, colonialism or commercial exploitation. Population-gathering is something television must do to survive economically; this need can be seen in other than catastrophic terms, and it has cultural, aesthetic and political consequences that are not necessarily evil. Population-gathering is fundamental to television as a transmodern teacher. (*Popular Reality*; *Uses of Television*)

PORTMEIRIONIZATION

Portmeirion is a slightly less than full-scale reproduction Mediterranean village, built by the architect Williams Clough Ellis in North Wales in the first half of the twentieth century. It was the setting for the cult TV show of the 1960s starring Patrick McGoohan, *The Prisoner*. Portmeirionization refers to the tendency in real towns to paint themselves up as a set, to present themselves as their own simulacrum, to change from a locality to a location. Places start to look real, authentic and genuine only when they approximate most accurately to their fictionalization on TV. (*Tele-ology*)

POWER VIEWING

On the model of power dressing, power viewing is assertive audienceship by TV viewers; it may describe hyper-active audience practices, such as fanship or active engagement in public critical responses to a text, where viewing is turned into a further creative or critical practice, or it can refer to a normal level of sophisticated media literacy, without which the common knowledge, embedded allusiveness and multiple semiosis of contemporary television doesn't make much sense. (*The Politics of Pictures*)

PROPAGANDA

A much maligned genre of address. Propaganda is campaigning communication, whether commercial (advertising) or political (elections etc.). It is widely held to be a dangerous form of communication, retaining a bad name from its association with the propaganda efforts of centralized bureaucracies from the Catholic church to Nazi, fascist and communist experiments in mass manipulation. The contemporary persuasion industries are widely denigrated among critics who express alarm at the ascendancy of advertising agencies, lobby groups, PR firms and professional 'spin doctors' in everyday politics. Equally, the susceptibility of populations to commercial exploitation is feared in relation to advertising. But in fact propaganda is a mode of communication which viewers have historically shown every sign of handling in a sophisticated or literate way as part of the repertoire of mass media – they know where they are with manipulative messages, whose generic, discursive form, including direct address, lack of narrative sequence, dissociation of image/verbal relations and persuasive rhetorics are remarkably close to avant-garde, experimental forms. Propaganda is the epistle on an industrial scale; person-to-person communication as junk-mail. (*The Politics of Pictures*)

PROTO-PHOTO

The realist-engraving and drawing of pre-photographic journalism, creating public literacy for photojournalism decades before it was technically feasible in the latter nineteenth century. (*The Politics of Pictures*)

PUBLIC SPHERE

See MEDIASPHERE, SEMIOSPHERE.

READER / READERSHIP

The public. (See, *passim*: *Tele-ology*, *The Politics of Pictures*, *Popular Reality*, *Uses of Television*.)

SEMIOSPHERE

The whole environment of sense-making, required in order to make any individual utterance possible. The term is modelled on the concept of the 'biosphere' and is very useful in post-Saussurian semiotics to understand how communication is founded on 'asymmetrical' dialogue rather than on the sign, single utterance or abstract language-rules. The semiosphere is the 'universe of the mind' according to Yuri Lotman (1990), whose term it is. See MEDIASPHERE. (*Popular Reality*)

SEMIOSIS

The general practice of sense-making. The object of study of semiotics.

SMILING PROFESSIONS

Professions where orientation to the audience, reader, viewer, public or consumer is the professional skill. The 'smiling professions' are concentrated in the commercial media, where audience maximization is associated with strategies and personalities intended as 'appealing' (in both senses of the word). 'Smiling' has extended from commercial into 'public service' media and 'newspapers of record'. More importantly, the smiling professions have extended socially beyond the media into government and education too (another instance of G-E-M integration), as citizens's charters, customer relations, persuasion-industries, market research and 'spin-doctoring' take hold as large-scale practices designed to bridge the gap between the administrative, control, regulatory and productive apparatus of a given society on the one hand, and its sovereign but anonymous, ultimately unknowable populations on the other. 'We' are glued together by the professional smile. See also KISS. (*The Politics of Pictures*; *Popular Reality*)

TEXTUAL SYSTEM (OF MODERNITY)

Textual systems, for instance journalism, television and literature, are very large-scale elaborate, historically evolving, socially organized forms of semiotic production, which include textmakers, texts and readerships. (*Popular Reality*)

TEXTUALITY

The empirical form taken by semiosis. The evidential archive of the cultural analyst.

THEORY SHOPPING

The 'method' of cultural studies: browsing, selecting and then using the appropriate theoretical framework for the task in hand. The term was coined by Paula

Amad and requires responsibility for theoretical adequacy to be taken by the analyst, not imputed to an absent (theoretical) authority; and it requires respect for the object of study's specificity, not the application of a predetermined theoretical framework (e.g. Marxism, psychoanalysis, Foucauldianism) irrespectively. (*Popular Reality*)

TRANSMODERN

Having pre-modern (e.g. classical/feudal), modern (e.g. scientific, industrial) and postmodern (e.g hyper-textual, commercial-consumerist) attributes at once. Television is the paradigm instance of a 'transmodern' medium. (*Uses of Television*)

TRANSMODERN TEACHING

Television uses pre-modern means (oral and visual modes) to communicate modern truths (rational progress towards freedom and comfort) to postmodern societies (made of consumers and audiences with mobile identities). (*Uses of Television*)

TRUTH, UNIVERSAL V. ADVERSARIAL

There are two kinds of truth in modern textual systems like TV and journalism: adversarial truth is arrived at by argumentation, opposition, conflict, producing a 'they' object; universal truth is knowledge of a 'we' identity or community. (*The Politics of Pictures; Popular Reality*)

TRUTH V. COMMUNICATION

Modern media, including television journalism, have to hold in tension the contradictory needs of telling the truth about the given topic or subject and communicating with an audience. Audiences have made no commitment to watch TV, or to watch a particular channel or segment at a given moment, so rhetorical and persuasive communicational strategies have to be evolved to hold their attention and interest. Meanwhile, the demands of the given story will have to be accommodated – the truth-seeking element of journalism and drama alike – and this may tend to the complex or not add up in the arithmetic of characterization + narrative = story. The trick in TV is to hold the demands of truth and communication in creative tension. (*The Politics of Pictures*)

223

WEDOM / THEYDOM

On the model of the 'dom' in 'kingdom' or 'Christendom', 'wedom' and 'they-dom' are domains of inclusion (wedom) and exclusion (theydom) in the characterization of communities in news and other media. (*The Politics of Pictures; Popular Reality*)

WINDSCREENWIPERISM

The opposite of Marshall McLuhan's notion of 'rearviewmirrorism'. Rearview-mirrorism occurs where a new technology or medium imitates the one it is destined to supplant. Early printed books looked like manuscripts; early television was viewed as if it were cinema; early concrete buildings looked like Tudor half-timbering. Windscreenwiperism, conversely, describes media forms that look into the future; for instance continuity on television was for decades ignored as the television that wasn't there, but windscreenwiperistically pointed to future generic forms that are now regarded as existant in their own right. (*Tele-ology*)

APPENDIX 2
Do–It–Yourself TV studies

Their [the people's] individuall imperfections being great, they are moreover enlarged by their aggregation; and being erroneous in their single numbers once hudled together, they will be error it self. For being a confusion of knaves and fools, and a farraginous [indiscriminate] concurrence of all conditions, tempers, sex, and ages; it is but natural if their determinations be monstrous, and many waies inconsistent with the truth.

(Sir Thomas Browne, 1650: 177)

What follows is a template for the practical teaching of television studies. It is not a syllabus or lesson plan, but a reasonably systematic working through of issues that newcomers to the study of television ought to think about as they go along. It is offered from the point of view of cultural and textual studies, since that is my specialist area and there are plenty of other publications to advise students on questions of political economy, audience ethnography, socio-psychology and all the other disciplinary approaches to television. What follows, then, is systematic, but not comprehensive. It is designed to intensify and harness curiosity about television, from the point of view of the viewer, by associating that viewpoint with the analytical procedures of TV studies, working through from a consideration of television's social and historical context, via some close encounters both textual and extra-textual, to a consideration of television's most important aspect – its relationships with its viewers. The idea is that television is only ever as dumb as the criticism brought to bear on it, so the better informed and the more generally accessible that criticism is, the better for television, for TV studies and for viewers.

I HISTORY OF A CULTURAL TECHNOLOGY OF LIVING

What is television? A look at the object of study from the point of view of the observer/viewer.

TV as a socio-personal phenomenon.   It is good to start with what students already know, and as viewers everyone is likely to be an expert in 'how to watch television'. What does this activity comprise? How is it done? How can it be made into 'knowledge' independent of the viewer? What kinds of skills are employed in watching TV? What cultural variations in viewing can be described based on the age, gender, ethnicity, class, region or taste of the viewer? For instance, try to map a

225

group's variety in: programme choices and preferences; time of day for most intensive viewing; number of people watching and relation to the viewer; how many TV sets in the home and where watched; relation between TV-watching and other activities like eating and talking; use of non-broadcast television like video and cable; rights to programme choice or use of the remote control by each member of a (family) viewing group.

TV and housing, suburban(al)ity. What are the connections between television and the domestic environment? How have they developed and changed over time and in different communities?

From unity to fragmentation, national culture to global/local networks and DIY citizenship. How has 'watching' developed and changed historically? Do audiences today watch television in the same way that their parents and grandparents did? Is there a 'history of looking'?

From class and quality to identity and exchange (Hartley, 1992b). What are the themes that 'drive' academic research and public debate about popular media, especially television? In this book, I've argued that the critical discourses that surrounded television in its early days were to do with issues of class and quality. Since then, issues of identity and 'semiotic self-determination' or 'DIY citizenship' are more important. Is this so?

II HISTORY OF DISCURSIVE APPROPRIATIONS

What is television as a formal object of study in academic/scholarly traditions?

TV as mass society: Frankfurt School to Foucault, psychology to literary theory;
TV as text: semiotics, anthropology, structuralism, postmodernism;
TV as audience: ethnography, political economy, consumerism;
TV and the pedagogical juggernaut (Ong, 1958): teaching TV.

III SOCIAL AND TEXTUAL POWER

If television has *social* power, but is only experienced by its viewers *textually*, how does it wield that power through its *textual features*? How does it connect with or differ from neighbouring media, from computer games to literary books?
TV among media:

PRINT = newspapers, books, magazines, etc.
SOUND = radio (speech and music), recorded music industry.
LIGHT = photography, cinema, television.

TV as pervasive popular power; socio-textual aspects of culture approached by reference to the most frequent complaints against TV:

SEX = *Drama*
VIOLENCE = *Actuality*
BAD LANGUAGE = *Ethics, morals, manners, norms* (Dening, 1992).

IV PRODUCTION

Starting from a socio-cultural focus on industrialization, the corporate production of culture and the social production of meaning, then narrowing to the production of television shows:

Cultural production:
- issues of authorship, intentionality, influence, creativity;
- 'production' of stars and personalities, social knowledges;
- *governmentality* and the discursive regulation of society; *censorship* and the governmental regulation of textuality;
- ownership, control, professionalization.

Corporate production:
1 Simulation Exercise: Win Your Own TV Franchise:
Convert a group of students into **TV-Fem** and/or **TV-Guy**, an organization preparing a franchise application for a TV station catering for women or men viewers. How would it be financed, promoted, programmed, scheduled? How would it appeal to its viewers, decide on programme purchases, set itself up in relation to other channels? Would it take advertising (would it ban any products)? Would it employ any gender-based policies of access or exclusion? What regulatory framework would TV-Fem/TV-Guy have to take into account? Are there any real-life stations on which it might model itself, e.g. Lifetime TV in the USA (cable station aimed at women); Imparja in Australia (owned by an Aboriginal community company, but broadcasting as a general commercial channel)?

Practical production:
An accomplishment in itself and as a technique for exploring issues in TV. Try:

1   No budget productions: actuality
Using 'found' (non-professional) locations, props and personnel, exercises are outlined using simple techniques: e.g. *Introductions* – saying hello and introducing each member of a group to camera (each person gives their name, home-town, current status and ambition). This 'single' message can be made to signify multiple meanings by changing framing, angle, lighting, sequence, etc. On each successive person-as-talent, vary:

- the framing from extreme close-up to very wide angle;
- the angle from looking down on the talent to looking up at them;
- the shot from static to one using tilts and pans (movement of the camera on a static base) and using tracking or hand-held shots (movement of the camera through the scene);
- the lighting from studio-saturation to a single source (e.g. a torch) in darkness or using available daylight;
- the scene from using one character speaking direct to camera, to a dialogue with music, or current affairs interview set-up with a two-shot;
- the take from short (do it news-fast) to long (make it lyrical or reflective); and from using one take per scene to cutting between multiple cameras.

After this has been done, analyze the different introductions to see what difference to their meaning, interest and impact has been made by purely technical and semiotic changes. Then attempt the same variety with a theme – 'The City,' 'Day in the life of' . . . anything from a pair of sneakers to a sister.

2 No budget productions: drama
No actors, no sets, etc. Use of found objects, locations and people. How to work to the strengths of non-professional actors (watch Humphrey Jennings's *Silent Village* (1941) for a brilliant example of this). How to cheat – making your local buildings look like 'New York'; using video for intimate-but-frank 'auto-ethnography' (in the style of the BBC's access slot *Video Nation*). Raid magazines like *National Geographic* or *Vogue* for visual ideas, designs, sets, graphics. Take a subject that is simple, but which you personally care about, and tell about it through dialogue: e.g. instead of an essay (written argument or description) on, say, 'vegetarianism' or 'home' set the arguments and feelings into a dialogue between two lovers in bed.

3 Making text do analysis
Scriptwriting in documentary and drama forms, within a brief which would simulate budgetary, timeslot and market considerations while allowing students to work with ideas they know and care about:

A documentary on *Bedrooms*;

A two-minute drama on *Men*.

(And then script a *documentary* on 'Men' and *drama* on 'Bedrooms')
Genre Exercise – on semiotic plenitude v. simplicity:

Take a music videoclip; in a class/group, isolate how many themes, visual elements, ideas, shots, sets, people, actions, words, story-lines, closures, etc. it contains. Develop these into a drama of the same length (i.e. two to four minutes). How much is left in? How much left out? What's the drama about? Is the message in the words, the music, or the bodies?

Now, or a different group simultaneously, do the same thing with a news clip.

V TEXT

Questions of genre, narrative, picture, sound and sequence. Textuality on television can be divided into two main worlds: *drama* (e.g. series, soap opera, movies, cartoons) and *actuality* (e.g. news, sport, current affairs, factual programming). Before embarking on the detailed analysis of these, however, note the large amount of what the Australian critic Frances Bonner has called 'ordinary television' that doesn't fit the two categories: e.g. continuity (i.e. channel IDs, trailers, announcements, promos, advertisements, national anthems); quiz shows, game shows, chat shows, breakfast and daytime magazine shows (often hybrids). And note also television's 'blivitousness' – how aspects of each main type have leaked into the other. Drama routinely uses 'real life' (archive footage, 'real' people, stories based on fact, etc.), while factual programming aspires to the status of drama at least in presentation, even in news segments. Analysis of the accepted distinctions between actuality and drama show them to be social and conventional, and sometimes based on the way they've been taken up in different academic disciplines; such distinctions are not based on any essential textual difference. For instance:

ACTUALITY : DRAMA
PUBLIC DOMAIN : PRIVATE DOMAIN
MALE : FEMALE
SOCIOLOGY/POLITICAL ECONOMY : ETHNOGRAPHY/TEXTUALITY
GOVERNMENTAL POLICY : EVERYDAY LIFE
TRUTH : EMOTION
etc. : etc.

Textual analysis of actuality:
1 TV news as an industrial commodity:
• News values (the routinely unexpected)
• Primacy of pictures (compare press and TV news)
• News as story (appeal to viewers)
• Competition between channels (different stations same news)

2 TV news as a generic form:
Visual elements:
• Studio anchor
• Graphics and design
• Actuality footage

Verbal elements:
• Institutional voices (reporters, anchors, media-commentators)
• Accessed voices (people not employed by the TV station: Hartley, 1982)

Narration:
- Plot (cause and effect)
- Characters (look for attribution of 'we' and 'they' attributes to news subjects)
- Dialogue (including how different stories work with each other)
- Camera point of view (is it *part* of the action, or observing it from *outside*?)
- Narrative point of view (does the script ascribe 'we' and 'they' identities?)
- Stereotypes, binary oppositions, 'us and them'

3 TV news as fictionalization of democracy:
- Representatives (talking heads in doorways)
- Vox-pops and interviews – the 'grab' and the 'bite' – orchestrated as the chorus of politics
- Policing the frontier between inside and outside 'our' culture
- Myths of us

4 TV news as a regime of truth:
- Impartiality, balance, neutrality – how is it done textually; on competing channels?
- Adversarial conflict (both sides of the story)
- The ideology of the eyewitness – *where* is the reporter?
- How TV fact is differentiated from TV fiction (generic use of music, slo-mo, eye-contact, etc.)

5 How to work through news texts analytically:
- Starting with what students know about: questions to elicit 'what's there':
- Picture/sound track relations (Hartley, 1992: Chapter 5)
- Sequence (editing)
- Ideology (story)
- Rhetoric (audience appeal)
- Mythicality (universal foundation myths)

Textual Analysis of TV Drama:
1 TV drama as an industrial commodity:
- Divisions of labour (above/below line costs; studio/OB production; producer/director/talent/crew, distribution/market mechanisms)
- Producer ideologies
- Mutation (spin-off, recombination, sequel)

Look at a successful drama series or serial: try to decide what one-sentence 'pitch' would have been needed to have it commissioned in the first place (e.g. 'hospital drama with sex'). What difference would it make to name the producer (e.g. Aaron Spelling, Michael Wearing); ditto the star (e.g. 'hospital drama with sex and Courtney Cox or Jimmy Smits')?

2 TV drama as a generic form:
- Series – action drama (the cop show); state of the nation or of morals (mini-series)
- Serials – sitcoms: analysis of life *within* families; soap opera of life *between* them
- Teleplays (one-off TV-movies) – compare with cinema movies

3 TV drama as actualization of popular reality:
- Emotional dilemma (construction of the discursive self)
- Rehearsing relationships (when your favourite character kisses, transgresses)
- Personal/social interface (love or war?)
- Epistemophilia (love of knowing) – how others live

4 TV drama as a regime of truth:
- Investigative drama (especially political thrillers)
- Dramatic conflict (impersonal opposites personalized as characters in struggle)
- Performance genres (actor as character, melodrama, mannerism, comedy)
- Realism: how TV drama is differentiated from TV actuality

5 How to work through drama texts analytically:
- Starting with what students know about (favourites: why?)
- Picture/sound track relations
- Sequence (editing)
- Ideology (story)
- Rhetoric (audience appeal)
- Mythicality (universal foundation myths)

VI READER

Audience studies. Ethnographic studies of everyday life and of different specialist audience types and activities (e.g. Gillespie, 1995). Students should know how to conduct their own ethnographies of TV audiences. Critical review of audience research. Understanding the use of statistics. Questions of generalizability, representativeness, sampling (Hammersley and Atkinson, 1989).

Audiences as fictional creations. Created by the institutions who wish to address them. Analyze how different the audience is understood to be in:

- commercial ratings research
- academic audience research
- government regulations

Audiences, public opinion and the public itself, as statistics in an economic model of society compared with audiences as images in media. Collect advertising images, art images and pictures from magazines and newspapers showing people interacting with TV. Analyze the images. For instance, when used as an accessory in fashion shoots, TV sets may be proposed as objects associated with solitary auto-eroticism or placed in scenes of urban dereliction, rather than being found in their familiar domestic environment. A visual aesthetic of the relation between the model and TV is suggested that differs markedly from TV's regular reputation. These photo-design appropriations are 'uses of TV' that have gone largely unanalyzed. Other images of audiences from advertising, news and graphics may be compiled to map out a visual (fantasy) typology of audiences. This can then be used to compare with traditional social-scientific (realist) images and representations of them. Questions to bear in mind would include the amount of difference or overlap between the artistic and realistic representations and to observe whether the TV audience is imagined differently in different genres, times, media, countries.

Specific audiences. How do people watch TV *as* specific audiences. What difference to the reception of the same show – news or drama – does it make if watched by audiences differentiated according to age, class, ethnicity, gender, nation, family-type? Why and how does the same show appeal (or not) *across* such demographic differences? Under this heading also comes questions of reading v. consumption; creative activity v. passive end-point; meaning v. ideology; teaching v. power.

Discourses organize practices. Distinctions between industrial production and consumption, or between subjects and objects, public and private, emotion and intellection, drama and actuality, have been influential in deciding how TV is instituted socially, and how it is studied. But such distinctions are also challenged and transgressed by TV and other media, and by this analysis.

TV as cultural pervasion. A form in which print, sound and light are distributed (in the form of market commodities) to the public (in the form of readers).

VII GO ON!

TV studies beyond the academy. Reviews, previews, regulation, market research; TV in pictures, art, ads, literature, public reputation, personal memory.

Further reading. Sources of information, ideas for further research and study; library catalogues, on-line research sources, books. It's a mistake to single people out, since good work will inevitably be overlooked, because the breadth, quality and seriousness of TV studies, the innovative, inspiring and interesting work that's been done, would take a book of its own to describe. So let's look at my shelf, not-quite at random. There's the ever-excellent work on American television of Lynn Spigel, for instance; the work on specific shows by Toby Miller (*The Avengers*); John Tulloch and Henry Jenkins (*Dr Who* and *Star Trek*); Julie D'Acci (*Cagney & Lacey*); Jostein Gripsrud (*Dynasty*); Jane Shattuc (*Oprah*); work on audiences by Henry Jenkins, the '*Remote Control*' group, Marie Gillespie; on producers by Todd Gitlin; the ground-breaking study of TV and race by Herman Gray; Karal Ann Marling's entertaining and erudite book on TV-related visual culture, from fashion to fridges, in 1950s America; the contribution to theory and explanation by the '*Console-ing Passions*' group and the collection on feminist TV criticism edited by Charlotte Brunsdon, Julie D'Acci and Lynn Spigel; retheorizations of television and the public sphere by Peter Dahlgren, work on television history by William Boddy, William Uricchio and others; myriad excellent individual studies in collected volumes and the journals, and in the massive but accessible *Encyclopedia of Television*, edited by Horace Newcomb. Look at the references section of this book (and others!); and catalogues of publishers specializing in or moving into TV studies: Routledge, Sage, Arnold, Minnesota, Indiana, Duke, Oxford, Cambridge, Allen & Unwin. Using Internet sources places unprecedented detail about individual shows within every student's reach; also virtual bookstores like Amazon.com.

Television as public knowledge.   Ask everyone in a group to supply a different daily, weekly or monthly publication from the high street newsstands; for instance:

- a national tabloid newspaper – *Daily Mail, Sun, USA Today*
- a national broadsheet newspaper – *The Independent, Washington Post*
- a regional newspaper – *Kalgoorlie Miner, South Wales Echo*
- a 'supermarket' weekly – from *Hello* and *Who Weekly* to *National Enquirer*
- an upscale weekly – *New Statesman, New Yorker*
- a TV weekly – *Radio Times, TV Times, TV Week, TV Guide*
- a teenage title – *More!, Bliss, Looks, Dolly, Girlfriend*
- a lad-mag – *Loaded, GQ, FHM, Sky*
- a volume-sales monthly – *Woman's Own, The Australian Women's Weekly*
- an upscale monthly – *Vogue, Elle, Frank, Harper's Bazaar, Marie Claire*
- an upscale monthly (version 1.2) – *The Face, I-D, Dazed and Confused, Trace*.

Sometimes one topic will ripple through all of the different news and magazine media, making for an interesting case study of public discourses about television and its audiences. As I write, just about every title in the above list (and a few more besides) has had something to say about the *Tellytubbies*. It can be instructive to follow one such story through different outlets to 'map' more general issues. Alternatively, search each news or magazine title for all references to television, including (p)reviews, celebrity spreads, pictures and gossip, TVs used in fashion sets, TVs in lifestyle/home improvement articles, advertising. What is the meaning of television in these different contexts? Is it 'the same' (e.g. as a prop in an upscale fashion-spread compared with a gossip feature)? What image of the reader/audience emerges in each case, in terms of their anticipated interests, idiom, desires and fears? What appears to be the *use* of television – in each of these publications, *to* each of these publications and *across* them, taken as a whole?

Go on! And watch a lot of television.

REFERENCES

Allen, Robert C. (ed.) (1995) *To Be Continued . . . Soap Operas Around the World*. London and New York: Routledge.

Ang, Ien (1996, first published 1984) 'The battle between television and its audiences'. In *Living Room Wars*. London: Routledge, 19–34.

Ariès, Philippe (1962) *Centuries of Childhood*. Trans. Robert Baldick. London: Jonathan Cape.

Arnold, Matthew ([1869] 1993) *Culture and Anarchy and Other Writings*. Edited by Stefan Collini. Cambridge: Cambridge University Press.

Attallah, Paul (1991) 'Of homes and machines: TV technology and fun in America'. *Continuum* 4: 2, 58–97.

Barker, Theo (ed.) (1975) *The Long March of Everyman 1750–1960*. Harmondsworth: Penguin, in association with André Deutsch and the BBC.

Barthes, Roland (1968) *Elements of Semiology*. London: Cape.

Barthes, Roland (1975) *S/Z*. London: Cape.

Bennett, Tony (1992) 'Useful culture'. *Cultural Studies* 6: 3, 395–408.

Berger, John (1972) *Ways of Seeing*. Harmondsworth: Penguin, in association with the BBC.

Bleuel, Hans Peter (1973) *Strength Through Joy: Sex and Society in Nazi Germany*. London and Sydney: Pan.

Bloustien, Gerry (1998) '"It's different to a mirror 'cos it talks to you". Teenage girls, video cameras and identity'. In Sue Howard (ed.) *Wired-Up: Young People and the Electronic Media*. London: UCL Press, 115–33.

Blumler, Jay and Katz, Elihu (1974) *The Uses of Mass Communications*. Beverly Hills: Sage.

Blumler, Jay and Katz, Elihu (eds) (1975) *The Uses and Gratifications Approach to Communications Research*. Beverly Hills: Sage.

Blumler, Jay and McQuail, Denis (1968) *Television in Politics: Its Uses and Influence*. London: Faber.

Boddy, William (1990) *Fifties Television: The Industry and Its Critics*. Urbana and Chicago: University of Illinois Press.

Braudel, Fernand (1958) 'Histoire et science sociale, la longue durée'. *Annales*, 725–53.

Brittain, William J. (1927) 'Television and its inventors'. In *Young Australia: Thirty-Sixth Annual Volume*. London: The Pilgrim Press.

Brooker, Will (1998) *Teach Yourself Cultural Studies*. London: Hodder.

Browne, Sir Thomas (1650) *Pseudoxia Epidemica: or, Enquiries into Very many Received Tenents, and Commonly Presumed Truths*. In *The Major Works*. Ed. C.A. Patrides (1977). Harmondsworth: Penguin.

Brunsdon, Charlotte, D'Acci, Julie and Spigel, Lynn (eds) (1997) *Feminist Television Criticism.* Oxford: Oxford University Press.

Chesterman, John and Galligan, Brian (1997) *Citizens without Rights: Aborigines and Australian Citizenship.* Cambridge: Cambridge University Press.

Clarissa Explains It All (1998) *Star Girl,* 11 February, 4–5 and 11 March, 8–9.

Cohen, Phil (1972) 'Subcultural conflict and working class community'. *Working Papers in Cultural Studies,* 2, 4–51.

Coleman, Terry (1976) *The Liners: A History of the North Atlantic Crossing.* Harmondsworth: Penguin.

Creative Camera (1982) 211, July/August.

Cross, Gary (1997) 'The suburban weekend: perspectives on a vanishing twentieth-century dream'. In Roger Silverstone (ed.) *Visions of Suburbia.* London and New York: Routledge, 108–31.

Curthoys, Ann (1991) 'Television before television'. Continuum 4: 2, 152–70.

D'Acci, Julie (1994) *Defining Women: The Case of Cagney and Lacey.* Chapel Hill, NC: University of North Carolina Press.

Dahlgren, Peter (1995) *Television and the Public Sphere.* London: Sage.

David, Elizabeth (1977) *English Bread and Yeast Cookery.* London: Allen Lane, Penguin Books.

Dening, Greg (1992) *Mr Bligh's Bad Language: Passion, Power and Theatre on the Bounty.* Cambridge: Cambridge University Press.

Die Olympischen-Spiele 1936 (1936) 'Wunder der Technik'. Cigaretten-Bilderdienst Altona-Bahrenfeld, Volume II.

Donzelot, Jacques (1980) *The Policing of Families.* London: Hutchinson.

Duby, Georges (ed.) (1988) *A History of Private Life: Revelations of the Medieval World.* Trans. Arthur Goldhammer. Cambridge, MA: Harvard University Press.

Dunkley, Chris (1985) *Television Today and Tomorrow: Wall-to-Wall Dallas?* Harmondsworth: Penguin.

Eco, Umberto (1972, first published in Italian, 1966) 'Towards a semiotic enquiry into the television message'. Trans. Paola Splendore. *Working Papers in Cultural Studies* 3, 103–21.

Eco, Umberto (1979) 'Can television teach?', *Screen Education* 31, 15–24.

Eco, Umberto (1981) *The Role of the Reader: Explorations in the Semiotics of Texts.* London: Hutchinson.

Eco, Umberto (1987) *Travels in Hyperreality.* Trans. William Weaver. London: Picador.

Ellis, John (1982) *Visible Fictions.* London: Routledge & Kegan Paul.

Enzensberger, Hans Magnus (1970) *Raids and Reconstructions: Essays on Politics, Crime, and Culture.* London: Pluto Press.

Ericson, Richard V., Baranek, Patricia M. and Chan, Janet B.L. (1987) *Visualizing Deviance: A Study of News Organization.* Milton Keynes: Open University Press.

Ericson, Richard V., Baranek, Patricia M. and Chan, Janet B.L. (1989) *Negotiating Control: A Study of News Sources.* Milton Keynes: Open University Press.

Ericson, Richard V., Baranek, Patricia M. and Chan, Janet B.L. (1991) *Representing Order: Crime, Law and Justice in the News Media.* Milton Keynes: Open University Press.

Felski, Rita (1995) *The Gender of Modernity.* Cambridge, MA: Harvard University Press.

Fiske, John (1987) *Television Culture.* London and New York: Routledge.

Fiske, John and Hartley, John (1978) *Reading Television.* London: Methuen.

Franklin, Annie and Franklin, Bob (1996) 'Growing pains: the developing children's rights movement in the UK'. In Jane Pilcher and Stephen Wagg (eds) *Thatcher's Children? Politics, Childhood and Society in the 1980s and 1990s.* London: Falmer Press, 94–113.

Frow, John (1995) *Cultural Studies and Cultural Value*. Oxford: Oxford University Press.

Frow, John (1997) *Time and Commodity Culture: Essays in Cultural Theory and Postmodernity*. Oxford: Oxford University Press.

Gerbner, George (1998) 'Stories of violence and the public interest'. In Kees Brants, Joke Hermes and Liesbet van Zoonen (eds) *The Media in Question: Popular Cultures and Public Interests*. London: Sage, 135–46.

Gibbs, Philip (1935) *England Speaks*. London: Heinemann.

Gidal, Tim (1982) 'Modern photojournalism – the first years'. *Creative Camera* 211, 572–9.

Gillespie, Marie (1995) *Television, Ethnicity and Cultural Change*. London: Routledge.

Gitlin, Todd (1983) *Inside Prime Time*. New York: Pantheon.

Gorham, Maurice (1951) 'Television: a medium in its own right?'. In Roger Manvell and R.K. Neilson Baxter (eds) *The Cinema 1951*. Harmondsworth: Penguin, 131–46.

Goulden, Holly and Hartley, John (1982) '"Nor should such topics as homosexuality, masturbation, frigidity, premature ejaculation or the menopause be regarded as unmentionable". English Literature, schools examinations and official discourses'. *LTP: Journal of Literature Teaching Politics*, 1, 4–20.

Gray, Herman (1995) *Watching Race: Television and the Struggle for 'Blackness'*. Minneapolis: University of Minnesota Press.

Gripsrud, Jostein (1995) *The Dynasty Years: Hollywood Television and Critical Media Studies*. London: Routledge.

Haebich, Anna (1988) *For Their Own Good: Aborigines and Government in the South West of Western Australia, 1900–1940*. Perth: University of Western Australia Press.

Hall, Stuart (1972) 'The social eye of *Picture Post*'. *Working Papers in Cultural Studies* 2, 70–120.

Hall, Stuart (1975) 'Between two worlds'. In Theo Barker (ed.) *The Long March of Everyman 1750–1960*. Harmondsworth: Penguin, in association with André Deutsch and the BBC, 273–94.

Hall, Stuart (1992) 'Cultural studies and its theoretical legacies'. In Lawrence Grossberg, Cary Nelson and Paula Treichler (eds) *Cultural Studies*. New York: Routledge, 277–94.

Hall, Stuart and Whannel, Paddy (1964) *The Popular Arts*. London, Melbourne, Sydney, Auckland, Bombay, Toronto, Johannesburg, New York: Hutchinson Educational.

Hall, Stuart, Chritcher, Chas, Jefferson, Tony, Clarke, John and Roberts, Brian (1978) *Policing the Crisis: Mugging, the State, and Law and Order*. London: Macmillan.

Hammersley, Martyn and Atkinson, Paul (1989) *Ethnography: Principles in Practice*. London: Routledge.

Harding, Gilbert (1953) *Along My Line*. London: Putnam & Co.

Hardy, Thomas (1930) *The Collected Poems of Thomas Hardy*. London: Macmillan.

Hartley, John (1982) *Understanding News*. London: Routledge.

Hartley, John (1987) 'Invisible fictions: television audiences, paedocracy, pleasure'. *Textual Practice* 1: 2, 121–38.

Hartley, John (1992a) *Tele-ology: Studies in Television*. London and New York: Routledge.

Hartley, John (1992b) 'Expatriation: useful astonishment as cultural studies'. *Cultural Studies* 6: 3, 449–67.

Hartley, John (1993) *The Politics of Pictures: The Creation of the Public in the Age of Popular Media*. London and New York: Routledge.

Hartley, John (1996) *Popular Reality: Journalism, Modernity, Popular Culture*. London: Arnold.

Hartley, John (1997) 'The sexualization of suburbia: the diffusion of knowledge in the postmodern public sphere'. In Roger Silverstone (ed.) *Visions of Suburbia*. London and New York: Routledge, 180–216.

Hartley, John (1998) '"When your child grows up too fast". Juvenation and the boundaries of the social in the news media'. *Continuum: Journal of Media & Cultural Studies* 12: 1, 9–30.

Hawkes, Terence (1973) *Shakespeare's Talking Animals*. London: Edward Arnold.

Hawkes, Terence (1977) *Structuralism and Semiotics*. London: Methuen.

Hebdige, Dick (1988) *Hiding in the Light: On Images and Things*. London: Comedia/Routledge.

Hechter, Michael (1976) *Internal Colonialism: The Celtic Fringe and British National Development, 1536–1966*. London: Routledge & Kegan Paul.

Hoggart, Richard (1958) *The Uses of Literacy: Aspects of Working-Class Life with Special Reference to Publications and Entertainments*. Harmondsworth: Penguin.

Hoggart, Richard (1960) 'The uses of television'. *Encounter* 76, January (vol. XIV, no. 1), 38–45.

Hoggart, Richard (1970) *Speaking to Each Other, Volume Two: About Literature*. Harmondsworth: Penguin.

Hoggart, Richard (1998) 'Forty years of cultural studies: an interview with Richard Hoggart, October 1997'. By Mark Gibson and John Hartley. *International Journal of Cultural Studies* 1: 1, 11–23.

Hopkinson, Tom (1982) '*Weekly Illustrated*: photojournalism's forgotten pioneer'. *Creative Camera* 211, 580–95.

Hunter, Ian (1988) *Culture and Government: The Emergence of Literary Education*. London: Macmillan.

Hunter, Ian (1994) *Rethinking the School: Subjectivity, Bureaucracy, Criticism*. Sydney: Allen & Unwin.

Innes, Harold (1951) *The Bias of Communication*. Toronto: University of Toronto Press.

Jenkins, Henry (1992) *Textual Poachers*. London: Routledge.

Kentley, Eric (1997) *Discover the Titanic*. Book and 3–D Model. London, New York, Moscow, Sydney: Dorling Kindersley Action Books.

Kuhn, Thomas (1970) *The Structure of Scientific Revolutions*. 2nd edn. Chicago: University of Chicago Press.

Laclau, Ernesto and Mouffe, Chantal (1985) *Hegemony and Socialist Strategy: Towards a Radical Democratic Politics*. Trans. Winston Moore and Paul Cammack. London: Verso.

Langton, Marcia (1993) *Well I Heard it on the Radio and I Saw it on the Television*. Sydney: Australian Film Commission.

Leavis, F.R. and Thompson, Denys (1933) *Culture and Environment: The Training of Critical Awareness*. London: Chatto & Windus.

Lebeau, Vicky (1997) 'The worst of all possible worlds?'. In Roger Silverstone (ed.) *Visions of Suburbia*. London and New York: Routledge, 280–97.

Lefebvre, Henri (1988) 'Toward a leftist cultural politics: remarks occasioned by the centenary of Marx's death'. In Cary Nelson and Lawrence Grossberg (eds) *Marxism and the Interpretation of Culture*. Urbana and Chicago: University of Illinois Press, 75–88.

Leslie, Norman (1993) *Black and White: Photographic Imagery and the Construction of Aboriginality*. Unpublished MA (Litt.Comm.) thesis, Murdoch University, Western Australia.

Lipsitz, George (1990) *Time Passages: Collective Memory and American Popular Culture*. Minneapolis: University of Minnesota Press.

Lotman, Yuri (1990) *The Universe of the Mind: a Semiotic Theory of Culture*. Trans. Ann Shukman. Bloomington and Indianapolis: Indiana University Press.

Lucy, Niall (1993) '(Don't) say "Cheese"'. *Continuum* 6: 2, 282–90.

Lumby, Catharine (1997) *Bad Girls: The Media, Sex and Feminism in the 90s*. Sydney: Allen & Unwin.

Macpherson, C.B. (1973) *Democratic Theory: Essays in Retrieval*. Oxford: Oxford University Press.

MacShane, Denis (1979) 'Reporting race'. *Screen Education* 31, Summer, 91–6.

Manvell, Roger (1944, revised 1946) *Film*. Harmondsworth: Penguin.

Marling, Karal Ann (1994) *As Seen on TV: The Visual Culture of Everyday Life in the 1950s*. Cambridge, MA: Harvard University Press.

Marshall, T.H. (1992, first published 1950) 'Citizenship and social class'. In T.H. Marshall and Tom Bottomore, *Citizenship and Social Class*. London: Pluto Press.

Mayhew, Henry (1968, first published 1862) *London Labour and the London Poor*. New York: Dover, 4 volumes: vols 1–3 *The London Street Folk*; vol 4 *Those That Will Not Work*.

McKay, George (ed.) (1998) *DiY Culture: Party and Protest in Nineties Britain*. London: Verso.

McLuhan, Marshall (1962) *The Gutenberg Galaxy*. London: Routledge & Kegan Paul.

McLuhan, Marshall (1964) *Understanding Media: The Extensions of Man*. London: Routledge & Kegan Paul.

McLuhan, Marshall (1967) *The Mechanical Bride*. London: Routledge & Kegan Paul.

McQuail, Denis, Blumler, Jay and Brown, J. (1972) 'The television audience: a revised perspective'. In Denis McQuail (ed.) *Sociology of Mass Communications*. Harmondsworth: Penguin, 135–65.

Medhurst, Andy (1995) 'Negotiating the gnome zone: versions of suburbia in British popular culture'. In Roger Silverstone (ed.) *Visions of Suburbia*. London and New York: Routledge, 240–68.

Media International Australia (1997) *Panic: Media, Morality, Culture* (themed issue), 85, November.

Mellencamp, Patricia (1992) *High Anxiety: Catastrophe, Scandal, Age, and Comedy*. Bloomington and Indianapolis: Indiana University Press.

Miller, Toby (1997) *The Avengers*. London: BFI Publishing.

Moran, Joe (1998) 'Cultural studies and academic stardom'. *International Journal of Cultural Studies* 1: 1, 67–82.

Morris, Meaghan (1990) 'Banality in cultural studies'. In Patricia Mellencamp (ed.) *Logics of Television: Essays in Cultural Criticism*. Bloomington and Indianapolis: Indiana University Press, 14–43.

Mulhern, Francis (1979) *The Moment of Scrutiny*. London: New Left Books.

Neville, A.O. (1944) *Australia's Coloured Minority*. Sydney: Currawong Publishing.

Newcomb, Horace (1974) *Television: The Most Popular Art*. New York: Doubleday, Anchor Books.

Newcomb, Horace (1987) *Television: The Critical View*. 4th edn. New York: Oxford University Press.

Newcomb, Horace (ed.) (1997) *Encyclopedia of Television* (Museum of Broadcast Communications). 3 Vols. Chicago and London: Fitzroy Dearborn Publishers.

O'Connor, Alan (ed.) (1989) *Raymond Williams on Television*. London and New York: Routledge.

O'Regan, Tom (1995) *Australian Television Culture*. Sydney: Allen & Unwin.

O'Sullivan, Tim, Hartley, John, Saunders, Danny, Montgomery, Martin and Fiske, John (1994) *Key Concepts in Communication and Cultural Studies*. 2nd edn. London and New York: Routledge.

Ong, Walter J., S.J. (1958) *Ramus, Method, and the Decay of Dialogue: From the Art of Discourse to the Art of Reason*. Cambridge, MA: Harvard University Press.

Orwell, George (1954, first published 1949) *Nineteen Eighty-Four*. Harmondsworth: Penguin.

Osborne, Sidney Godolphin (1853) 'Immortal Sewerage'. In Viscount Ingestre (ed.) *Meliora: or, Better Times to Come*. London: John W. Parker & Son [new impression published by Frank Cass & Co., 1971], pp. 7–17.

Paine, Thomas (1792) *Rights of Man: Being an Answer to Mr Burke's Attack on the French Revolution*. Ed. Hypatia Bradlaugh Bonner (1937 edn). London: Watts & Co.

Player, Robert [Robert Furneaux Jordan] (1977) *Let's Talk of Graves, of Worms, and Epitaphs*. Harmondsworth: Penguin.

Priestley, J.B. (1977, first published 1934) *English Journey: Being a Rambling but Truthful Account of What One Man Saw and Heard and Felt and Thought during a Journey through England during the Autumn of the Year 1933*. Harmondsworth: Penguin.

Ray, Robert B. (1995) *The Avant-Garde Finds Andy Hardy*. Cambridge, MA: Harvard University Press.

Richards, I.A. (1924) *Principles of Literary Criticism*. London: Routledge & Kegan Paul.

Rorty, Richard (1989) *Contingency, Irony, and Solidarity*. Cambridge: Cambridge University Press.

Rubinstein, David and Stoneman, Colin (1972) 'Introduction'. In David Rubinstein and Colin Stoneman (eds) *Education for Democracy*. 2nd edn. Harmondsworth: Penguin Education, 7–13.

Ruskin, John (1907 [1849]) *The Seven Lamps of Architecture*. London: J.M. Dent; New York: E.P. Dutton.

Sahlins, Marshall (1976) *Culture and Practical Reason*. Chicago: Chicago University Press.

Saussure, Ferdinand de (1974 [1915]) *Course in General Linguistics*. London: Fontana.

Screen Education (1979) 'Editorial'. Screen Education 31, Summer, 1–2.

Seiter, Ellen, Borchers, Hans, Kreutzner, Gabriele and Warth, Eva-Maria (eds) (1989) *Remote Control: Television, Audiences, and Cultural Power*. London and New York: Routledge.

Shattuc, Jane (1996) *The Talking Cure: Women and TV Talk Shows*. New York: Routledge.

Sinfield, Alan (ed.) (1983) *Society and Literature 1945–1970*. London: Methuen.

Spigel, Lynn (1992) *Make Room for TV: Television and the Family Ideal in Postwar America*. Chicago: Chicago University Press.

Spigel, Lynn and Curtin, Michael (eds) (1997) *The Revolution Wasn't Televised: Sixties Television and Social Conflict*. New York: Routledge.

Stretton, Hugh (1974) *Housing and Government*. Sydney: Australian Broadcasting Corporation.

Sussex, Elizabeth (1975) *The Rise and Fall of British Documentary*. Berkeley: University of California Press.

Taylor, John (1991) *War Photography: Realism in the British Press*. London: Routledge.

Trigger, David (1998) 'Citizenship and indigenous responses to mining in the Gulf country'. In Nicholas Peterson and Will Sanders (eds) *Citizenship and Indigenous Australians: Changing Conceptions and Possibilities*. Cambridge: Cambridge University Press.

Tulloch, John and Jenkins, Henry (1995) *Science Fiction Audiences: Watching Dr Who & Star Trek*. London: Routledge.

Turnbull, Sue and Bowles, Kate (1995) *Tomorrow Never Knows: Soap on Australian Television*. Canberra: Australian Film Institute.

Uricchio, William (1992) 'Television as history: representations of German television broadcasting 1935–1944'. In Bruce Murray and Christopher Wickham (eds) *Framing the Past: The Historiography of German Cinema and Television*. Carbondale: Southern Illinois University Press, 167–96.

Uricchio, William (1998) 'Television, film and the struggle for media identity'. Film History 10: 2, 118–27.

Vonnegut, Kurt (1987) *Galapagos*. London: Grafton Books.

Wark, McKenzie (1994) *Virtual Geography: Living With Global Media Events*. Bloomington and Indianapolis: Indiana University Press.

Wark, McKenzie (1997) *The Virtual Republic: Australia's Culture Wars of the 1990s*. Sydney: Allen & Unwin.

Williams, Gwyn Alf (1975) 'True-born Britons'. In Theo Barker (ed.) *The Long March of Everyman 1750–1960*. Harmondsworth: Penguin, in association with André Deutsch and the BBC, 59–81.

Williams, Raymond (1958) *Culture and Society*. Harmondsworth: Penguin.

Williams, Raymond (1961) *The Long Revolution*. Harmondsworth: Penguin.

Williams, Raymond (1968, first published 1962) *Communications*. 2nd edn. Harmondsworth: Penguin.

Williams, Raymond (1974) *Television: Technology and Cultural Form*. London: Fontana.

Williams, Raymond (1977) *Marxism and Literature*. Oxford: Oxford University Press.

Winston, Brian (1995) *Claiming the Real: The Documentary Film Revisited*. London: BFI Publishing.

Wolfe, Tom (1968) 'What if he is right?'. In *The Pump House Gang*. New York: Bantam Books, 107–33.

INDEX